Peter Ga
Editc

The Leadership
Hubris Epidemic

Biological Roots and Strategies
for Prevention

palgrave
macmillan

Editor
Peter Garrard
St George's, University of London
London, UK

ISBN 978-3-319-86115-9   ISBN 978-3-319-57255-0   (eBook)
https://doi.org/10.1007/978-3-319-57255-0

This Palgrave Macmillan imprint is published by Springer Nature
The registered company is Springer International Publishing AG
The registered company address is: Gewerbestrasse 11, 6330 Cham, Switzerland

The Leadership Hubris Epidemic

Foreword

The publication of Lord Owen's book 'In Sickness and in Power' (Owen 2008) brought to public attention details of the biographies of some world leaders in a way that exposed their health and personality problems as well as the disastrous consequences of some of their decisions. However, it was Owen and Davidson's (2009) description of the disorder Hubris Syndrome that attracted the greatest interest, not only from professionals and experts, but also from the general public. Although the phenomenon of hubristic behaviour had been recognised in the leadership literature for a long time, the idea that some politicians had suffered from an actual disorder, which could be described in formal, medical terminology, was novel, perhaps even shocking. Whether Hubris Syndrome justifies inclusion in the classification system of psychiatric disorders remains to be seen, the phenomenon being more one of personality change or trait—occurring when a leader becomes dangerously overconfident and develops an excessive degree of pride—than an actual psychiatric disorder.

It has since become clear that Hubris Syndrome is at least as rife in the world of business as that of politics and that the actions of many senior investment bankers and Wall Street market financiers had been significant contributing factors to the global financial crisis of 2008. Hubris has been witnessed in senior executives in crucial leadership positions such as in Lehman Brothers, the Royal Bank of Scotland, HBOS and Enron (Garrard and Robinson 2016). The financial world was shocked to learn the fall of Bill Gross, the legendary investor known as the 'bond king', whose behaviour had become increasingly erratic, and personality prone to arrogance and an unwillingness to listen or accept criticism. Hubris Syndrome has also been presented as organisational phenomenon, and the Deep Water Horizon oil spill in the Gulf of Mexico has been attributed, at least in part, to corporate hubris at British Petroleum (Sadler-Smith et al. 2016).

The growing interest in hubristic leadership led to the formation, in 2011, of the charity The Daedalus Trust <www.daedalustrust.com> (see footnote). The name was taken from the Greek myth (most famously retold in Book VIII of Ovid's *Metamorphoses*), in which Daedalus fashioned two pairs of wings using bird feathers strung together with thread and wax, to enable him and his son Icarus to escape from imprisonment by the Cretan King Minos. Before setting off, Daedalus warned his son Icarus to keep flying a middle course to avoid being too close to either the moisture of the sea or the heat of the sun. The exuberant Icarus, however, flew towards the sun, and when the wax in his wings melted, he crashed into the sea and drowned.

The aims of the Daedalus Trust have been to raise public awareness of the dangers of personality change associated with the exercise of power, whether individual or collective, and in all walks of life, including business, politics, the military and public services, and to draw attention to the effect of hubris on decision-making, and the grave problems that can ensue.

'The Leadership Hubris Epidemic: biological roots and strategies for prevention' is the second book to be published under the auspices of Daedalus Trust. The contents of this book and its 2016 predecessor 'The Intoxication of Power: interdisciplinary insights', edited by Peter Garrard and Graham Robinson, both emerged from academic activity sponsored or commissioned by the Daedalus Trust, which included workshops, research cafes, conferences, and research projects. The book draws on the complex, multidimensional problem of hubris, its toxic effect on individuals and organisations and its potential for serious harmful consequences.

The contents of the present book are divided into three parts: focusing in turn on possible mechanisms by which the brain (and body) may give rise to Hubris Syndrome, its effects on certain groups and organisations, and finally possible preventative measures that could counteract its potentially catastrophic consequences. The neurobiological roots, which include cognitive, psychological and neuroendocrine mechanisms, are explored in the opening part.

In Chap. 1, Prof. Garrard (a neurologist and neuroscientist researching neurodegenerative disorders) draws attention to similarities between the Hubris Syndrome and some forms of the personality change that is seen in people with frontotemporal dementia. This suggestion, which is backed up by neuroanatomical evidence and the neuroscience of addiction, supports the contention (first put forward by Owen and Davidson in their 2009 paper) that Hubris Syndrome is likely to be underpinned by change at a biological level. A different level of analysis of this putative biological basis is put forward by the well-known trader-turned-neuroscientist, John Coates, and his co-workers in Chap. 2, who report their findings that the concentrations of circulating signalling compounds (hormones) are closely correlated with patterns of decision-making in financial markets. A key result was the differential effects on mood and confidence of acute and chronic exposure to hormones. There is a possibility that acutely elevated steroids may optimise performance on a range of tasks but chronically elevated steroids may promote irrational risk–reward choices. This hypothesis suggests that both the irrational exuberance and profound pessimism that were observed during market bubbles and crashes may be mediated by steroid hormones. A corollary of the research discussed by the authors is that age and sex composition among traders may affect inherent levels of instability in financial markets.

The stimulation received from frequent winning situations encourages continued contesting of more and more difficult challenges, leading to the phenomenon of the 'winner effect', which is analysed by Iain Robertson (Professor of Neuropsychology at Trinity College Dublin) in Chap. 3. Power relationships influence cognitive and emotional function via systematic changes in the brain's approach and avoidance systems, which in turn are linked to the neurotransmitters dopamine and noradrenaline. There might also be individual and gender differences in the quality and quantity of power motivation and how these can be assessed.

The book's second part concentrates on the environmental factors that have been implicated in the emergence of Hubris Syndrome in all forms of leadership. The pivotal role of the leaders' personality interacting with organisational environments and structures is emphasised in Chap. 4 by Prof. Adrian Furham (whose academic career as an organisational and applied psychologist at University College London has resulted in the publication of over fifty books on management and workplace psychology). The process of interaction between personality and environment is thought to be in determining success, hubris or failure.

The military is not immune from disastrous leadership, suggests Colonel J.W. Dagless in Chap. 5, as he offers an insight into the phenomenon of 'toxic leadership' in the Armed Forces. Military leaders can be selfish and self-serving individuals who crush the morale of subordinates and units. Toxic leadership can have devastating effect in the military and there is general acceptance that this phenomenon should be curtailed whenever possible, preferably without the imposition of corrosive bureaucratic fiats.

Concentrating power in the hands of a few people risks the development of hubris and other dysfunctional leadership practices. In Chap. 6, Prof. Dennis Tourish—another prolific contributor to the scientific study of leadership—stresses that business leaders are often prone to develop hubris because they tend to get too little critical feedback on their decision-making, but surround themselves by coteries of flattering admirers. Looking at the banking crises in recent years and beyond, it seems that such conventional leadership practices produce dysfunctional leaders, ineffective organisations and disempowered employees.

Chapters in the book's third part draw attention to factors and techniques that can mitigate the harmful effects of hubris. In Chap. 7, the occurrence of the syndrome in world leaders, the transformation of charisma to hubris and the critical role of the trusted adviser ('toe-holder') in the prevention of dangerous overconfidence are presented by The Rt. Hon. Lord Owen (who, as Dr. David Owen, was a Member of the United Kingdom Parliament for over twenty-six years and served as Foreign Secretary between 1977 and 1979). It was Owen who, with the psychiatrist Dr. Jonathan Davidson, developed the concept of Hubris Syndrome as an acquired personality disorder in 2009.

Extreme, potentially derailing Hubris Syndromes in leaders and managers as they rise up the career ladder is inevitable, argues Gillian Hyde—Chief Psychologist with Psychological Consultancy Ltd (PCL)—in Chap. 8. At the same time, as the opportunities for restraint become fewer, colleagues become less likely to advise or criticise. The challenge is to find ways to help leaders create influential partnerships in their everyday working lives and to motivate them to perceive the need for such a relationship before their Hubris Syndrome becomes excessive.

Practical, precautionary measures in the form of mentoring proto-cols designed to prevent and ameliorate the effects of hubris in business and beyond are discussed by Karen Otazo in the book's final chapter. Dr. Otazo is an experienced adviser to corporations and illustrates the problems and solutions that can arise in these environments with exam-ples from her own practice.

Manifestations of phenomena resembling Hubris Syndrome have been reported in many other walks of life in addition to politics, bank-ing and business. In the world of aviation, fatal accidents have occurred when wrong decisions were made by captains whose position of power on the flight deck inhibited other crew members from challenging his decisions (Helmreich et al. 1999). Failures of leadership in medicine have been cited as causes of clinical errors in hospitals, particularly 'hyperacute' areas such as intensive care units, emergency rooms and operating theatres, where the most senior clinical specialist has auto-matically assumed command, even in the presence of other members of staff who are better qualified to deal with specific problems (Sundar et al. 2007). Atul Gawande (2014) attributed the medicalisation of old age and failure to accept that the end of life is not 'curable' to medi-cal hubris. And even earlier, Winkler (1987) described an 'intellectual celebrity syndrome', in which fêted experts seek to popularise serious ideas or influence contemporary events. The latter can result in concepts being transmitted to the general public in a distorted and unusable framework. Diamandis (2013) coined the term 'Nobelitis' to describe the behaviour of some Nobel Prize winners following their award. Some Nobel Prize laureates seem to undertake projects or accept positions beyond their capabilities feeling that they hold some superpowers to go on and benefit the world with bigger and better achievements. The Editor tells me that Daniel Glaser (Director of the Science Gallery at King's College London) once referred to this phenomenon in conversation as the 'Fallacy of Universal Competence'—a neat encapsulation of the problem.

Increased awareness of hubris has led to the term not always being used appropriately. A common misconception is that hubris is indistinguishable from narcissism. On the contrary, narcissism is expressed with a blatantly attention seeking, grandiose sense of self-importance, a persistent and burdensome search for admiration and lack of empathy (Kets de Vries 2016). Excessive narcissism might lead to or coexist with hubris, but the two are fundamentally distinct, the latter characterised by overconfidence, over ambition, arrogance and excessive pride. Hubris has also been described as an occupational hazard and the possibility that leaders may be selected precisely because they displayed such tendencies: so long as they perform successfully, such Hubris Syndrome would not be perceived as demonstrating hubris.

The publication of this book has further advanced the knowledge on hubris and the underlined factors involved in its manifestation, possible causes and potential preventative measures. More effort is needed to produce robust evidence base on individual and collective hubris and on the effects of a predisposing personality to the exposure to power. Some of the issues that can potentially be explored include the following questions: How can hubristic be distinguished from visionary leadership? What characteristics are shared by successful and hubristic leaders? Where is hubris most prevalent and dangerous? Is hubris a natural consequence of the isolation and chronic stress that many successful leaders experience, or of lasting biological or personality patterns? Is hubris associated with particular forms of social organisation? Might some ways of organising increase or mitigate the risk of hubris?

How have social organisations been able to protect themselves from hubristic leaders? What are the wider societal and institutional implications of hubristic Hubris Syndrome in the current social, political and economic climate? The recognition of hubris as a problem is an urgent issue for all organisations including business, banking, military, judicial and all walks of life. While many regulations and procedures are put in place, the impact of personality of senior leaders should be seriously examined and taken into consideration. Organisations should encourage to promote institutional conditions and enforceable rules of governance, Hubris Syndrome and dialogue that might facilitate the development and maintenance of positive practices to mitigate the onset of Hubris. Participation in organisational decision-making processes, together with enforceable rules on decision-making might reduce the risk of potentially disastrous decisions while improving the quality in the implementation of effective organisational decisions.

Nick Bouras
Emeritus Professor of Psychiatry
King's College London
London, UK

Note

1. In June 2017 the Daedalus Trust decided to merge with another charity—the Maudsley Philosophy Group—whose aims are broader but complementary to its own. Building on this new structure, the Daedalus Trust will continue to disseminate discussion and research into leadership and its disorders through meetings, publications and electronic media, including its website <www.daedalustrust.com>.

References

Diamandis, E. P. (2013). Nobelitis: A common disease among Nobel laureates? Clin Chem Lab Med, *51*(8), 1573–1574.

Garrard, P., & Robinson, G. (Eds.). (2016). *The intoxication of power*. London: Palgrave McMillan.

Gawande, A. (2014). *Being mortal: medicine and what watters in the end*. Metropolitan Books.

Helmreich, R. L., Merritt, A. C., & Wilhelm J. A. (1999). The evolution of crew resource management in commercial aviation. *International Journal of Aviation Psychology, 9*(1), 19–32.

Kets de Vries, M. (2016). *Sex, money, happiness and death. The quest for authenticity*. London: Springer.

Owen, D., & Davidson, J. (2009). Hubris syndrome: An acquired personality disorder? A study of US presidents and UK prime ministers over the last 100 years. *Brain, 132*, 1396–1406.8.

Owen, D. (2016). *In sickness and in power: Illness in heads of Government, Military and Business Leaders since 1900*. Methuen Publishing. First published 2008.

Sadler-Smith, E., Akstinaite, V., Robinson, G., & Wray, T. (2016). Hubristic leadership: A review. *Leadership*.

Sadler-Smith, E., & Robinson, G. (in press). http://www.daedalustrust.com/anti-hubris-toolkit-takes-important-step-2016/

Sundar, S., Pawlowski, J., Blum, R., Feinstein, D., & Pratt, S. (2007). Crew resource management and team training. *Anaesthesiology Clinics, 25*(2), 283–300.

Winkler, J. T. (1987). The intellectual celebrity syndrome. *Lancet, 329*(8530), 450. (February 21).

Contents

Editor and Contributors

About the Editor

Peter Garrard is Professor of Neurology and Deputy Director of the Molecular and Clinical Sciences Research Institute at St George's, University of London. His specialist clinical and research area is the neurodegenerative dementias, on which he has written and lectured extensively and which he manages clinically at a regional cognitive neurology clinic at St George's Hospital in London. Professor Garrard has an interest in language disorders associated with dementia and other brain diseases, including Hubris Syndrome, in which he described a characteristic set of language changes. Along with his numerous scientific publications, he co-edited (with Graham Robinson) 'The Intoxication of Power: interdisciplinary insights' published by Palgrave in 2013, on behalf of the Daedalus Trust. Professor Garrard is a Trustee of the Maudsley Philosophy Group, with which the Daedalus Trust merged in 2017.

Contributors

Nick Bouras is Emeritus Professor of Psychiatry at the Institute of Psychiatry, Psychology and Neuroscience at King's College London. He is currently Programme Director of Maudsley International. Professor Bouras' research has focused on health service-related issues, evaluation of multi-professional training methods and social and biological determinants of behaviour. He was a founding member of the Daedalus Trust.

John Coates is the founder of Dewline Research. He was previously a research fellow at the University of Cambridge, and before that a trader for Goldman Sachs and Deutsche Bank, where he developed techniques for valuing and arbitraging the tails of probability distributions, and for trading low-probability events such as financial crises. Dr. Coates now researches the biology of gut feelings, risk taking and stress. His book *The Hour Between Dog and Wolf: How Risk Taking Transforms Us, Body and Mind* was shortlisted for the Financial Times/Goldman Sachs Business Book of the Year, and the UK Wellcome Trust Science Prize.

John W. Dagless joined the Army in 1997 and was commissioned into the Royal Signals. During his military career, he has served in a wide variety of roles, including operational deployments in Kosovo, Mozambique, Sierra Leone, Northern Ireland, Iraq and Afghanistan. While attending the Advanced Command and Staff Course at the United Kingdom's Defence Academy, he wrote a Defence Research Paper on toxic leadership in the military. Since the paper's publication, John has supported the Defence Master Class series, assisted at Beckett House Leadership Centre and currently presents on the topic of negative leadership traits to the Army's General Staff course and Generalship programme. His paper has been published across Defence and was incorporated into the Army's new Leadership Doctrine, released in October 2016. He continues to study and write on leadership.

Adrian Furnham has been Professor of Psychology at University College London since 1992 and held scholarships and visiting professorships at, among others, the Universities of New South Wales, the

West Indies, Hong Kong and KwaZulu-Natal. Professor Furnham has also been a Visiting Professor of Management at Henley Management College and Adjunct Professor of Management at the Norwegian School of Management. Prof. Furnham has written over 1200 scientific papers and 85 books and is a regular contributor on national and international radio and television.

Mark Gurnell is Clinical SubDean and Honorary Consultant Physician in the University of Cambridge School of Clinical Medicine and has special clinical and scientific expertise in metabolic and endocrine disorders. He has a long-standing cross-disciplinary collaboration with the Judge Business School, studying the endocrine and neural basis of financial decision-making.

Gillian Hyde is a Chartered Psychologist with more than 25 years' experience and has particular expertise in assessing leadership derailment and creating personality assessments. Her work encompasses in-depth individual assessments, consulting on the management of extreme personality characteristics for individual and team development and researching derailment patters within organisations. She also designs tailor-made assessment solutions for clients and is an expert trainer on the Hogan Development Survey. Gillian is Chief Psychologist at Psychological Consultancy Ltd., where her client work ranges from one-to-one executive coaching to creating and validating bespoke assessment systems.

Dr. Karen Otazo received her BA and MA in Linguistics at the City University of New York. She focused on the way that one's native language shapes one's thinking which shapes one's view of how the world works. In the process, she learned a half dozen languages. After receiving a doctorate in Human Resources Development from the University of Northern Colorado, Karen moved into corporate roles in two multi-national, oil companies. In lengthy assignments in China and Indonesia, she acted as an executive coach and thinking partner for senior leaders, so that they were prepared to coach local leaders to replace them. In 1997, she started her Global Leadership Network in London, UK servicing Europe, Asia and the states. Her publications

xviii   Editor and Contributors

include: The Truth About Being a Leader, The Truth about Managing Your Career, The No Time for Theories Series for Executives (co-author), 21 Steps: An Anthology for Women Leaders (Editor of Karen Otazo's Global Leadership Network contributions), Profiles of Leadership (Podcasts), and Political Leadership Blogging @A Leadership Coach Perspective on Facebook.

Lord David Owen qualified in medicine, practising neurology and carrying out neuroscience research at St Thomas's Hospital, London, before entering politics. He held several Government posts including those of Minister of Health and Foreign Secretary, and was the leader of the Social Democratic Party between 1983 and 1987, and now sits in the House of Lords as an independent social democrat. Between 1992 and 1995, he was EU peace negotiator during the Yugoslav Wars. Lord Owen's writing on the subject of Power and Hubris stimulated the formation of the Daedalus Trust, a charity that promotes discussion and research into personality changes associated with the exercise of power. He was Chairman of the Trust from 2011 to 2017, when it became part of the Maudsley Philosophy Group.

Ian H. Robertson is Professor Emeritus at Trinity College Dublin, and Co-Director of the Global Brain Health Institute. He has expertise in both clinical psychology and neuroscience, applying the results of his scientific research to the pressures of everyday life. His previous books, Mind Sculpture, The Mind's Eye and The Winner Effect, have been translated into many languages. His most recent book, 'The Stress Test: How pressure can make you stronger and smarter', was published by Bloomsbury Press in 2016. Professor Robertson is recognised as one of the world's leading researchers in neuropsychology.

Zoltan Sarnyai is a Professor and Director of the Psychiatric Neuroscience Laboratory at James Cook University, Australia, with an active research programme in the neurogiological mechanisms of stress and psychiatric disorders, including drug addiction, schizophrenia and depression. He did postdoctoral work at Harvard Medical School, before holding an independent research position at Rockefeller University, New York. Prior to his current appointment, he was

University Lecturer in Parmacology at the University of Cambridge and Fellow of Pembroke College.

Dennis Tourish is Professor of Leadership and Organisation Studies at the University of Sussex. He is the editor of the journal Leadership, a Fellow of the Leadership Trust Foundation and a Fellow of the Lancaster Leadership Centre. His main research interests are in critical leadership studies, leadership effectiveness, leadership development and organisational communication. He has co-written or co-edited eight books. He has extensive experience of consultancy and executive education with a range of public and private sector organisations and is interviewed frequently on radio and television about his research.

List of Figures

List of Tables

Part I
Biology

1

Frontotemporal Dementia: A Clue to the Biological Basis of Hubris Syndrome?

Peter Garrard

1 Introduction

When, at 3:30 pm on October 30th 1990, Prime Minister Margaret Thatcher made a statement to the House of Commons on the European Council, which she had attended in Rome a few days earlier, her written statement was factual almost to the point of dryness, contrasting markedly with the robust opposition to the Council's federalist agenda that she had conveyed in earlier statements to the press. The statement covered agricultural trade negotiations, the Hungarian economy, the situation in the Gulf, and finally the Council's preparations for forthcoming intergovernmental conferences on economic, monetary and political union. On the latter, Mrs. Thatcher reported that she had "...reserved the United Kingdom's position on, for example, extension of the Community's powers into new areas, greater powers for the European Parliament in the legislative sphere, defining European citizenship,

P. Garrard (✉)
St. George's, University of London, London, UK
e-mail: pgarrard@sgul.ac.uk

© The Author(s) 2018
P. Garrard (ed.), *The Leadership Hubris Epidemic*,
https://doi.org/10.1007/978-3-319-57255-0_1

and a common foreign and security policy. All these are issues for discussion at the intergovernmental conference itself rather than to be settled in advance."

In the unscripted debate that followed, her performance took on a strikingly different character, famously described by the Parliamentary sketch-writer Hugo Young (1998) as "...leaping with rage, ringing round the chamber, startling even those who in eleven years had much experience of the Thatcher vocabulary on Europe. 'No! No! No!' she bawled, her eyes seemingly directed to the fields and seas, the hills and the landing-grounds, where the island people would never surrender." Owen (2012), who witnessed the debate from the opposition benches, recalled his impression of Mrs Thatcher as 'on an emotional high... the adrenalin ... pumping round her system as she handbagged every federalist proposal' and cites the event as marking the emergence of 'full-blown hubris'.

The events marked the culmination of an increasingly domineering pattern in Thatcher's leadership style, the onset and time-course of which appears to have been reflected in the language that she used during parliamentary debate (Garrard et al. 2014a, b). They also exposed the deep ideological rifts at the heart of her Cabinet and led within weeks to her decision to resign from office. Against the background of her astonishing political success over the preceding decade, this period of the Thatcher premiership also marked out a paradigm case of what Owen and Davidson (2009) described in clinical terms as 'Hubris Syndrome'—a distinctive change in personality brought about by the acquisition and prolonged tenure of significant power.

Owen and Davidson (2009) argued that a pattern of exuberant overconfidence, isolation, and narcissism was also associated with the periods in office of three other British Prime Ministers—Tony Blair (1997–2007), Neville Chamberlain (1937–1940) and David Lloyd George (1916–1922), and one US President, George W. Bush (2001–2009). Although the observed Hubris Syndrome changes overlapped to some extent with the personality disorders that are described in the Diagnostic and Statistical Manual of Mental Disorders (DSM), specifically the Antisocial, Histrionic and Narcissistic varieties, there were also distinctive elements, identifiable from historical records, which occurred repeatedly in these individuals. The distinctive features included: a tendency to 'identify with the nation'; adoption of the 'royal we'; restlessness and impulsivity; and an unshakeable belief that their decisions and actions are accountable to an authority higher than that of equally well-placed colleagues or the collective voice of public opinion. Perhaps the best known example of the last of these was the comment made by Blair looking back on his Iraq policy during a television interview in March 2006: 'In the end' he said, 'there is a judgement that, I think if you have faith about these things then you realize that judgement is made by other people... and if you believe in God, it's made by God as well'.

What are we to make of the biological basis for these recurrent and distinctive Hubris Syndrome phenomena? It is widely accepted that cognitive states (such as the formation of memories and the experience of emotions) are not only subjectively felt but can in principle be described at the level of a neurobiological event. John Coates and his co-authors Mark Gurnell and Zoltan Sarnyai (Chap. 2 of this volume) argue persuasively that the event or events in question consist of alterations in the responsiveness of neuronal circuits caused by changes in their hormonal environments. Using the 'winner effect' (the competitive enhancement produced by the experience of success) as a paradigm case, Iain Robertson (Chap. 3) puts forward the related proposal that personality traits may develop as a result of local biological alterations that take place in response to specific types of experience. The changes in marking, colouring and size, as well as behaviour, that accompany any change in the ecological status of a male fish from the family Chichlidae, represent an extreme example of the transformations of which this psycho-biological continuum is capable. Although not explored in depth in this volume, the biology of addiction may also be relevant to a neural account of personality change. When a novel motivational state is encoded by the brain's dopamine-mediated reward system a new predisposition to act (or 'trait') may be said to have emerged, and proponents of the psychometric school regard such predispositions ('traits') as the fundamental units of personality (see, e.g. Eysenck (1953), Cattell (1965) and Allport (1937)).

The central thesis of the present chapter, however, is that personality change can also result from changes to the physical integrity of the brain. At first sight this assertion may seem to hark back to simplistic notions of the brain as an interconnected series of functional units ('modules'), first articulated in the phrenology movement of the late nineteenth century. More informed interpretations of functional architecture at both neural and cognitive levels, however, can fully reconcile 'lesion based' accounts of cognitive impairment with state- or system-based accounts put forward in the following two chapters. So these are not competing accounts so much as descriptions of different pathways to a common outcome—the fundamental transformation of one personality into another.

The most celebrated example of personality change following brain injury is that of Phineas Gage, the American railway construction foreman whose prefrontal cortex was destroyed by a metal rod, which he was using to pack gunpowder into a hole. When the gunpowder accidentally ignited, the rod was propelled upwards like a bullet, piercing Gage's left cheek and travelling up through his brain, before emerging out of the top of his skull. (If you think you have a strong enough stomach, perform a Google image search on 'Phineas Gage'.) Improbably, the physical effects of this devastating injury were minimal; the surface wounds healed effectively with a minimum of surgical intervention, and there were no impairments to the power or dexterity of the limbs. In consequence, he was before long able to return to work. The damage to the inferior frontal regions of Gage's brain, however, resulted in dramatic changes to his personality. From one who was '…looked on by those who know him as a shrewd, smart business man, very energetic and persistent in executing all his plans of operation' his behaviour turned into that of a man who was '…fitful, irreverent, indulging at times in the grossest profanity… manifesting but little deference from his fellows, impatient of restraint or advice when it conflicts with his desires, at times pertinaciously obstinate, yet capricious and vacillating, devising many plans of future operations, which are not sooner arranged than they are abandoned in turn for others appearing more feasible.' (Quotations taken from the case report published by John Harlow, the provincial physician who treated Gage's injuries (Harlow 1868)).

Industrial accidents resulting in focal penetrating injuries such as Gage's are vanishingly uncommon in the modern era, though are still caused by gunshot wounds sustained by both military and civilian victims, and result in similar changes in judgement, social and ethical propriety, which may remain remarkably isolated from their effects on more traditional aspects of cognition. See, for instance, Damasio's case history of a 'modern day Phineas Gage' in whom inability to take decisions in his own long-term interest despite preservation of razor-sharp analytical abilities, followed damage to the same, inferior regions of his frontal cortex (Damasio 2008).

Diffuse traumatic brain injuries are more frequently recognised and often give rise to personality change in the context of a more widespread pattern of neurological and physical (orthopaedic) disability. In neurological practice, however, when isolated and insidious personality change is reported the underlying cause is most likely to be some form of neurodegenerative process.

2   The Frontotemporal Dementia Spectrum

There is an unhelpful tendency in the media to refer to Alzheimer's disease and dementia as if they mean one the same thing. Alzheimer's disease is, to be sure, a common *cause* of dementia but is no more synonymous with that clinical state than influenza is with the state of having a fever. Although in both examples the assumption of equivalence would result in a correct diagnosis most of the time, it would also lead to a substantial error rate and (at least in the fever scenario) a great many avoidable deaths from other treatable causes of infection. The stakes are perhaps not quite so high in the case of cognitive impairment, but a good clinician will always consider treatable alternatives before diagnosing a progressive and incurable disease—a piece of clinical common sense that is reflected in recommendations of expert bodies (such as the UK National Institute of Clinical Excellence and the American Academy of Neurology), that brain imaging and blood tests including for vitamin deficiency, thyroid status and certain forms of chronic infection should be included in the workup of a patient with suspected dementia.

Even when (as is almost always the case) these simple screening tests prove to be negative, the spectrum of possible neurodegenerative causes includes too wide a range of distinct pathological processes for Alzheimer's to be assumed by default. Again, the organised clinical mind recognises heuristic boundaries marking out the territories of rarer conditions: Creutzfeldt Jakob Disease when progression is unusually rapid; one of a growing number of genetic mutations when a patient has close relatives who are similarly affected; and in someone with symptom onset before the age of 60, one of the frontotemporal dementias.

The clinical spectrum of frontotemporal dementia is broad and encompasses a range of difficulties and disabilities that are distinct from those seen in patients with Alzheimer's disease. Alzheimer's typically begins with increasing difficulty forming new memories, leading to a failure to keep track of changes over days, hours, or even smaller intervals. Frontotemporal dementia, on the other hand, is heralded by difficulties in the domains of either the use of language or of 'social cognition'. These two faculties are broadly dependent on the integrity of neural systems located in frontal and temporal regions of the brain. Language problems are easily recognised, both by patients—who experience increasing difficulties with speech production and/or word language comprehension—and clinicians, who distinguish between syndromes of fluent and nonfluent 'progressive aphasia'. In contrast, progressive disruption of social and emotional cognition gives rise to much subtler clinical phenomena, which are seldom fully recognised by patients in spite of their perplexing and alarming effects on family members. Changes may also be invisible to clinicians, particularly at mild stages or when very slowly progressive.

2.1   Quantifying Cognitive Disability

An aggregate index of measurable cognitive skills can be usefully equated with some overall index of intelligence. Membership of the 'society for bright people' Mensa, for instance, is open to individuals whose scores on a battery of problem solving tests exceed those of 98%

of the overall population. Although the tests that contribute to the calculation of such a measure (normally referred to as the intelligence quotient (IQ)) are designed to be socially and culturally neutral, the extent to which the ability to solve a novel problem depends on pure reasoning, as opposed to education and accumulated experience, is still much debated, as is the objective status of the quality that is so measured.

It is less controversial, however, to use this type of test to compare different aspects of an individual's intellectual abilities one with another (i.e. to characterise their relative cognitive strengths and weaknesses), against population norms, or serially over time, as a means of describing the clinical profiles of performance that match those seen in different types of dementia. For instance, the syndromes of fluent and non-fluent aphasia may be identified using tests of vocabulary comprehension and production tasks such as reading words and naming pictures, and repeating words or sentences. Other patients may show isolated difficulties learning and recalling new information, and these individuals often go on to develop dementia due to Alzheimer's disease. Those who experience difficulties in solving visual tasks that most people find easy may be suffering from the syndrome of posterior cortical atrophy.

'Social cognition' is a more difficult set of abilities to define, and changes in it are predictably more challenging to detect and measure. When changes do take place they normally become apparent first to patients' spouses or children, and sometimes to friends who have known them over years or decades. These witnesses often report that they are seeing the emergence of a 'different personality'. Disturbing as this may be, the term 'personality' remains clinically problematic: it has no universally agreed definition; the features that distinguish one 'personality type' from another may be subtle, and as a result not only selectively recognised, but even differentially valued. This is not to say that the term is meaningless: in life, personality can be operationalised with reference to the set of stable dispositions that may, for instance, support a prediction about someone's response to an event, challenge, or set of circumstances. We would neither expect nor wish to see Caspar Milquetoast commanding a platoon of soldiers, nor Sherlock Holmes counselling the recently bereaved. We want our diplomats to be diplomatic and our leaders to be decisive.

Yet when Penny comments to Sheldon in *The Big Bang Theory* "How can you not be happy? You're tall, thin and famous. Oh my God. I'm jealous of Sheldon!" the line works partly because the nature of Sheldon's unique brand of social awkwardness is both difficult to pin down, and compatible with normal (or in Sheldon's case ludicrously superior) intellectual capability while at the same time rendering him vulnerable and pitiable. And the same sense that 'something is not quite right' about the way a patient with suspected FTD behaves may be the only clinical clue to there being anything seriously wrong. I teach my clinical students and specialist trainees that it can be revealing to examine the effect that a consultation has on *them personally*: finding the encounter unusually enjoyable, hard work, or uncomfortable may be indicative, respectively, of disinhibition, apathy or obsessionality— the major dimensions in which personality changes in frontotemporal dementia are described.

Disinhibition is characterised by the emergence of increased familiarity, particularly with strangers, and often accompanied by a jocularity and mental energy that, when mild and unfamiliar, may be considered engaging, even attractive or flattering. It is not unusual for (usually male) patients with this phenotype to be accompanied to the clinic by a second wife or partner, who later came to recognise the changed personality pattern as unstable and maladaptive. Friendliness and lack of inhibitions quickly become embarrassing, as social rules and sensitivities become invisible and behaviour ever more childlike. Impulsivity develops, and complaints and Police involvement often follow.

The onset of apathy is commonly mistaken for an episode of depression, and treated with a sequence of antidepressant drugs. Unlike depression, however, apathy does not resolve but instead deepens, with taciturnity, emotional unresponsiveness and insensitivity to the needs or feelings of others, becoming dominant characteristics.

The obsessionality dimension comprises perhaps the most complex set of traits. Patients may become fixated on particular activities, television shows, musical genres or even individual tunes. There is low tolerance of novelty and an impatience to return to the comfort of the established routine. Activities take precedence over the needs or desires of others, to whom patients display a distressing lack of concern. Most patients with this variety of Frontotemporal dementia resist participating in clinical assessments, as they cannot understand the purpose of them, and when they do attend may appear restless and resentful. Together with the absence of any overt sense of interpersonal engagement their attitude is easily misconstrued as one of hostility.

3   'Hubris Syndrome' Variant FTD

The above sketches of the three most recognisable behavioural phenotypes of FTD may give the impression that patients with this form of dementia can easily be categorised as either disinhibited/impulsive, apathetic or obsessional, but this turns out to be doubly untrue. In the first place, a patient may start with features of predominant disinhibition, only to turn more apathetic as the spread of neuropathology begins to involve new brain regions. And secondly, like colours in a landscape painting such traits, whilst individually recognisable when examined close-to, usually co-exist with other features to produce a compound aggregate that makes each individual patient unique. The central contention of this chapter is that there is a commingling of traits that uniquely causes the patient to develop features of the Hubris Syndrome.

Look again at some of the descriptive terms that I used above to describe the clinical characteristics of disturbance along each of the main behavioural dimensions: the social confidence that initially makes the disinhibited sufferer an attractive prospect as a mate; the impulsivity that prevents proper, careful evaluation of a situation before a decision is taken; and the erosion of the capacity to listen to and understand the needs of others. These exact same deficiencies—albeit in the context of a struggling organisation rather than of a degenerating brain—typify some of the core features of Hubris Syndrome as originally postulated by Owen and Davidson. Impulsivity itself forms part of symptom 12, while intolerance of the advice of others is central to symptom 7 (excessive confidence in their own judgment and contempt for the advice or criticism of others); in many FTD cases there is a lack of insight (symptom 11: 'loss of contact with reality; often associated with progressive isolation') that can be profoundly disturbing and is often significantly harmful to their welfare (cf. symptom 14: 'Hubristic incompetence'). An appeal to the divine for judgement is not seen, though hyperreligiosity does develop as a distinctive feature in a subgroup of patients (Miller et al. 2001).

So, in principle, a cocktail of impulsivity, confidence and insightlessness may give rise to a 'Hubris Syndrome phenotype' of FTD. The following case history should show that this theoretical phenotype can indeed be identified in practice.

AB was in her early fifties when I first met her in my cognitive neurology outpatient clinic, but changes in her behaviour and personality had been noted several years earlier by both her husband and her employer (a company chief executive to whom AB had been a trusted, and highly valued, PA for more than a decade). She had originally been referred to the company's occupational health department because of problems (noted by others but ignored by herself) transitioning to new, electronically-based working practices in place of the paper diaries and meticulously kept notebooks on which she had previously relied.

Around the same time her husband was noticing that she had developed a tendency to 'stubborn and unreasonable' behaviour that he had never before known in her. She became a stickler for rules and regulations, delighting in both obeying them and criticising others for not doing so. She had also developed a tendency to highly uncharacteristic displays of disinhibition (such as dancing to music in public places) that were completely out of character for her. A diagnosis of reactive depression was made, and she was given counselling and drugs, but her difficulties failed to improve. I requested a magnetic resonance imaging brain scan, which revealed marked and assymetric loss of volume in both frontal and both temporal lobes, with the greater emphasis on right hemisphere structures.

Inevitably, the clinical situation progressed: she became harshly critical of people close to her, particularly when they tried to offer her advice. It was not long before AB was forced to leave her job, a turn of events that she completely failed to understand, and against which she forcefully protested. She developed a sweet tooth and stereotyped dietary preferences for fried chicken and fish, which she had to eat every day at exactly the same time. She became restless and unpredictable, and engaged only reluctantly with care staff, whom she treated abruptly and contemptuously. Continuous supervision and eventually institutional care became unavoidable after AB developed features of hypersexuality and public exhibitionism, and was taken into Police custody on several occasions before being transferred to specialist residential accommodation.

There can be little doubt that AB's behavioural abnormalities developed in response to the accumulation of neurodegenerative changes in her brain: the evolution was gradual to the point of imperceptibility; the core features of disinhibition and rigidity dominated the change in personality; there was no response to antidepressant medication; and she remained stubbornly unaccepting of any problems and any reason not to carry on working, until late into her disease course. (I lost touch with AB after she was admitted to a residential home specialising in young onset dementia in a different part of the United Kingdom, but it is unknown for insight to return, once lost, in these circumstances).

What is also apparent, however, is a marked similarity between the overall *Gestalt* of AB's new personality and the features that are typical of leaders with Hubris Syndrome: she showed no hint of apathy as long as I knew her, remaining restless (as well as reckless and impulsive) throughout the first few years of her illness. She was, moreover, convinced that she was always in the right about everything, and was unable to understand why others were so incompetent in comparison to her: when I interviewed her without her husband she focused intently on his organisational and intellectual deficiencies, and when I interviewed her husband alone he told me that AB found me an incompetent and ill-informed doctor. Hypersexuality has occasionally been discussed in the context of hubristic leadership, and examples of sexual indiscretion coming to light after hubristic incompetence has led to a fall from grace (and immunity from adverse publicity) are not hard to find.

I would therefore argue that the overlap between these two clinical entities is not coincidental, but rather reflects a dysfunction in a common set of brain structures that, when functioning normally, ensure effective self-monitoring, particularly in response to the reactions of other people. The critical difference being, of course, that in one disorder the dysfunction is reversible, while in the other it is relentlessly progressive. As to what these critical brain structures may be, it is worth going into the pathological anatomy of FTD in a little more detail, to understand how the behavioural changes may arise.

4   Neuropathology and Neuroanatomy of FTD

Understanding of the molecular processes that cause disruption in neurodegenerative conditions has advanced rapidly over that past decade: many of the common dementia pathologies result from the deposition of structurally altered proteins that accumulate in healthy tissue in the form of insoluble aggregates, such as the amyloid plaques and neurofibrillary tangles seen in Alzheimer's disease, or the intracellular deposits of altered tau protein that cause neuronal dysfunction and death in some forms of FTD. It is usually assumed that these pathological processes accumulate over a period of time measured in years or even decades, and that mild cognitive disruption occurs when there is still a relatively low pathological load. It is also generally accepted that the location of these early changes determines the clinical patterns that emerges in the early clinical stages and that, as pathology accumulates, neuronal cells cease to function, die and disappear, resulting in the process of initially localised, but eventually global, brain atrophy.

By contrast, a neural account of the processes by which the brain supports particular types of cognitive ability seems a long way off, though the study of patients with brain damage remains one of the most informative ways of gaining relevant insights. All clinical syndromes involving cognitive decline occur when one or more of the neural systems that contribute to higher levels of cerebral function begin to operate at a suboptimal level. The contribution that a system or systems make to the achievement of a goal determines the effects that its impairment will have on the performance of a task that depends on the goal in question. To illustrate this point with a concrete example: the task of expressing a spoken opinion in a public place will be impaired if the would-be speaker is unable to achieve the goal of sufficient confidence, or if he lacks knowledge of the grammatical structure or the sounds and meanings of the words in the language in which he aims to communicate. A sudden failure of articulacy could result from any one or any combination of these goals not being achieved, which in turn could be due to failure at the level of one or more neural systems. A skilful observer may be able to distinguish between candidate mechanisms by reasoning from more fine-grained characteristics of the performance, and even form a conjecture as to the location of the damaged region within the brain. This may seem like a coarse level of resolution, but it characterises most of what we know of the neuroanatomical basis of brain function at this higher, cognitive level.

5   Defining and Identifying Clinical Subtypes

Many clinical observations take place at this automatic 'pattern recognition' level, and this is especially likely to occur when the to-be-recognised patterns have variable and compound characteristics, as has already been argued to be the case in behavioural variant FTD. As exposure to new clinical examples accumulates a process of learning takes place, which leads to the creation of a 'model' in which cases are more or less similar to one another. Groups of instances will emerge that are similar to those within the same 'cluster' and very dissimilar from others. The model may then start to become organised around these clusters, the existence of which will begin to exert a process of attraction on new instances, such that similarity is defined in an increasingly 'top-down' fashion. A well-developed model may support the formation of prototypical examples of each cluster, the salient features of which should remain relatively constant across observers.

The above model, based on experiential learning, is not formed with reference to the similarity of an instance to a pre-existing 'gold standard'. Rather, the model's dimensions and their values in individual instances emerge as a result of repeated exposure to examples. This process contrasts with the sort of clinical instinct or 'nose' that develops in other situations and leads to rapid recognition of a condition whose presence is later confirmed using an objective test (such as a stroke or heart attack).

In both of the above examples of the development of clinical knowledge there are striking similarities to types of formal computational models that are defined in the field of machine learning (Bishop 2006). In the former case, the emergence of clusters from similarities and differences among training examples, would be driven by 'unsupervised learning' algorithms. In the latter, the ability to classify a new instance as a member of one or another class on the basis of a set of example class members, is a form of 'supervised learning'. The comparison is, of course, intentional, and is partly meant to illustrate of how expert knowledge can be (and is increasingly becoming) instantiated in computational systems that can be continuously updated on the basis of newly acquired data.

A fully generalizable machine learning model of FTD would naturally entail the existence of a common and reproducible language of description, to ensure that all clinical observations are of equivalent value (that is, not weighted by prior assumptions about their importance). Many large research-oriented clinical institutes have developed checklists of symptoms that can be endorsed by a patient's relative or carer, to create a cognitive profile of the patient and as a means of monitoring and identifying salient changes at serial clinical assessments. The questionnaire used in the St. George's clinic covers symptoms that are relevant to both cognitive and social domains, and is reproduced at the end of this chapter. The Neuropsychiatric Inventory (NPI) is a more widely used instrument, and has an exclusive focus on symptoms in the social domain, which overlap with many of the features of psychosis and other psychiatric conditions, and may additionally have the potential to capture instances of hubristic behaviour disorders, such as the Hubris Syndrome and the putative Hubris Syndrome presentation of FTD (Cummings 1997).

The NPI consists of twelve major symptom types, within each of which the informant is asked to endorse one or more examples. For instance, the very first section deals with the phenomenon of delusional beliefs, and lists the following possible scenarios, which the informant is invited to endorse (or, alternatively, confirm to be absent):

1. Does the patient believe that he/she is in danger, or that others are planning to hurt him/her?
2. Does the patient believe that others are stealing from him/her?
3. Does the patient believe that his/her spouse is having an affair?
4. Does the patient believe that unwelcome guests are living in his/her house?
5. Does the patient believe that his/her spouse or others are not who they claim to be?
6. Does the patient believe that his/her house is not her/her home?
7. Does the patient believe that family members plan to abandon him/her?
8. Does the patient believe that television or magazine figures are actually present in the home?
9. Does the patient believe any other unusual things that I haven't asked about?

Similar choices attach to the remaining symptoms, namely: hallucinations; agitation/aggression; depression/dysphoria; anxiety; elation/euphoria; apathy/indifference; disinhibition; irritability/lability; aberrant motor Hubris Syndrome; sleep and appetite/eating disorders. Each one of the multiple scenarios that are suggested under these headings may be endorsed for frequency and severity.

6   Machine Learning Approaches to Understanding Clinical Subtypes in FTD

If we assume that the above inventory of personality changes forms at least a subset of those that are observable in all cases of the Hubris Syndrome variant of FTD, then an unsupervised machine learning model may naturally identify clusters of similarly affected patients simply by virtue of their similarities within the feature space. Such an approach has been used to look for symptom combinations that characterise different forms of dementia. Bozeat et al. (2000), for example, subjected symptom questionnaire data to a data reduction procedure (principal components analysis) that identified groups of complaints that tended to occur together. They identified four robust clusters, which represented stereotypic or compulsive behaviours, self-monitoring ability, mood disturbance, and impairment of insight. A similar methodology has not been used (or at least not reported) to look for symptom clusters specifically within populations of FTD patients. This may be partly because systematic study on a large enough scale of patients with behavioural variant FTD is hampered by the relative rarity of the condition (its prevalence is estimated as being around 15 cases per 100,000 population (Ratnavalli et al. 2002)), and the reluctance of some patients and their families to take part in such observational research.

When data does become available in sufficient quantities to support this approach, we will not only be able to infer clinically useful information about how such patients should best be categorised, but also to relate the resulting symptom clusters to regional patterns of brain degradation. The latter aim necessitates a further statistical step in which correlations are sought between measures of severity in some cognitive domain and the extent of physical degradation within small parcellations of structural data (voxels) comprising an image of a set of normal and diseased brains. When these correlations form regional (i.e. *spatial*) clusters it can be assumed that the regions involved are critical to the cognitive domain or task used in the correlation analysis. Relative difficulty with speech production would, for instance, be expected to show a cluster of correlations in the inferior frontal region of the left cerebral hemisphere. In a recent and relevant application of these techniques, Hornberger et al. (2011) showed that abnormalities in the medial orbitofrontal regions of the prefrontal cortex of patients with bvFTD (highlighted in Fig. 4) correlated significantly with a tendency to disinhibition. In addition to disinhibition data derived from the NPI, Hornberger et al. examined patients' performance on a test of the ability to suppress (i.e. inhibit) an impulse to initiate an 'obvious but incorrect' response. They administered the Hayling test (Burgess and Shallice 1997), which requires the subject to supply the final word of a sentence with a word unconnected to its meaning. For example, after hearing the sentence fragment 'He posted the letter without a…', 'STAMP' is so overwhelmingly the most probable closing word that the temptation to utter it requires effortful suppression, to allow the instruction ('complete this sentence with a word *unconnected* to its meaning') to be followed, and

NPI – disinhibition frequency

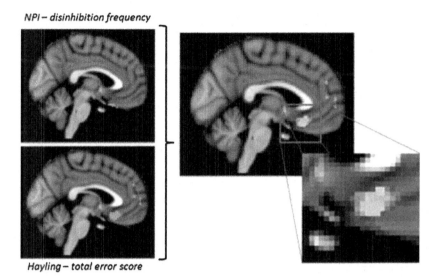

Hayling – total error score

Fig. 1 Overlap between areas of grey matter atrophy correlating with total error score on the Hayling test and areas correlating with the reported frequency of disinhibition in the Neuropsychiatric Inventory, in patients with behavioural variant FTD [From: Hornberger et al. Brain (2011). Reproduced by permission of the author.]

a word such as 'KANGAROO' produced instead. The coloured areas in Fig. 1 indicate that volume loss in both orbitofrontal regions is significantly correlated with these measures of disinhibition. Hornberger et al.'s findings provide additional evidence that these areas may be critical to the emergence of the disinhibited FTD phenotype described above.

7   A 'Hubris Syndrome' BvFTD Phenotype?

I began this chapter by describing some of the striking behavioural changes that support a diagnosis of the acquired personality disorder that has come to be known as Hubris Syndrome. I then went on to explore the concept of personality, to describe some of the circumstances under which brain damage may result in personality change, and how an understanding of the anatomy of these physical changes and their relationship with clusters of abnormal clinical subtypes can inform an understanding of how personality comes to be represented, and distorted, at the neural level. This line of enquiry leads naturally to the question of whether the cluster of behavioural features that appear in Hubris syndrome, similar to the single case that I described from my personal clinical experience, may be more routinely identified in a subset of patients with FTD. Finding a 'Hubris Syndrome-like phenotype' of FTD would provide strong supportive evidence for a neurological origin, or at least a neurological component, for the phenomenon. Moreover, it may allow the dysfunctional systems involved in HS to be identified, such that those vulnerable to developing the syndrome could be more readily identified, and rational approaches to ameliorating its effects developed.

It may not be coincidental that many of the neural structures that undergo progressive erosion in the context of FTD are implicated in dysfunction within the dopamine-mediated reward pathways that develop in patients with pathological addictions to alcohol, drugs or gambling (Berke and Hyman 2000), or those who develop impulse control disorders in response to traumatic brain injury or exposure to drugs that act centrally at dopamine receptors (Weintraub et al. 2010). It is also worth noting that the development of both addiction and the Hubris Syndrome are subject to susceptibility effects, rather than an inevitable consequence of exposure to certain substances or to extreme power. In that case, it is conceivable that the sense of reward that is surely induced by the successful exercise of power—by Tony Blair after Kosovo, for example, or Margaret Thatcher as she approached the end of her long period in office—could exert a powerful distorting effect on an individual's judgement, leading them to prioritize repeated achievement of the reward over short and long term goals that may be more important to their personal (and political) survival. Under this analysis, power would be analogous to a drug and Hubris syndrome to an addiction, to which certain personality types (perhaps disproportionally represented among those who are driven to seek office) are dangerously susceptible.

8   Questions for Future Research

A systematic, unbiased approach is required involving large numbers (probably several hundreds) of patients with behavioural variant FTD, whose symptoms have been documented using a common clinical vocabulary, is required to determine whether a Hubris Syndrome-like state or symptom cluster emerges regularly in the early stages of the condition, and if so, with what frequency it does so. Unsupervised machine learning algorithms, such as cluster analyses, could be employed to identify groups of symptoms that often co-occur, and the personality dimensions along which these clusters lie scrutinised for their similarity to the Hubris Syndrome phenotype. It would be hypothesised that among the dimensions to emerge disinhibition would be a very powerful one, as disinhibition is a common and dominant clinical feature of the condition. Similarly with apathy, which would probably dominate a different dimension and account for a considerable proportion of the overall variability of the data. Impulsivity would also be likely to be reflected by the co-occurrence of a particular symptom subset, whilst others may be describable in terms of extreme overconfidence, loss of insight, and possibly even a contemptuous disregard for the advice of others.

The delineation of these major dimensions would create a multidimensional 'feature space' within which the clinical features of each individual case could be plotted. A portion of the space would correspond to the clinical features of the Hubris Syndrome variant of FTD, and my anecdotal case described above would be found within this region. The number of other cases within this region of the space would provide an estimate of how frequently the subtype comes to clinical attention. If sufficient cases also had MR imaging available, then neuroanatomical associations between a position on any dominant dimension and atrophy within a particular region could also be sought, providing insights into the neural structures whose integrity is important in the regulation of different forms of behaviour and different types of personality. Any overlap between the regions correlating with the 'hubristic symptom dimensions' and the frontal-subcortical 'reward' circuits that are known to become dysregulated in patients with different forms of addiction, would represent additional evidence of a common mechanism underlying both states, and could eventually lead to the development of targeted treatments to prevent or reverse the deleterious effects of such traits. Genetic variants (such as the possession of one or more copies of variant forms of the gene encoding the enzyme Catechol-O-methyltransferase, which may have mechanistic significance in a subgroup of FTD patients) could also be looked for across patients occupying different regions of symptom space, with a view to creating a risk profile for FTD subtypes, and hence identifying those at greatest risk of Hubris Syndrome before it was able to do very much damage.

Appendix

The St. George's cognitive symptom questionnaire

References

Allport, G. W. (1937). *Personality: A psychological interpretation*. New York: H. Holt and Company.

Berke, J., & Hyman, S. E. (2000). Addiction, dopamine and the molecular mechanisms of memory. *Neuron, 25*, 515–532.

Bishop, C. M. (2006). *Pattern recognition and machine learning*. New York: Springer.

Bozeat, S., Gregory, C. A., Lambon Ralph, M. A., & Hodges, J. R. (2000). Which neuropsychiatric features distinguish frontal and temporal variants of frontotemporal dementia from Alzheimer's disease? *Journal of Neurology, Neurosurgery and Psychiatry, 69*, 178–186.

Burgess, P., & Shallice, T. (1997). *The Hayling and Brixton tests*. Thurston, Suffolk: Pearson.

Cattell, R. B. (1965). *The scientific analysis of personality*. Baltimore: Penguin Books.

Cummings, J. L. (1997). The Neuropsychiatric Inventory: Assessing psychopathology in dementia patients. *Neurology, 48*, S10–S16.

Damasio, A. (2008). *Decartes' error: Emotion, reason and the human brain*. London: Vintage Books.

Eysenck, H. J. (1953). The scientific study of personality. *British Journal of Statistical Psychology, 6*, 1–59.

Garrard, P. (2014a). On the linguistics of power (and the power of linguistics). In P. Garrard & G. Robinson (Eds.), *The intoxication of power*. London: Palgrave Macmillan.

Garrard, P., Rentoumi, V., Lambert, C., & Owen, D. (2014b). Linguistic biomarkers of Hubris Syndrome. *Cortex, 55*, 167–181.

Harlow, J. M. (1868). Recovery from the passage of an iron bar through the head. *Publications of the Massachussetts Medical Society, 2*, 327–347.

Hornberger, M., Geng, J., & Hodges, J. R. (2011). Convergent grey and white matter evidence of orbitofrontal cortex changes related to disinhibition in behavioural variant frontotemporal dementia. *Brain, 134*, 2502–2512.

Miller, B. I., Seeley, W. W., Mychack, P., Rosen, H. J., Mena, I., & Boone, K. (2001). Neuroanatomy of the self: Evidence from patients with frontotemporal dementia. *Neurology, 57*, 817–821.

Owen, D. (2012). *Hubris Syndrome: Bush, Blair and the intoxication of power*. London: Methuen.

Owen, D., & Davidson, J. (2009). Hubris Syndrome: An acquired personality disorder? A study of US presidents and UK prime ministers over the last 100 years. *Brain, 132*, 1396–1406.

Ratnavalli, E., Brayne, C., Dawson, K., & Hodges, J. R. (2002). The prevalence of frontotemporal dementia. *Neurology, 58*, 1615–1621.

Weintraub, D., Koester, J., & Potenza, M. N. (2010). Impulse control disorders in Parkinson disease: A cross-sectional study of 3090 patients. *Archives of Neurology, 67*, 585–595.

Young, H. (1998). *The blessed plot: Britain and Europe from Churchill to Blair*. Oxford: Macmillan.

2

From Molecule to Market

John Coates, Mark Gurnell and Zoltan Sarnyai

1 Introduction

Emotions are commonly viewed as subcortical eruptions impairing the rational guidance of behaviour. However, certain authors (e.g. Damasio 1994; LeDoux 1996; Loewenstein et al. 2001) have disputed this contrast, suggesting that rationality by itself would be overwhelmed and directionless were information not emotionally tagged for significance. Nonetheless, lapses of rationality continue to be blamed on emotional interference. This is especially true of irrational risk-reward choices made during financial market bubbles and crashes, choices considered by many as instances of irrational exuberance and pessimism overwhelming rational economic agency (Shiller 2005). However, there are

J. Coates (✉)
Dewline Research, London, UK

M. Gurnell · Z. Sarnyai
University of Cambridge, Cambridge, UK

Z. Sarnyai
James Cook University, Townsville, Australia

© The Author(s) 2018
P. Garrard (ed.), *The Leadership Hubris Epidemic*,
https://doi.org/10.1007/978-3-319-57255-0_2

grounds for believing that the emotions of euphoria and fear displayed in markets may be more accurately described as shifts in confidence and risk preferences, caused by elevated levels of steroid hormones.

Steroids are a class of hormone, hormones being chemical messengers sent from one part of the body or brain to another, bringing about a change in the target tissue. The major classes of hormones include amines (such as adrenaline and noradrenaline), peptides and proteins (such as oxytocin and leptin) and steroids (such as testosterone, oestradiol and cortisol). Steroids are lipids cleaved from cholesterol by a series of enzymatic modifications, with the major sites of bio-synthesis being the gonads and the adrenal cortex, although some neurosteroids, such as pregnenolone, can be synthesized directly by neurons and glial cells in the brain (Baulieu 1997).

Steroids constitute a particularly influential class of hormones because of their range of action. With receptors in almost every nucleated cell in the body, they affect growth, metabolism, immune function, mood, memory, cognition and behaviour. Steroids are of special interest for the study of emotions and economic behaviour because they help coordinate body and brain in archetypical situations, such as fight, flight, mating, feeding, search and struggle for status. Because they are known to respond powerfully to such social situations, steroid hormones may provide an important missing link in the emerging field of neuroeconomics between economic events and brain processes. Here, we review the relevant literature on two steroids that may help provide this link—testosterone and cortisol.

2   Steroid Hormones

2.1   Testosterone and the Hypothalamic-Pituitary-Gonadal Axis

Testosterone is produced by the Leydig cells of the testes, in smaller quantities by the ovaries, and by the adrenal cortex in both sexes. The sex steroids, testosterone and oestrogen, are regulated by a series of glands acting in concert—the hypothalamic–pituitary–gonadal (HPG)

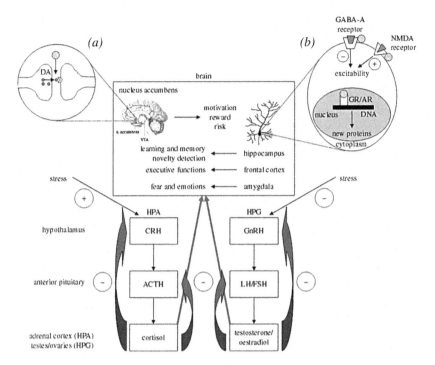

Fig. 1 Schematic representation of the HPA and HPG axes and their effects on brain function. **a** Effects of steroid hormones on dopaminergic neurotransmisson in the nucleus accumbens; **b** genomic and non-genomic effects of steroids in the brain; for more details see text. *GABA* g-aminobutyric acid; *NMDA* N-methyl-D-aspartate; *GR* glucocorticoid receptor; *AR* androgen receptor; *plus* stimulatory effect; *minus* inhibitory effect; *dotted circles* steroid hormones (either glucocorticoid or testosterone); *grey-shaded* symbols cognate ligands for other receptors

axis (Fig. 1). Sex steroids orchestrate reproductive function, regulating spermatogenesis in males, the menstrual cycle in females and sexually relevant and other forms of motivated behaviours in both genders (Reichlin 1998). Gonadotrophin-releasing hormone (GnRH), synthesized by a small group of neurons in the hypothalamus, is transported axonally to the median eminence where it is released in a pulsatile manner into the hypothalamic–pituitary portal circulation (a network of blood vessels connecting the hypothalamus with the pituitary gland). GnRH then acts on the anterior pituitary gonadotrophs—cells responsible for the production of luteinizing hormone (LH) and follicle-stimulating hormone (FSH). When LH and FSH are released into the bloodstream in response to GnRH stimulation, they travel to the gonads—the ovaries in females and the testes in males.

In females, carefully coordinated actions of LH and FSH facilitate follicular maturation and subsequent ovulation in response to rising oestrogen levels. Progesterone levels rise in the second half (luteal phase) of ovulatory cycles, and help maintain the corpus luteum. In males, FSH is a critical regulator of spermatogenesis, while LH stimulates the production of testosterone. Reactivation of the HPG axis at puberty, and the consequent secretion of testosterone, causes maturation of the reproductive organs and development of secondary sexual characteristics. Testosterone has marked anabolic effects, promoting development of the musculature and increased bone growth, and contributing, with pituitary-derived growth hormone, to a rapid increase in height at puberty (the so-called 'growth spurt'). Oestrogen, progesterone and testosterone—together with inhibin, which is produced by the gonads in response to FSH action—inhibit the production and release of GnRH, LH and FSH in order to maintain the homeostasis of the system, with the HPG axis being subject to tight feedback control at all levels (Reichlin 1998).

As well as controlling the female menstrual cycle and male spermatogenesis, gonadal steroids also affect sexual behaviour (Vadakkadath et al. 2005). Importantly, they have been shown to exert both organizational and activational effects. The former refers to the fact that sexual differentiation of the brain can be permanently altered by the presence or absence of sex steroids at key stages in development. For example, administration of androgens to female rats within a few days of birth results in long-term virilization of behaviour. Conversely, neonatal castration of male rats causes them to develop as females (Phoenix et al. 1959; Breedlove and Hampson 2002). Similar, but less complete, virilization of female offspring has been demonstrated following androgen administration in non-human primates. Brain development in the absence of sex steroids follows female lines, but is switched to the male pattern by exposure of the hypothalamus to androgen at a key stage of development. After puberty, androgens cause a feeling of well-being, an increase in physical vigour and increased libido. Testosterone's contribution to aggression and other forms of impulsive and risk-taking behaviours remains the subject of intense debate, and we return to this literature below.

2.2 Cortisol and the Hypothalamic-Pituitary-Adrenal Axis

Cortisol, the main human glucocorticoid, is produced and regulated by the hypothalamic–pituitary–adrenal (HPA) axis (Fig. 1). This axis is critical to maintaining normal physiological homeostasis, and it regulates diverse processes, including metabolism, cardiovascular biology, immune function/inflammatory responses and cognitive function—indeed disorders of cortisol secretion (e.g. Addison's disease—cortisol deficiency; Cushing's syndrome—cortisol excess) are associated with considerable excess morbidity and mortality if left untreated. The system operates in a hierarchical manner similar to the HPG axis. Corticotropin-releasing hormone (CRH) is produced by neurons in the paraventricular nucleus of the hypothalamus, which project to the base of the hypothalamus, the median eminence. In response to a stressful stimulus, CRH is released from axon terminals into the hypothalamic–pituitary portal circulation, and reaches the anterior pituitary where it promotes the synthesis and secretion of adrenocorticotropic hormone (ACTH) by pituitary corticotrophs. ACTH then travels through the bloodstream to reach the adrenal glands (situated bilaterally above the kidneys) where it stimulates the synthesis and release of adrenal glucocorticoid hormones (cortisol in humans and other primates, corticosterone in rodents; Buckingham 1998) and adrenal androgens (e.g. dehydroepiandrosterone (DHEA)).

Glucocorticoids play a key role in helping the body adapt to changing circumstances in both its internal and external environments. Biologically, glucocorticoids facilitate the mobilization of resources to meet demand, including effects on intermediary metabolism, carbohydrate and protein metabolism, as well as acting as potent regulators of our endogenous 'defence' mechanisms, including the innate and adaptive immune responses (Buckingham 1998). Owing to their highly lipophilic nature, they can enter the brain easily and exert widespread effects on emotions, cognition, and the response to stress (de Kloet 2000).

However, chronic, as opposed to acute, elevation of circulating gluco-corticoids may have a number of adverse effects on the body and brain. In its most extreme form (i.e. Cushing's syndrome), hypercortisolism may lead to excessive weight gain (especially abdominal fat), muscle wasting, severe metabolic dysfunction (with resistance to the action of insulin and in some cases overt diabetes mellitus), hypertension, impaired wound healing and enhanced susceptibility to opportunistic infections. Similarly, prolonged supraphysiological glucocorticoid expo-sure may have deleterious effects on the brain, leading to depression and in extreme cases psychosis, as well as atrophy of the hippocampus, a brain region playing a central role in learning and memory (Sapolsky et al. 2000). Therefore, in order to avoid the undesirable consequences of glucocorticoid excess, the HPA axis is tightly regulated by a sensitive negative feedback loop, similar to that operating in the HPG axis: when glucocorticoid levels are high, CRH and ACTH secretion are downreg-ulated: as cortisol levels subsequently fall, feedback inhibition of hypo-thalamic–pituitary function is removed and CRH and ACTH secretion increase, which in turn restores adrenal cortisol production.

2.3   Steroid Receptors: Mechanism of Action of Steroid Hormones

The principles governing the interactions of steroid hormones with their cellular receptors are the same for adrenal and gonadal-derived sex steroids (Gurnell et al. 2017) and will be considered together for the purpose of this review. Steroid hormones are highly lipid soluble: they easily enter cells through the outer membrane. Once inside the cell, they bind to high-affinity receptors that belong to the nuclear receptor superfamily of ligand-gated transcription factors. For steroid hormones such as cortisol, oestrogen and testosterone, this process of binding to their receptors occurs outside of the nucleus in the cyto-plasm. Hormone-bound receptor then traffics into the nucleus where it seeks out, and interacts with, specific regions of the DNA to control the rate at which target genes are 'switched on' (activation) or 'switched off' (repression) (Fig. 1) (Tsai and O'Malley 1994; Funder 1997). In so doing, steroid hormones are able to increase or decrease the rate at which the cell synthesizes new proteins, and in this way change the structure and/or function of the cell, and the tissues made up of these cells.

These nuclear receptor-mediated events are relatively slow, usually taking several hours, and reflect the need for up- or downregulation of new protein synthesis. However, steroids also exert effects that can be observed within seconds, and these effects cannot be explained by the classic, genomic mechanisms. Instead, steroid hormones appear to act in a non-genomic manner to more rapidly alter cellular function (Falkenstein et al. 2000). Steroid receptors have been found in extranuclear sites in the hippocampus and in many other brain regions (McEwen and Milner 2007). These membrane-associated receptors are connected to a number of intracellular signalling pathways, such as growth factor signalling, kinases and phosphatases, to influence cell function or indirectly alter gene expression in order to support functional and structural plasticity of the nervous system (McEwen and Milner 2007). Furthermore, a particular subclass of steroid hormones, the neuro-active steroids (metabolites of the peripheral steroidogenic pathway, e.g. pregnenolone and DHEA and their sulphated forms (DHEAS)), together with neurosteroids (i.e. those produced by neurons de novo), can rapidly alter neural excitability by acting as allosteric modulators on neurotransmitter-gated ion channels, such as the g-aminobutyric acid type A (GABA-A) and N-methyl-D-aspartate (NMDA) receptors in the brain (Fig. 1). In this way, steroids are able to influence emotions and mood within a narrow time frame (Baulieu 1997).

2.4   Androgens, Glucocorticoids and Brain Function

Recent work in neuroscience and economics has begun to elucidate how various brain regions process decisions and behaviours that violate the tenets of rational choice theory. Among these are the amygdala, which has been associated with framing effects (De Martino 2006) and ambiguity aversion (Hsu et al. 2005); the nucleus accumbens, associated with irrational risk-seeking (Matthews et al. 2004; Kuhnen and Knutson 2005); and the insula, associated with irrational risk aversion (Kuhnen and Knutson 2005) and the rejection of monetary reward in the ultimatum game (Sanfey et al. 2003). The brain is a major target of steroid hormone action, with cortisol, testosterone and oestradiol (Dreher et al. 2007) regulating neural function in many regions that are now recognized to be involved in economic decision-making (such as the prefrontal cortex and hippocampus) as well as regions implicated in irrational or emotional response to financial cues (such as the amygdala and nucleus accumbens). The powerful effects of steroids on these key brain regions raise the possibility that the irrationality or emotionality displayed in financial decisions may be significantly influenced by the levels of steroid in the body.

Corticosteroids—glucocorticoid and mineralocorticoid produced by the adrenal cortex—have dense receptor fields in the brain, as first demonstrated by McEwen and colleagues, who showed specific accumulation of 3H-corticosterone in the rat hippocampus (McEwen et al. 1968). Glucocorticoids bind to both glucocorticoid (GR) and mineralocorticoid receptors (MR), the latter of which has 10-fold higher affinity for its ligand than the GR (Reul and de Kloet 1985). MRs maintain basal activity of the axis, whereas GRs enhance negative feedback when corticosterone levels rise in response to a stressor. While the GR has a widespread expression pattern throughout the brain, MR expression is mostly restricted to limbic brain regions such as the hippocampus, amygdala, the septum and some cortical areas (de Kloet et al. 1998), regions critically involved in learning and memory, modulation of emotional responses and inhibition of behaviour.

For the purpose of this article, the key neural target regions considered with respect to glucocorticoid action are the hippocampus, amygdala and the pre-frontal cortex (McEwen 2007). The hippocampus is essential for novelty detection and for the formation of declarative memory, underlying the conscious acquisition and recollection of facts and events (Scoville and Milner 1957). The prefrontal cortex, on the other hand, plays a key role in working memory, the cognitive mechanism that allows us to keep small amounts of information active for a limited period of time. The amygdala is particularly concerned with fear and emotions and mediates fear-conditioned memories.

The diverse actions of cortisol on human cognitive functions depend, among other factors, on the amount of hormone released, the length of exposure to cortisol, the emotional salience of the situation and the brain areas involved in dealing with the task. Low doses of glucocorticoids impair prefrontal, working memory, whereas high-dose or long-term administration results in an impairment in declarative (hippocampal) memory (Lupien et al. 2007). Furthermore, sustained elevation of corticosterone, or chronic stress, leads to plastic remodelling of neuronal structure in the hippocampus, amygdala and prefrontal cortex, as well as profound changes in functional plasticity, e.g. long-term potentiation (McEwen and Chattarji 2004; Liston et al. 2006). Specifically, chronic stress, through the activation of the HPA axis, decreases the number of apical dendrites of the CA3 pyramidal neurons of the hippocampus and increases the number of dendritic branches in the central nucleus of the amygdala (McEwen and Chattarji 2004). Furthermore, chronic stress induces a selective impairment in attentional set-shifting and a corresponding retraction of apical dendritic arbors in the medial prefrontal cortex (mPFC). In stressed rats, but not in controls, decreased dendritic arborization in the mPFC predicts impaired attentional set-shifting performance (Liston et al. 2006). Consistent with results obtained in rodents, psychosocial stress in humans selectively impairs attentional control and disrupts functional connectivity within a frontoparietal network that mediates attention shifts (Liston et al. 2009). These stress-induced, and perhaps glucocorticoid-mediated, changes in neuroplasticity may underlie altered cognitive functions, such as impaired attention, novelty detection and risk assessment, as well as anxiety and facilitated consolidation of emotionally negative memories, that are typical of chronic stress.

Cortisol, as well as testosterone, may crucially influence economic decision-making through its effects on the nucleus accumbens (or ventral striatum), a main forebrain target of the mesolimbic dopaminergic system. Dopaminergic neurotransmission in the nucleus accumbens underlies motivation and reward-related behaviours such as drug self-administration and reward prediction (Ikemoto and Panksepp 1999; Schultz 2000). One study also found the nucleus accumbens to fire in anticipation of irrational risk-seeking choices in a financial choice task (Kuhnen and Knutson 2005). Both corticosteroids and testosterone profoundly influence dopamine transmission in this region (Piazza and Le Moal 1997; Sarnyai et al. 1998; Frye et al. 2002). Both hormones are self-administered by experimental animals, indicating their reinforcing properties (Piazza et al. 1993; Sato et al. 2008).

Evidence of the 'rewarding property' of testosterone is also provided by the finding that it can stimulate a conditioned place preference when administered to rats (Schroeder and Packard 2000; Frye et al. 2002).

In humans there is evidence that anabolic steroids are addictive (Kashkin and Kleber 1989). It is thought that the rewarding properties of testosterone derive from the effect it and its metabolites, dihydrotestosterone and 3a-androstanediol, have of increasing dopamine release in the shell of the nucleus accumbens (Frye et al. 2002).

Cortisol has a complex pattern of effects on the nucleus accumbens. The activation of the HPA axis appears to be critically involved, through CRF and glucocorticoids, in different aspects of drug reward (Sarnyai et al. 2001). Acute stress increases extracellular dopamine levels, whereas chronic stress blunts the dopamine response and further inhibits dopamine outflow (Cabib and Puglisi-Allegra 1996). Chronic stress, through elevated corticosterone, appears to result in an increased dopamine D2 receptor density selectively in the shell of the nucleus accumbens (Lucas et al. 2007). D2 receptors are inhibitory autoreceptors that dampen dopamine release from the pre-synaptic terminal. Similarly, we have shown that chronic corticosterone treatment upregulates the binding of the dopamine transporter, which is responsible for the termination of dopamine's effect in the synapse, in the same brain region (Sarnyai et al. 1998). Others have shown long-lasting desensitization of dopamine receptor signalling caused by chronic stress (Choy et al. 2009). Therefore, it can be hypothesized that chronic stress induces an allostatic attenuation of the mesolimbic dopaminergic system, possibly due in part to persistent corticosterone elevation.

3   Steroid Hormones and Risk-Taking

3.1   Testosterone and Risk-Taking

Testosterone mediates sexual behaviour as well as competitive encounters, so there are prima facie reasons for believing it could also affect financial risk-taking. Research into how it may do so is, however, in its infancy. Much of the work on the cognitive and behavioural effects of androgens has instead studied humans taking anabolic steroids, studies that are pharmacological rather physiological because the steroids are taken in supra-physiological doses (Kashkin and Kleber 1989); or the work has studied animal behaviour, thus leaving open the question of the results' applicability to humans (Sapolsky 1997). The animal studies, besides those examining sexual behaviour, have focused largely on the effects of testosterone on mating, guarding and territorial aggression, and on competitions for rank within a social hierarchy. This research has been elegantly synthesized by the biologist John Wingfield in his highly influential challenge hypothesis.

According to the challenge hypothesis, testosterone in males rises to a minimum level required for sexual behaviour; it will continue to rise beyond this level only when males are confronted with an intruder or a social challenge, the increased testosterone promoting aggressive behaviour (Wingfield et al. 1990). The insights gained from the challenge hypothesis, and from animal hormone studies more generally, have been applied to human behaviour (Archer 2006), but often with questionable success. Many studies, for example, could not determine whether testosterone caused aggression or the other way round; others found testosterone levels were poor predictors of who subsequently became aggressive (Sapolsky 1997; Monaghan and Glickman 2001); still others did not distinguish between aggressive and non-aggressive risk-taking (Vermeersch et al. 2008). One problem with these studies stems from the fact that in humans, as in some non-human primates, higher cognitive functions refract the effects of testosterone, which in smaller brained animals are more deterministic. Furthermore, the dependent variables in these studies, such as aggression, dominance, or status seeking, often cannot be defined or measured in humans with any objectivity, leading to marginally significant experimental results and contradictory findings between papers (Archer et al. 1998).

Studies of steroids and financial risk-taking promise to overcome many of these difficulties. To begin with, financial variables, such as profit, variance of returns, volatility of the market, can be defined objectively and measured precisely. Furthermore, the competitive behaviour Wingfield and his colleagues observed in animals may manifest itself in humans, not so much in aggressive encounters as in competitive economic behaviour. Through its known effects on dopamine transmission in the nucleus accumbens, testosterone may well have its most powerful effects in humans by shifting their utility functions, state of confidence or financial risk preferences.

We began testing this hypothesis by setting up a series of experiments on a trading floor in the City of London (Coates and Herbert 2008). We chose to study professional traders because real risk-taking, with meaningful consequences, seemed most likely to trigger large endocrine reactions. Our hypothesis and predictions were based on the challenge hypothesis as well as a closely related model, the winner effect (see below). Biologists working with these models have noticed that two males entering a fight or contest experience androgenic priming in the form of elevated testosterone levels. Moreover, the winning male emerges with even greater levels of testosterone, the loser with lower ones. The orders of magnitude of these hormone swings can be large: Monaghan and Glickman (2001) report that in a competition for rank among recently introduced rhesus monkeys, the winning male emerged with a 10-fold increase in testosterone, while the loser experienced a drop to 10% of baseline levels within 24 hours, and these new levels for both winner and loser persisted for several weeks. This reaction may make sense from an evolutionary point of view: in the wild, the loser of a fight is encouraged to retire from the field and nurse his wounds while the winner prepares for new challenges to his recently acquired rank.

A similar result has been found in experiments with humans (Gladue et al. 1989). Athletes, for example, experience the same androgenic priming before a sporting contest, and a further increase in testosterone after a win. This experiment has been repeated for a number of different events, including tennis (Booth et al. 1989) and wrestling (Elias 1981), as well as less physical contests such as chess (Mazur et al. 1992). It has also been found that the rising and falling levels of an athlete's testosterone can be mimicked by fans: Bernhardt et al. (1998) took testosterone samples from fans during a World Cup match in which Brazil defeated Italy. Both sets of fans went into the game with elevated testosterone, but afterwards the Brazilian fans' testosterone levels rose while those of the Italians fell.

The role of these elevated testosterone levels is further explored in an animal model known as the 'winner effect'. In this model, winning in an agonistic encounter can itself contribute to a later win (Chase et al. 1994; Oyegbile and Marler 2005), an effect that is independent of (i) an animal's resource-holding potential (RHP), i.e. the physical resources it can draw on in an all-out fight, (ii) its motivation, i.e. the value of the resource in dispute, or (iii) its aggressiveness (Hurd 2006). It is not known if the win imparts information to winner and loser about their respective resources (Hsu and Wolf 2001; Rutte et al. 2006) or whether it has physiological effects. This latter possibility is suggested by experiments in which elevated testosterone has been found to contribute to further wins (Trainor et al. 2004; Oyegbile and Marler 2005). Another possibility not fully considered in the literature is that higher testosterone, through its beneficial effects on the cardiovascular system and muscle mass, may effectively increase an animal's RHP, or, through its effects on confidence and risk-taking, may increase an animal's motivation or aggressiveness (Neat et al. 1998). Whatever the mechanism, a winner, with heightened testosterone levels, may proceed to the next round of competition with an advantage. This positive feedback loop, in which victory raises testosterone which in turn raises the likelihood of later victories (Fig. 2), may help account for winning and losing streaks in round-robin animal competitions that establish a social hierarchy (Dugatkin and Druen 2004).

We examined the relevance of the challenge hypothesis and winner effect models to the financial markets (Coates and Herbert 2008) by looking for evidence that traders experience an increase in testosterone when they enjoy an above-average win in the markets. To do so, we sampled steroids from 17 young male traders, taking saliva samples

Fig. 2   Schematic representation of a winner effect mediated by testosterone

twice a day, at 11.00 and 16.00, over a period of eight consecutive business days. Hormone readings are notoriously noisy owing to the pulsatile nature of their production and release into the blood stream, hence our protocol of repeated sampling to help separate 'signal' from 'noise'. The traders were engaged in high-frequency trading, meaning that they positioned securities, mostly futures contracts in European and US bond and equity markets, in sizes up to £1 billion, but held their positions for a short period of time—several minutes, and sometimes mere seconds. They rarely positioned trades overnight, and they did not let winning or losing positions run for long.

We discovered that these traders did indeed have significantly higher testosterone levels on days when they made an above-average profit. We could not determine from this correlation whether the profits were raising hormone levels or vice versa, but since we took two samples per day, we could examine how morning testosterone levels were related to afternoon profits and losses (P&Ls). To do so, we looked at the days when each trader's 11.00 testosterone levels were above his median level during the study, these days showing testosterone levels a modest 25%

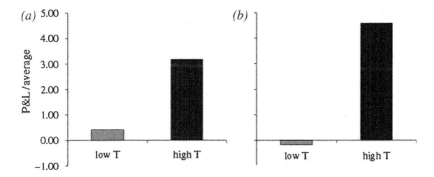

Fig. 3 P&L on low- and high-testosterone days. **a** P&L made between 11.00 and 16.00 for 17 traders on days when their testosterone levels were above their median level during the study ('high T') and on the rest of the days ('low T') ($n = 17$, paired t-test $p = 0.008$; Cohen's $d = 0.97$). P&Ls for each trader were standardized by dividing them by their 1-month average daily P&L. Standardized P&Ls were then averaged across all 17 traders, **b** Afternoon P&L for experienced traders only, i.e. ones with more than 2 years trading experience ($n = 10$, paired t-test $p = 0.005$; Cohen's $d = 1.37$)

higher than on the other days. We found that on days of high morning testosterone, the traders returned an afternoon profit (Fig. 3a) that was almost a full standard deviation higher than on 'low-testosterone' days. Interestingly, this relationship was even stronger among experienced traders (Fig. 3b), i.e. those who had traded for longer than 2 years, suggesting that testosterone, at moderate levels, was not having its effect by encouraging overly risky behaviour but was instead optimizing performance, at least with respect to high-frequency trading.

The effects of androgens on high-frequency trading were also evident in a second experiment, one that looked at a surrogate marker of pre-natal androgen exposure—the second to fourth digit (finger length) ratio (2D:4D) (Coates et al. 2009). As mentioned above, there are two distinct periods and types of hormone action—organizational effects of pre-natal steroids on the foetus and activational effects of circulating steroid on the adult. Androgens surge between the ninth and 18th week of gestation, masculinizing the foetus and exerting developmental changes on the body and brain that are permanent (Cohen-Bendahana et al. 2005). After the 19th week, androgen production subsides, spikes again briefly in the neonate and then drops back to low levels until the onset of puberty. At puberty, androgen production increases, activating the circuits created earlier in life by pre-natal hormone exposure. According to the organizational/activational model of hormone action (Phoenix et al. 1959), the sensitivity of adults to changes in circulating testosterone is a function of the amount of pre-natal androgen to which they were exposed (Meaney 1988; Breedlove and Hampson 2002).

Importantly, the amount of pre-natal androgen an individual was exposed to can be estimated because it leaves traces throughout the adult body, traces often measured by paediatricians looking for effects of environmental hormone disruptors on newborn infants. 2D:4D is the most convenient measure for studies (McIntyre 2006). A lower 2D:4D ratio is thought to indicate higher levels of pre-natal testosterone exposure (Manning et al. 1998; Brown et al. 2002). Consistent with this, men on average have lower ratios than women. We sampled 2D:4D from a total of 44 traders, including 14 from the first study, and found that it predicted both the traders' P&Ls over a 20-month period and the number of years they had survived in the business. It also predicted, in line with the organizational/activational model, the sensitivity of the trading performance of the original 14 traders to increases in circulating testosterone: the lower the trader's 2D:4D, the more money he made when his testosterone levels rose.

Pre-natal testosterone appears, therefore, to predict long-term success in high-frequency trading, a style of trading requiring quick physical and cognitive reactions. However, there are grounds for believing that in other types of trading, especially those permitting more time for analysis and a longer holding period, or ones that do not make such physical demands, the correlation may weaken and even reverse sign (Coates et al. 2009). The market, it appears, selects for biological traits but these traits may vary between market segments.

The two trading floor experiments described here raise troubling questions about the efficient markets hypothesis. If, as this hypothesis assumes, markets are random, then we should not be able to predict relative trading performance by means of biological traits. Yet, our results suggest that higher levels of circulating testosterone predict short-term profitability and higher levels of pre-natal testosterone predict long-term profitability, at least in the segment of the market inhabited by high-frequency traders. The implication seems to be that the markets are not efficient or that they select for traits other than rational expectations (De Bondt and Thaler 1987; Shiller 2005; Blume and Easley 2006).

This leads us to another important question: how could testosterone exert its effects on profitability? Field studies such as those reported above do not allow us to establish a causal relationship between testosterone and profits, merely a predictive relationship, albeit a strong one. To establish causality, one needs pharmacological manipulation. Some studies administering testosterone esters to eugonadal males have found significant but weak effects on mood and aggressiveness (Bhasin et al. 2001; O'Connor et al. 2004), although they were not examining financial tasks. However, converging evidence from other lines of research suggests that androgen may affect confidence and risk preferences. For example, administered testosterone promotes confidence and fearlessness in the face of novelty, a result observed in both animals (Boissy and Bouissou 1994) and humans (Hermans et al. 2006). Furthermore, in a between-subjects study of male students playing an investment game, testosterone levels correlated with risk preferences (Apicella et al. 2008). This study also examined 2D:4D and risk preferences, finding a significant correlation among Swedish Caucasians but not in a more ethnically heterogeneous population, the difference in results being accounted for by the fact that ethnic population is an important confound for 2D:4D.

Intriguingly, there is another potential path of causation between testosterone and trading profits. Trading, it is not often appreciated, is a physical activity, a demanding one, so the important effects of testosterone may be physical rather than cognitive. High testosterone levels or increased androgenic effects, for example, can increase vigilance and visuomotor skills such as scanning and speed of reactions (Salminen et al. 2004; Falter et al. 2006), qualities that may help traders to spot and trade price discrepancies before others arbitrage them away (Coates et al. 2009). Elevated testosterone levels have also been found to increase an animal's search persistence (Andrew and Rogers 1972) and, during search, to focus visual attention while decreasing distraction by irrelevant stimuli (Andrew 1991). These last traits may be of particular importance in high-frequency trading because this form of trading requires lengthy periods of visuomotor scanning and quick reactions.

An increase in confidence or risk preferences, as found in some studies, would tend to increase a trader's position size; an increase in search persistence the frequency of trading; an increase in reaction times the chances of getting to a trade before others. Given that the traders in our study had a positive expected return, i.e. they usually made money, larger positions or more frequent trades would translate into higher daily profits. However, we cannot at this point say by which route these effects travelled, that is, whether testosterone was having its effect by augmenting the effort, speed, confidence or risk preferences of the traders.

3.2   Cortisol and Risk-Taking

A review of research on cortisol and financial risk-taking is necessarily brief as there is almost no work done on this subject. Van Honk et al. (2003) looked at the cortisol levels of people playing the Iowa Gambling Task and found that they correlated with risk aversion. In our own studies, we hypothesized that cortisol, as a stress hormone, would increase as traders lost money. This seemed a reasonable assumption, but our experiment did not find evidence to support it, as we observed no relationship between trading losses, even above-average ones, and cortisol levels. However, caution is needed before extrapolating these findings, as the style of trading and the risk management practices on this trading floor prevented traders from losing large sums of money. Had they not done so, or had we sampled in a different setting, for example in an investment bank where traders position interest rate or credit risk for longer periods of time, and had these traders entered a sustained losing streak, it is likely they would have experienced high levels of stress and cortisol.

However, we did note a potentially more interesting finding—that cortisol was rising with uncertainty. Early research on stress and cortisol, especially the pioneering work of Hans Selye, focused on how cortisol production reacts to actual bodily harm. But later research found that the HPA axis can respond more robustly to expected harm and that the size of the response is an increasing function of the uncertainty over timing. For example, an animal receiving a shock at regular intervals or after a warning tone may have normal cortisol levels at the end of an experiment; in contrast, an animal receiving the same quantity of shock will experience rising cortisol levels as the timing of the shocks becomes more and more unpredictable, reaching a maximum when the timing becomes random (Levine et al. 1989). Animals can have a similarly elevated HPA response when exposed to situations of novelty (Erikson et al. 2003) or uncontrollability (Swenson and Vogel 1983; Breier et al. 1987). Uncertainty, novelty and uncontrollability can perhaps be reduced to a common denominator of uncertainty; all three describe a situation in which an animal finds it increasingly difficult to predict what may happen and what actions will be required. The necessity of being prepared for the unexpected signals to the body, via cortisol, that catabolic metabolism may be needed. As it transpires, 'uncertainty', 'novelty' and uncontrollability' aptly describe the financial markets and the environment in which traders find themselves on a daily basis.

To examine the effect of uncertainty on traders' HPA axes, we looked at the risk faced by each trader, as measured by the variance of his P&L, over the course of the study (Coates and Herbert 2008). We found a highly significant correlation with cortisol that once again displayed a large effect size. Variance in P&L is a measure of the uncertainty or uncontrollability a trader has just lived through; but we also wanted to measure how uncertain the traders were about upcoming events in the market, such as the release of important economic statistics. To do so, we used the implied volatility of the Bund futures contract (a future on German Government bonds), which was the security most widely traded by the traders in the study. Bond options require for their pricing the market's estimate of the future variance of the underlying asset, so option prices provide an objective measure of the market's collective uncertainty. Here, again we observed a very high and significant correlation between the traders' daily cortisol levels, averaged from all traders, and the market's uncertainty regarding upcoming market moves. Our results raise the possibility that while testosterone codes for economic return, cortisol codes for risk.

Our experiment represents only the mere beginning of research into the role of cortisol in financial decision-making. To underline our belief in the critical importance of this hormone, we should point out that the cortisol fluctuations we observed were large. In the normal course of a day, cortisol, like testosterone, peaks in the morning and falls over the course of the day. Between our sampling times, cortisol levels would be predicted to fall by approximately 40%, yet in many of our subjects it rose, in some cases by as much as 500%. Similar-sized cortisol fluctuations were also observed between days. What purpose do changes of this magnitude serve? Cortisol, as highlighted above, marshalls glucose for immediate use, and it promotes anticipatory arousal and a focused attention (Erikson et al. 2003). We speculate therefore that traders, when expecting a market move, would benefit from such an acute increase in cortisol, as it prepares them for the money-making opportunities that increased volatility brings.

3.3   Steroids and Impaired Risk-Taking

If market volatility or the variance in the traders' P&L were to remain high, cortisol levels could also remain elevated for an extended period. Chronically elevated cortisol levels, as we have seen, can have the opposite effect on cognitive performance as acute levels. Cortisol displays an inverted U-shaped dose–response curve, according to which performance on a range of cognitive and behavioural tasks is optimized at moderate levels, while being impaired at lower and higher levels (Fig. 4) (Conrad et al. 1999). As cortisol levels rise past the optimal point on the dose–response curve, they may begin to impair trading performance, specifically by promoting irrational risk aversion. Chronically elevated cortisol levels increase CRH gene transcription in the central nucleus of the amygdala thereby promoting fear (Corodimas et al. 1994), anxiety (Shephard et al. 2000; Korte 2001) and the tendency to find risk where perhaps none exists (Schulkin et al. 1994; McEwen 1998). They may also alter the types of memory recalled, causing a person to selectively recall mostly negative precedents (Erikson et al. 2003). Lastly, chronic stress, as we have seen, downregulates dopamine transporters, receptors and downstream signalling molecules in the nucleus accumbens, and may thereby alter risk-related behaviours. All these effects would tend to decrease a trader's appetite for risk.

When might conditions of chronic stress occur in the markets? Bear markets and crashes are notable for their extreme levels of volatility, the

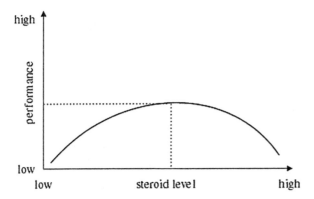

Fig. 4 Inverted *U-shaped* dose–response curve relating cortisol levels to cognitive function, such as performance, on a spatial navigation or declarative memory task

protracted subprime mortgage crisis being a notable example, with the VIX, an index of implied volatilities on the New York Stock Exchange, rising from 12% before the crisis to a high of 80% 18 months later. It seems likely that cortisol levels among traders threatened for so long with historic levels of uncertainty would have increased and perhaps remained elevated for a prolonged period of time. Under such circumstances, the steroid may have contributed to the extreme levels of risk aversion observed among traders. Indeed, extended periods of uncertainty and uncontrollable stress can promote a condition known as 'learned helplessness', in which persons, and animals, lose all belief in their ability to control or influence their environment (Kademian et al. 2005). Under these circumstances, traders could become price insensitive and fail to respond to lower asset prices or interest rates, thereby rendering monetary policy ineffective. In short, rising cortisol levels among traders and investors may promote risk aversion during a bear market, exaggerating the market's downward move.

Could testosterone work in the opposite direction, encouraging irrational risk-taking during a bull market? This is a difficult question. Moderate levels, as described above, may promote effective risk-taking among animals and high-frequency traders. But higher levels may indeed carry increased costs such as encouraging excessive risk-taking.

In studies related to the challenge hypothesis and the winner effect, animal behaviourists have found that the higher a male's testosterone level (either on account of the breeding season, an agonistic encounter or an experimental implant), the more often he fights, the large the area he patrols or the more often he ventures into the open (Marler and Moore 1988; Beletsky et al. 1995). These habits can lead to loss of fat stores (i.e. nutritional reserves), neglect of parenting duties, frequent wounds and increased predation (Dufty 1989; Wingfield et al. 2001). High-testosterone males end up paying a stiff price for their risk-taking in the form of a higher rate of mortality. We do not know if traders can experience rises in endogenous testosterone sufficient to encourage analogous forms of over-confidence and irrational risk-taking analogous forms of over-confidence and irrational risk-taking. The traders we observed experienced only moderate increases, although one trader, who enjoyed a 5-day winning streak during which he made over twice his daily average P&L, experienced a 75% increase in mean daily testosterone. It is known that cortisol can rise to extreme levels, and for extended periods of time; but research on the costs of high physiological levels of testosterone in humans is rare. Nonetheless, some studies have found that physiological levels of testosterone are indeed correlated with risky behaviour (Booth et al. 1999), sensation seeking (Daitzman and Zuckerman 1980) and the size of offers rejected in the Ultimatum Game, rejections often considered as violations of economic rationality (Van den Bergh and Dewitte 2006; Burnham 2007). Other studies with users of anabolic steroids, or subjects administered pharmacological doses of testosterone, have found evidence of manic behaviour (Pope and Katz 1988; Pope et al. 2000). In one study, researchers administered testosterone to a group of women playing the Iowa Gambling Task (van Honk et al. 2004) and found that it shifted risk preferences to such an extent that the women switched from playing the low variance and positive expected-return decks of cards to the high variance but negative expected-return decks. A similar result was found in a physiological study in which the performance of young males on the Iowa Gambling Task was negatively correlated with their testosterone levels (Reavis and Overman 2001). These study results suggest that elevated levels of testosterone could at some point begin to impair rational financial decision-making.

4 Conclusions

Taken together, the findings surveyed in this review suggest the possibility that economic agents are more hormonal than is assumed by theories of rational expectations and efficient markets. These theories assume, for example, that prices in financial markets accurately reflect all available information. But a trader's interpretation of information may not be stable: a trader with high levels of testosterone may see only opportunity in a set of facts; while the same trader with chronically elevated cortisol may find only risk. Furthermore, risk preferences may not be stable. If traders are subject to a financial variant of the winner effect, such that rising levels of testosterone increase their appetite for risk during a bull market, and rising levels of cortisol decrease their appetite for risk during a bear market, then steroid hormones may shift risk preferences systematically across the business cycle. This effect, even if confined to a small number of people, could destabilize the financial markets (Camerer and Fehr 2006). The hypothesis of steroid feedback loops exaggerating market moves raises the further possibility that the emotions of irrational exuberance and pessimism (what the economist John Maynard Keynes called 'animal spirits') commonly blamed for financial instability may in fact be steroid-induced shifts in confidence and risk preferences. This is not to say hormones cause bubbles and crashes; advances in technology, for example, caused the bull markets of 1920s and the Dotcom era, but hormones may exaggerate moves once under way.

The study of hormonal influences is, we believe, an important step in the ongoing project, beginning with behavioural economics and continuing with neuroeconomics, of showing how the body influences economic decisions, frequently pushing economic agents, for good or ill, away from rational choice. The research, moreover, carries intriguing policy implications: if hormones affect risk-taking, then perhaps financial markets can be made more stable by having a greater endocrine diversity in the financial industry. How do we achieve endocrine diversity? Hormone levels change over the course of our lives, with testosterone and oestrogen declining, and cortisol increasing; so young and old have markedly different endocrine profiles. The sexes as well have very different endocrine systems. Market stability is served by opinion diversity; so it may be served as well by having more balance in the banks between young and old, men and women. One does not need to argue that one group is better than others for this policy to work; merely different (Dreher et al. 2007). However, there are grounds for thinking that women may be less 'hormonally reactive' when it comes to financial risk-taking. For example, women have only 5–10% of the circulating levels of testosterone of men, and they have not been exposed to the same organizing effects of pre-natal androgens. Furthermore, some studies have found that women's HPA axes are less reactive to stressors stemming from a competitive situation (Stroud et al. 2002). Their greater presence in the ranks of money managers may therefore help dampen hormonal swings in the market.

Lastly, the endocrine system may be the missing link in the new field of neuroscience and economics, connecting market events to brain processes (Caldu´ and Dreher 2007). If research in endocrinology, especially work done with animal models, were to be wedded to recent developments in neuroscience and economics, we could begin to approach a unified scientific subject, from molecule to market (McEwen 2001).

References

Andrew, R. (1991). The development and integration of behaviour. In P. Bateson (Ed.), *Essays in honour of Robert Hinde* (pp. 171–190). Cambridge, UK: Cambridge University Press.

Andrew, R., & Rogers, L. (1972). Testosterone, search behaviour and persistence. *Nature, 237,* 343–346.

Apicella, C., Dreber, A., Campbell, B., Gray, P., Hoffman, M., & Little, A. (2008). Testosterone and financial risk preferences. *Evolution and Human Behavior, 29,* 384–390.

Archer, J. (2006). Testosterone and human aggression: An evaluation of the challenge hypothesis. *Neuroscience and Biobehavioral Reviews, 30,* 319–345.

Archer, J., Birring, S., & Wu, F. (1998). The association between testosterone and aggression among young men: Empirical findings and a meta-analysis. *Aggressive Behavior, 24,* 411–420.

Baulieu, E. (1997). Neurosteroids: Of the nervous system, by the nervous system, for the nervous system. *Recent Progress in Hormone Research, 52,* 1–32.

Beletsky, L., Gori, D., Freeman, S., & Wingfield, J. (1995). Testosterone and polygyny in birds. *Current Ornithology, 12,* 141.

Bernhardt, P. C., Dabbs, J., Fielden, J., & Lutter, C. (1998). Changes in testosterone levels during vicarious experiences of winning and losing among fans at sporting events. *Physiology & Behavior, 65,* 59–62.

Bhasin, S., et al. (2001). Testosterone dose-response relationships in healthy young men. *American Journal of Physiology. Endocrinology and Metabolism, 281,* 1172–1181.

Blume, L., & Easley, D. (2006). If you are so smart why aren't you rich? Belief selection in complete and incomplete markets. *Econometrica, 74,* 929–966.

Boissy, A., & Bouissou, M. (1994). Effects of androgen treatment on behavioural and physiological responses of heifers to fear-eliciting situations. *Hormones and Behavior, 28,* 66–83.

Booth, A., Shelley, G., Mazur, A., Tharp, G., & Kittok, R. (1989). Testosterone, and winning and losing in human competition. *Hormones and Behavior, 23,* 556–571.

Booth, A., Johnson, D., & Granger, D. (1999). Testosterone and men's health. *Journal of Behavioral Medicine, 22,* 1–19.

Breedlove, S., & Hampson, E. (2002). Behavioral endocrinology. In J. Becker, S. Breedlove, D. Crews, & M. McCarthy (Eds.), (2nd ed., pp. 75–114). Cambridge, MA: MIT Press.

Breier, A., Albus, M., Pickar, D., Zahn, T. P., Wolkowitz, O. M., & Paul, S. M. (1987). Controllable and uncontrollable stress in humans: Alterations in mood and neuroendocrine and psychophysiological function. *American Journal of Psychiatry, 144,* 1419–1425.

Brown, W., Hines, M., Fane, B., & Breedlove, M. (2002). Masculinized finger length patterns in human males and females with congenital adrenal hyperplasia. *Hormones and Behavior, 42,* 380–386.

Buckingham, J. (1998). Stress and the hypothalamo-pituitary-immune axis. *International Journal of Tissue Reactions, 20,* 23–34.

Burnham, T. (2007). High-testosterone men reject low ultimatum game offers. *Proceedings of the Royal Society of London B: Biological Sciences, 274,* 2327–2330.

Cabib, S., & Puglisi-Allegra, S. (1996). Different effects of repeated stressful experiences on mesocortical and meso-limbic dopamine metabolism. *Neuroscience, 73,* 375–380.

Caldu, X., & Dreher, J. (2007). Hormonal and genetic influences on processing reward and social information. *Annals of the New York Academy of Sciences, 1118,* 43–73.

Camerer, C., & Fehr, E. (2006). When does 'economic man' dominate social behavior? *Science, 311,* 47–52.

Chase, I. D., Bartolomeo, C., & Dugatkin, L. A. (1994). Aggressive interactions and inter-contest interval: How long do winners keep winning? *Animal Behaviour, 48,* 393–400.

Choy, K., de Visser, Y., & van den Buuse, M. (2009). The effect of 'two-hit' neonatal and young-adult stress on dopaminergic modulation of prepulse inhibition and dopamine receptor density. *British Journal of Pharmacology, 156,* 388–396.

Coates, J. M., & Herbert, J. (2008). Endogenous steroids and financial risk taking on a London trading floor. *Proceedings of the National Academy of Sciences of the United States of America, 105,* 6167–6172.

Coates, J. M., Gurnell, M., & Rustichini, A. (2009). Second-to-fourth digit ratio predicts success among high-frequency financial traders. *Proceedings of the National Academy of Sciences of the United States of America, 106,* 623–628.

Cohen-Bendahana, C., van de Beeka, C., & Berenbaum, S. (2005). Prenatal sex hormone effects on child and adult sex-typed behavior: Methods and findings. *Neuroscience and Biobehavioral Reviews, 29,* 353–384.

Conrad, C., Lupien, S., & McEwen, B. (1999). Support for a bimodal role for type II adrenal steroid receptors in spatial memory. *Neurobiology of Learning and Memory, 72,* 39–46.

Corodimas, K., LeDoux, J., Gold, P., & Schulkin, J. (1994). Corticosterone potentiation of learned fear. *Annals of the New York Academy of Sciences, 746,* 392–393.

Daitzman, R., & Zuckerman, M. (1980). Disinhibitory sensation seeking, personality and gonadal hormones. *Personality and Individual Differences, 1,* 103–110.

Damasio, A. R. (1994). *Descartes' error: Emotion, reason, and the human brain.* New York, NY: Grosset/Putnam.

De Bondt, W., & Thaler, R. (1987). Further evidence on investor overreaction and stock market seasonality. *The Journal of Finance, 42,* 557–581.

de Kloet, E. R. (2000). Stress in the brain. *European Journal of Pharmacology, 405,* 187–198.

de Kloet, E. R., Vreugdenhil, E., Oitzl, M. S., & Joels, M. (1998). Brain cor-
ticosteroid receptor balance in health and disease. *Endocrine Reviews, 19,*
269–301.

De Martino, B., Kumaran, D., Seymour, B., & Dolan, R. (2006). Frames,
biases and rational decision-making in the human brain. *Science, 313,*
684–687.

Dreher, J.-C., Schmidt, P. J., Kohn, P., Furman, D., Rubinov, D., & Berman,
K. F. (2007). Menstrual cycle phase modulates reward-related neural func-
tion in women. *Proceedings of the National Academy of Sciences of the United
States of America, 104,* 2465–2470.

Dufty, A. M. (1989). Testosterone and survival: A cost of aggressiveness?
Hormones and Behavior, 23, 185–193.

Dugatkin, L., & Druen, M. (2004). The social implications of winner and
loser effects. *Proceedings of the Royal Society of London B: Biological Sciences
(Suppl.)* 271, S488–S489.

Elias, M. (1981). Serum cortisol, testosterone, and testosterone-binding globu-
lin responses to competitive fighting in human males. *Aggressive Behavior, 7,*
215–224.

Erikson, K., Drevets, W., & Schulkin, J. (2003). Glucocorticoid regulation
of diverse cognitive functions in normal and pathological emotional states.
Neuroscience and Biobehavioral Reviews, 27, 233–246.

Falkenstein, E., Tillmann, H., Christ, M., Feuring, M., & Wehling, M.
(2000). Multiple actions of steroid hormones—A focus on rapid, non-
genomic effects. *Pharmacological Reviews, 52,* 513–556.

Falter, C., Arroyo, M., & Davis, G. (2006). Testosterone: Activation or organization of spatial cognition? *Biological Psychology, 73,* 132–140.

Frye, C., Rhodes, M., Rosellini, R., & Svare, B. (2002). The nucleus accumbens as a site of action for rewarding properties of testosterone and its
5alpha-reduced metabolites. *Pharmacology Biochemistry and Behavior, 74,*
119–127.

Funder, J. W. (1997). Glucocorticoid and mineralocorticoid receptors: Biology
and clinical relevance. *Annual Review of Medicine, 48,* 224–231.

Gladue, B., Boechler, M., & McCaul, K. D. (1989). Hormonal response to
competition in human males. *Aggressive Behavior, 15,* 409–422.

Gurnell, M., Burrin, J., & Chatterjee, K. (2017). Principles of hormone
action. In D. Warrell, T. Cox & J. Firth (Eds.), *Oxford textbook of medicine*
(5th ed.). Oxford: Oxford University Press.

Hermans, E., Putman, P., Baas, J., Koppeschaar, H., & van Honk, J. (2006). A single administration of testosterone reduces fear-potentiated startle in humans. *Biological Psychiatry, 59,* 872–874.

Hsu, Y., & Wolf, L. (2001). The winner and loser effect: What fighting behaviours are influenced? *Animal Behaviour, 61,* 777–786.

Hsu, M., Bhatt, M., Adolphs, R., Tranel, D., & Camerer, C. (2005). Neural systems responding to uncertainty in human decision-making. *Science, 310,* 1680–1683.

Hurd, P. (2006). Resource holding potential, subjective resource value, and game theoretical models of aggressiveness signaling. *Journal of Theoretical Biology, 241,* 639–648.

Ikemoto, S., & Panksepp, J. (1999). The role of nucleus accumbens dopamine in motivated behavior: A unifying interpretation with special reference to reward-seeking. *Brain Research Reviews, 31,* 6–41.

Kademian, S., Bignante, A., Lardone, P., McEwen, B., & Volosin, M. (2005). Biphasic effects of adrenal steroids on learned helplessness behavior induced by inescapable shock. *Neuropsychopharm, 30,* 58–66.

Kashkin, K., & Kleber, H. (1989). Hooked on hormones? An anabolic steroid addiction hypothesis. *Journal of the American Medical Association, 262,* 3166–3170.

Korte, S. (2001). Corticosteroids in relation to fear, anxiety and psychopathology. *Neuroscience and Biobehavioral Reviews, 25,* 117–142.

Kuhnen, C., & Knutson, B. (2005). The neural basis of financial risk taking. *Neuron, 47,* 763–770.

LeDoux, J. E. (1996). *The emotional brain: The mysterious underpinnings of emotional life.* New York: Simon & Schuster.

Levine, S., Coe, C., & Wiener, S. G. (1989). Psychoneuroendocrinology of stress: A psychobiological perspective. In F. Bush & S. Levine (Eds.), *Psychoendocrinology* (pp. 341–377). New York: Academic Press.

Liston, C., Miller, M. M., Goldwater, D. S., Radley, J. J., Rocher, A. B., Hof, P. R., et al. (2006). Stress-induced alterations in prefrontal cortical dendritic morphology predicts selective impairments in perceptual attention set-shifting. *Journal of Neuroscience, 26,* 7870–7874.

Liston, C., McEwen, B., & Casey, B. (2009). Psychosocial stress reversibly disrupts prefrontal processing and attentional control. *Proceedings of the National Academy of Sciences of the United States of America, 106,* 912–917.

Loewenstein, G., Weber, E., & Hsee, C. (2001). Risk as feelings. *Psychological Bulletin, 127,* 267–286.

Lucas, L. R., Wang, C. J., McCall, T. J., & McEwen, B. (2007). Effects of immobilization stress on neurochemical markers in the motivational system of the male rat. *Brain Research, 1155,* 108–115.

Lupien, S. J., Maheu, F., Tu, M., Fiocco, A., & Schramek, T. E. (2007). The effects of stress and stress hormones on human cognition: Implications for the field of brain and cognition. *Brain and Cognition, 65,* 209–237.

Manning, J., Scutt, D., Wilson, D., & Lewis-Jones, D. (1998). 2nd to 4th digit length: A predictor of sperm numbers and concentrations of testosterone, luteinizing hormone and oestrogen. *Human Reproduction, 13,* 3000–3004.

Marler, C. A., & Moore, M. C. (1988). Evolutionary costs of aggression revealed by testosterone manipulations in free-living male lizards. *Behavioral Ecology and Sociobiology, 23,* 21–26.

Matthews, S., Simmons, A., Lane, S., & Paulus, M. (2004). Selective activation of the nucleus accumbens during risk-taking decision making. *NeuroReport, 15,* 2123–2127.

Mazur, A., Booth, A., & Dabbs, J. (1992). Testosterone and chess competition. *Social Psychology Quarterly, 55,* 70–77.

McEwen, B. (1998). Stress, adaptation, and disease: Allostasis and allostatic load. *Annals of the New York Academy of Sciences, 840,* 33–44.

McEwen, B. (2001). From molecules to mind: Stress, individual differences, and the social environment. In A. Damasio et al. (Eds.), Unity of knowledge: The convergence of natural and human science. *The Annals of the New York Academy of Sciences, 935,* 42–49.

McEwen, B. (2007). Physiology and neurobiology of stress and adaptation: Central role of the brain. *Endocrine Reviews, 87,* 873–904.

McEwen, B., & Chattarji, S. (2004). Molecular mechanisms of neuroplasticity and pharmacological implications: The example of tianeptine. *European Neuropsychopharmacology, 14,* S497–S502.

McEwen, B., & Milner, T. (2007). Hippocampal formation: Shedding light on the influence of sex and stress on the brain. *Brain Research Reviews, 55,* 343–355.

McEwen, B., Weiss, J. M., & Schwartz, L. S. (1968). Selective retention of corticosterone by limbic structures in rat brain. *Nature, 220,* 911–912.

McIntyre, M. (2006). The use of digit ratios as markers for perinatal androgen action. *Reproductive Biology and Endocrinology, 4,* 10.

Meaney, M. (1988). The sexual differentiation of social play. *Trends in Neurosciences, 11,* 54–58.

Monaghan, E. P., & Glickman, S. E. (2001). Hormones and aggressive behavior. In J. B. Becker, S. M. Breedlove, & D. Crews (Eds.), *Behavioural endocrinology* (pp. 261–287). Cambridge, MA: MIT Press.

Neat, F., Huntingford, F., & Beveridge, M. (1998). Fighting and assessment in male cichlid fish: The effects of asymmetries in gonadal state and body size. *Animal Behaviour, 55,* 883–891.

O'Connor, D., Archer, J., & Wu, F. (2004). Effects of testosterone on mood, aggression, and sexual behavior in young men: A double-blind, placebo-controlled, cross-over study. *Journal of Clinical Endocrinology and Metabolism, 89,* 2837–2845.

Oyegbile, T., & Marler, C. (2005). Winning fights elevates testosterone levels in California mice and enhances future ability to win fights. *Hormones and Behavior, 48,* 259–267.

Phoenix, C., Goy, R., Gerall, A., & Young, W. (1959). Organizing action of prenatally administered testosterone propionate on the tissues mediating mating behavior in the female guinea pig. *Endocrinology, 65,* 369–382.

Piazza, P. V., & Le Moal, M. (1997). Glucocorticoids as biological substrate of reward: Physiological and pathophysiological implications. *Brain Research Reviews, 25,* 259–372.

Piazza, P., Deroche, V., Deminie`re, J. M., Maccari, S., Le Moal, M., & Simon, H. (1993). Corticosterone in the range of stress-induced levels possesses reinforcing properties: Implications for sensation-seeking behaviours. *Proceedings of the National Academy of Sciences of the United States of America, 90,* 11738–11742.

Pope, H., & Katz, D. (1988). Affective and psychotic symptoms associated with anabolic steroid use. *American Journal of Psychiatry, 145,* 487–490.

Pope, H., Kouri, E., & Hudson, J. (2000). Effects of supraphysiologic doses of testosterone on mood and aggression in normal men: A randomized controlled trial. *Archives of General Psychiatry, 57,* 133–140.

Reavis, R., & Overman, W. (2001). Adult sex differences on a decision-making task previously shown to depend on the orbital prefrontal cortex. *Behavioral Neuroscience, 115,* 196–206.

Reichlin, S. (1998). Neuroendocrinology. In J. D. Nelson, H. M. Kronenberg, & P. P. Larson (Eds.), *Williams textbook of endocrinology* (10th ed., pp. 165–248). Philadelphia, PA: N. B. Saunders.

Reul, J. M., & de Kloet, E. R. (1985). Two receptor systems for corticosterone in rat brain: Microdistribution and differential occupation. *Endocrinology, 117,* 2505–2511.

Rutte, C., Taborsky, M., & Brinkhof, M. (2006). What sets the odds of winning and losing? *Trends in Ecology & Evolution, 21,* 16–21.

Salminen, E., Portin, R., Koskinen, A., Helenius, H., & Nurmi, M. (2004). Associations between serum testosterone fall and cognitive function in prostate cancer patients. *Clinical Cancer Research, 10,* 7575–7582.

Sanfey, A., Rilling, J. K., Aronson, J. A., Nystrom, L. E., & Cohen, J. D. (2003). The neural basis of economic decision-making in the ultimatum game. *Science, 13,* 1755–1758.

Sapolsky, R. (1997). *The trouble with testosterone: And other essays on the biology of the human predicament.* New York: Simon & Schuster.

Sapolsky, R. M., Romero, L. M., & Munck, A. U. (2000). How do glucocorticoids influence stress responses? Integrating permissive, suppressive, stimulatory, and preparative actions. *Endocrine Reviews, 21,* 55–89.

Sarnyai, Z., McKittrick, C. R., McEwen, B., & Kreek, M. J. (1998). Selective regulation of dopamine transporter binding in the shell of the nucleus accumbens by adrenalectomy and corticosterone replacement. *Synapse, 30,* 334–337.

Sarnyai, Z., Shaham, Y., & Heinrichs, S. C. (2001). The role of corticotropin-releasing factor in drug addiction. *Pharmacological Reviews, 53,* 209–243.

Sato, S. M., Schulz, K., Sisk, C., & Wood, R. (2008). Adolescents and androgens, receptors and rewards. *Hormones and Behavior, 53,* 647–658.

Schroeder, J., & Packard, M. (2000). Role of dopamine receptor subtypes in the acquisition of a testosterone conditioned place preference in rats. *Neuroscience Letters, 282,* 17–20.

Schulkin, J., McEwen, B. S., & Gold, P. W. (1994). Allostasis, amygdala, and anticipatory angst. *Neuroscience and Biobehavioral Reviews, 18,* 385–396.

Schultz, W. (2000). Multiple reward signals in the brain. *Nature Reviews Neuroscience, 1,* 199–207.

Scoville, W. B., & Milner, B. (1957). Loss of recent memory after bilateral hippocampal lesions. *Journal of Neurochemistry, 20,* 11–21.

Shephard, J. D., Barron, K. W., & Myers, D. A. (2000). Corticosterone delivery to the amygdala increases corticotropin-releasing factor mRNA in the central amygdaloid nucleus and anxiety-like behavior. *Brain Research, 861,* 288–295.

Shiller, R. (2005). *Irrational exuberance.* New York: Doubleday.

Stroud, L., Salovey, P., & Epel, E. (2002). Sex differences in stress responses: Social rejection versus achievement stress. *Biological Psychiatry, 319,* 318–327.

Swenson, R., & Vogel, W. (1983). Plasma catecholamine and corticosterone as well as brain catecholamine changes during coping in rats exposed to stressful footshock. *Pharmacology Biochemistry and Behavior, 18,* 689–693.

Trainor, B. C., Bird, I. M., & Marler, C. A. (2004). Opposing hormonal mechanisms of aggression revealed through short-lived testosterone manipulations and multiple winning experiences. *Hormones and Behavior, 45,* 115–121.

Tsai, M.-J., & O'Malley, B. W. (1994). Molecular mechanisms of action of steroid/thyroid receptor superfamily members. *Annual Review of Biochemistry, 63,* 451–486.

Vadakkadath Meethal, S., & Atwood, C. S. (2005). The role of hypothalamic-pituitary-gonadal hormones in the normal structure and functioning of the brain. *Cellular and Molecular Life Sciences, 62,* 257–270.

Van den Bergh, B., & Dewitte, S. (2006). Digit ratio (2D:4D) moderates the impact of sexual cues on men's decisions in ultimatum games. *Proceedings of the Royal Society B, 273,* 2091–2095.

van Honk, J., Schutter, D., Hermans, E., & Putman, P. (2003). Low cortisol levels and the balance between punishment sensitivity and reward dependency. *NeuroReport, 14,* 1993–1996.

van Honk, J., Schuttera, D. J. L. G., Hermansa, E. J., Putmana, P., Tuitena, A., & Koppeschaar, H. (2004). Testosterone shifts the balance between sensitivity for punishment and reward in healthy young women. *Psychoneuroendocrinology, 29,* 937–943.

Vermeersch, H., T'sjoen, G., Kaufman, J. M., & Vincke, J. (2008). The role of testosterone in aggressive and non-aggressive risk-taking in adolescent boys. *Hormones and Behavior, 53,* 463–471. doi:10.1016/j.yhbeh.2007.11.021.

Wingfield, J. C., Hegner, R. E., Dufty, A. M., & Ball, G. F. (1990). The 'challenge hypothesis': Theoretical implications for patterns of testosterone secretion, mating systems, and breeding strategies. *American Naturalist, 136,* 829–846.

Wingfield, J. C., Lynn, S., & Soma, K. (2001). Avoiding the 'costs' of testosterone: Ecological bases of hormone-behavior interactions. *Brain, Behavior and Evolution, 57,* 239–251.

3

The Winner Effect—The Neuropsychology of Power

Ian H. Robertson

1 Introduction

I am going to start with a mystery and it is about a fish. Among the cichlid fish of Lake Tanganyika, there are males and females, but there are two types of males: there is the T fish and the NT fish. Sometimes, however, something quite remarkable happens; within the course of one to seven days, Mr. NT turns into Mr. T, in every respect (Fernald 2003). This is quite important because apart from being more handsome, brightly-coloured, bigger, he is also more aggressive, he is also sexually highly fertile: a group of cells in his brain that produce a sex hormone called *gonadotropin-releasing hormone* swell to eight times their previous, NT size during the transformation. That is the mystery I am leaving you with just now, and I will give you the answer at the end of the chapter.

I.H. Robertson (✉)
Trinity College, Dublin, Ireland

© The Author(s) 2018
P. Garrard (ed.), *The Leadership Hubris Epidemic*,
https://doi.org/10.1007/978-3-319-57255-0_3

If you are familiar with Rodin's famous sculpture 'The Kiss' you may not have noticed that the figures turn rightward towards each other during the embrace. It turns out that this is a feature of real life too: a German researcher called Onur Güntürkün, who went to a number of airports in Europe and America and counted the direction in which people were kissing, found that in the majority of cases they behaved as in Rodin's kiss, by kissing to the right (Gunturkun 2003). It also turns out that if you have goalkeepers under pressure, i.e. when behind in a penalty shootout, they dive to the right 71% of the time (Roskes et al. 2011).

2   Approach and Avoidance

What does this have to do with power and the topic of hubris? Approach and avoidance are the two fundamental biological impulses underpinning all our behaviour as animals. It is about survival: we want to approach certain things—for food and for sex—and we want to avoid certain things, to avoid being eliminated (Gray 1987). The approach system is closely linked to the dopamine (reward) system of the brain (Wacker et al. 2013), which tends to activate left frontal areas more than the right (Davidson 1992). Electrical brain recordings (EEG) show that people who are being made to think or remember a situation when they had power over someone, for instance sitting on an interview panel or in another position of power, activate the brain's left-lateralised *approach* system (Boksem et al. 2012). This motivation to approach explains why Rodin's statues—and indeed embracers the world over—strain slightly to the right, driven by the increased activity in the left frontal lobes of their brains.

Mike Tyson, World Heavyweight Boxing Champion, was convicted of rape in 1992 and spent three years in prison. When he came out he was no longer World Champion, Frank Bruno was. What do you do if you have been eating bad food under fluorescent lights for three years, and you are no longer the champion? What is the recipe? Don King, who was the promoter, had the same recipe that all American boxing promoters had had for at least 100 years, a recipe which is not about diet. What Mike Tyson needed was *tomato cans*. I have no idea why, actually, the American boxing fraternity have this concept of a tomato can. A tomato can in this context is a boxer, for instance, Peter McNeely Jr, a Boston Irishman, who was the first contender whom Mike Tyson was set to fight in Las Vegas a few months after he got out of prison. A tomato can is someone you are bound to beat because he is so much worse than you. And this happened. People paid a large number of dollars to see Mike Tyson fight, which lasted only 89 seconds before the first tomato can was defeated. Then the second one, Buster Mathis, a few months later in Philadelphia, lasted three rounds before being defeated as well.

What has this got to do with power and hubris? It is to do with the "Winner Effect", a phenomenon that pertains across all of biology and which is the title of my book on the subject (Robertson 2012). What it means is, if you win one contest even against an artificially weakened opponent, or against a "tomato can", your chances of winning the next contest against a much stronger opponent are statistically increased. The American boxing fraternity knew this for 100 years yet it did not hit science until 1951 when a mathematical biologist called Landau, who was trying to understand the rise of authoritarian dictatorships such as Hitler and Mussolini, tried to work out how pecking orders, or hierarchies in animals developed and were maintained. He created through purely mathematical modelling equations where he put in variables like body size, testosterone levels, size of the group, but mathematically he could never get a stable hierarchy. Hierarchies emerged, but they constantly shifted, changed and reformed (Landau 1951a). Then he discovered in his second paper (Landau 1951b) that there was one variable he could put into the mathematical equation which gave him stable hierarchies, and that was a little rule that said, if you have a minor contest against one member of the group, and you win it, this causes a small increase in your chances of winning the next contest. This is the Winner Effect. It was not demonstrated empirically until 1967, in the green sunfish (McDonald et al. 1968). If you put a small green sunfish in the same tank as a big green sunfish, then the experience of bullying the little green sunfish gave the bigger fish a much better chance of becoming dominant when he subsequently went into another tank with an equal sized sunfish.

We also know from the work of John Coates and Joe Herbert on London financial traders, that testosterone is linked to winning, and, in his case, winning trades; profit levels are higher on days when testosterone levels are greater (Coates and Herbert 2008). There is a similar phenomenon in sport: in the 1994 World Cup, Italy were in the final with Brazil, and Roberto Baggio missed the penalty resulting in Italy losing. Researchers took saliva samples in the group of Italian and Brazilian fans before and after the game, and what they found was: in the fans, the testosterone levels of the Brazilian people went up, and of the Italian fans, went down (Bernhardt et al. 1998). Think about it. We are talking here perhaps about the biggest pharmacological experiment ever done, about mass manipulation of the hormones of 100 million Brazilians and of 60 million Italians. So our contest with other people changes our biology fundamentally. We tend to think of our biology changing us, but actually our social relationships constantly, every day, change our biology.

3   Power

Finally we have come to power. Bertrand Russell wrote an entire book about power, arguing that the fundamental entity in social science is power in the same sense that energy is the fundamental concept in physics (Russell 1938). Karl Marx clearly knew this, but it is something that neuropsychologists like myself have only stumbled upon relatively recently: the fact is that we are a group species and the main determinants, even greater than those of genetics, of our cognitive and emotional functions, are our relationships with other people. And power is one of the fundamental elements of such relationships.

Let me just give you a little quiz for yourself for you to do in your own head. Think of a boss in whom power went to his or her head. Just mentally go through whether any of the following applied to them. Did they change, to become more pushy, selfish? Did they like having an impact on underlings, not just by making them frightened, or shocking them, but also making them grateful? Did they start to see people as objects, in terms of how useful they are? Did they develop a tunnel vision? Did they become sexually primed? Did they become hypocritical, having difficulty in seeing things from other people's points of view? Were they disinhibited, making would-be jokey comments that are not funny to the person on the receiving end? These are all demonstrated effects of even small amounts of imagined power in ordinary people (Robertson 2012).

There is one other such effect of power that comes not from experimental studies, but rather through studies of people who are bosses in real life, from Nathanael Fast and colleagues (Fast and Chen 2009). They showed that if you promote someone into a position in which they feel inadequate *and* they have power, they are likely to behave in a bullying fashion to underlings, the result of a toxic combination of inadequacy and power.

Does then power turn us into selfish, hypocritical bullies who see other people as objects? Not necessarily. Consider examples of people given power who have changed in some or all of these domains: strategic vision, decisive, goal-focused, healthy appetite for risk, handled stress well, smart, upbeat, bold and inspiring? These are also effects of power on the brain. How can that be? What lies behind this two-edged sword of power? It can make people selfish and hypocritical, or it can make them smart, bold and inspiring. The evidence is that, like many of the brain's other chemical messengers, there is an inverted U shape function for the neurotransmitter most linked to power—dopamine: too little dopamine activity in the brain's reward network and the brain underperforms, while too much distorts judgment and emotions. There is therefore a delicate balance, a sort of "Goldilocks Zone" where the biological effects of power on the brain cause positive changes, without tilting the brain into the sort of distorted behaviour that we know as "hubris".

So how do you try to ensure that people in power can hit this Goldilock's zone and get all the benefits of power? Power's effects on the dopamine system means that it has certain antidepressant properties, it emboldens you, permits you to see the wood rather than the trees, and contributes to charisma. A charismatic person has the capacity to see a future alignment of events that other people cannot see, and power actually is a sort of drug that helps your brain do that. We know from David Owen's fundamental work about leaders who developed the Hubris Syndrome that there is, in a manner of speaking, a change in behaviour, a complete change in demeanour that he has documented happens to some British leaders including Margaret Thatcher and Tony Blair (Owen and Davidson 2009). Here is a segment of a BBC interview conducted by Michael Parkinson with Tony Blair.

> Blair: In the end, there is a judgement that… well, I think if you have faith about these things, then you realise that judgement is made by other people and also by…
>
> Michael Parkinson: Sorry - what do you mean by that? Sorry…
>
> Blair: I mean, by other people, by… if you believe in God, it's made by God as well…

In June 2003, former US President George W Bush told Palestinian Prime Minister Abu Mazen that God had told him to invade Iraq (BBC 2005). Blair clearly felt that there was a greater power involved and that he was, in some way, anointed in terms of the weighty decisions he had to make. This is a feature of hubris. One of the symptoms is messianic manner, but the thing about power, the real victim of power, is the ego. And if the ego swells to that extent it becomes so hungry that it cannot bear to think of itself as being secondary or subservient to higher laws or principles or people. So it is a very common thing—Julius Caesar had himself made a demi-god while he was still alive. John Paul Getty, believed himself to be the reincarnation of Emperor Hadrian (Getty 2003). Picasso had himself called the 'Sun' by his staff, while he called himself the King. So this sense of specialness that comes from this narcissistically swollen ego, that is the greatest risk of power.

4 Antidotes to Power's Effects on the Brain

So can we forecast who is going to succumb to it? The great psychologist David McClelland identified power as one of the three great motivators of human beings, the others being affiliation and achievement (McClelland 1987). At the base of power motivation there is always a personal egotistical aspect to this, the sheer pleasure of being in charge, of calling the shots. McClelland calls this P (personal) power motivation.

You can assess how much motivation people have for power by their free speech and their natural language. This was done in Tony Blair's case assessing his power motivation by using Prime Minister's Questions in Parliament (Dyson 2006), where in the free speech, researchers look for linguistic themes of carrying out strong psychologically or physically forceful actions. One can reliably code this in free speech and give people a score on how much power motivation they have. It turns out that this measure of power motivation has strong biological correlates, with high power motivation resulting in higher and more prolonged testosterone surges in competitive situations than is the case in people with lower levels of power motivation. High power motivation individuals find losing stressful and secrete the stress hormone testosterone, while the reverse is true for people with low power motivation—they are inclined to find winning stressful (Schultheiss et al. 1999; Wirth et al. 2006)! Some people, in other words find that dominating other people is stressful rather than rewarding, a process that, according to McClelland, is largely unconscious. Other sophisticated analysis comparing the speech patterns of leaders with and without hubris such as Blair, Thatcher and Major has been carried out by Garrard and colleagues (Garrard et al. 2014).

There is, however, a second dimension to power motivation, which is where a person still wants to have control over other things, but wants it for the benefit of the group and not purely for egotistical, "P" power reasons. This is called S (social) power (Winter 1973). Where there exists an appetite for power, there is always a P power, egotistical power, aspect to it. But in addition, people vary in how much S (social) power they have. And S power can be measured in the speech by, reliably, the extent to which people use negatives such as not and don't in their free speech. These are signs of internal constraints on behaviour that moderate the biological effects of P power (Wirth et al. 2006). If you compare the power motivation of George Bush and Barack Obama, both have equally high appetites for power, but George Bush is very low in the S power while Barack Obama is high on the S power (Kusari 2010). Why is that important?—because S power acts as an antidote to the testosterone-driven, potentially addictive surges of power. One finds smaller and less sustained testosterone surges to dominating other people if one has a combination of P power and S power (Wirth et al. 2006). The interesting thing is women have, on average, higher levels of S power than men, and therefore may be somewhat protected against the Hubris Syndrome, although certainly not completely (Chusmir 1986).

5   The Mystery Solved

I will now return to the cichlid fish. Why does Mr NT turn into Mr T in every respect? Here is the answer. One of the downsides of being a T fish is you are brightly coloured. In the shallow waters of Lake Tanganyika you are therefore more visible to gulls and more likely to be taken out the water. The reason you are called a T fish is because you have territory. When you are plucked out of the water your territory becomes vacant, so a NT fish sees the territory—by merely having territory, and is biologically, in every respect, transformed; within a week, the colour, size, behaviour, fertility and everything else is changed. So that is the influence of environment over biology. Does this happen in humans? Perhaps it does: Oscar winners live an average four years longer than Oscar nominees (Redelmeier and Singh 2001). Four years is the increase in life-span you will get if you cure all cancers, so this is a huge effect. Nobel Prize winners live an average one and a half years longer than Nobel nominees (Rablen and Oswald 2008). So perhaps something like the T fish effect does happen in humans Our power relationships certainly are the fundamental dictators of who we are, including the very stuff of our brains.

References

BBC. (2005). Available from: http://www.bbc.co.uk/pressoffice/pressreleases/stories/2005/10_october/06/Bush.shtm.

Bernhardt, P. C., et al. (1998). Testosterone changes during vicarious experiences of winning and losing among fans at sporting events. *Physiology & Behavior, 65*(1), 59–62.

Boksem, M. A. S., Smolders, R., & De Cremer, D. (2012). Social power and approach-related neural activity. *Social Cognitive and Affective Neuroscience, 7*(5), 516–520.

Chusmir, L. H. (1986). Personalized vs. socialized power needs among working women and men. *Human Relations, 39*(2), 149–159.

Coates, J. M., & Herbert, J. (2008). Endogenous steroids and financial risk taking on a London trading floor. *Proceedings of the National Academy of Sciences, 105*(16), 6167–6172.

Davidson, R. J. (1992). Anterior cerebral asymmetry and the nature of emotion. *Brain and Cognition, 20*(1), 125–151.

Dyson, S. B. (2006). Personality and foreign policy: Tony Blair's Iraq decisions. *Foreign Policy Analysis, 2*(3), 289–306.

Fast, N. J., & Chen, S. (2009). When the boss feels inadequate power, incompetence, and aggression. *Psychological Science, 20*(11), 1406–1413.

Fernald, R. D. (2003). How does behavior change the brain? Multiple methods to answer old questions. *Integrative and Comparative Biology, 43*(6), 771–779.

Garrard, P., et al. (2014). Linguistic biomarkers of Hubris Syndrome. *Cortex, 55,* 167–181.

Getty, J. P. (2003). *As I see it: the autobiography of J. Paul Getty.* Los Angeles: Getty Publications.

Gray, J. A. (1987). The neuropsychology of emotion and personality. In S. M. Stahl, S. D. Iverson, & E. C. Guinote (Eds.), *Cognitive Neurochemistry* (pp. 171–190). Oxford: OUP.

Gunturkun, O. (2003). Human Hubris Syndrome: Adult persistence of head-turning asymmetry. *Nature, 421,* 711.

Kusari, F. (2010). Predicting American presidential election outcomes based on candidates' power, affiliation and achievement motives, in Graduate School of Applied and Professional Psychology, Rutgers University.

Landau, H. G. (1951a). On dominance relations and the structure of animal societies: 1. Effect of inherent characteristics. *Bulletin of Mathematical Biophysics, 13,* 1–19.

Landau, H. G. (1951b). On dominance relations and the structure of animal societies: II. Some effects of possible social factors. *Bulletin of Mathematical Biophysics, 13,* 245–262.

McClelland, D. C. (1987). *Human motivation.* Cambridge: CUP Archive.

McDonald, A. L., Heimstra, N. W., & Damkot, D. K. (1968). Social modification of agonistic behaviour in fish. *Animal Behaviour, 16*(4), 437–441.

Owen, D., & Davidson, J. (2009). Hubris syndrome: An acquired personality disorder? A study of US Presidents and UK Prime Ministers over the last 100 years. *Brain, 132*(5), 1396–1406.

Rablen, M. D., & Oswald, A. J. (2008). Mortality and immortality: The Nobel Prize as an experiment into the effect of status upon longevity. *Journal of Health Economics, 27*(6), 1462–1471.

Redelmeier, D. A., & Singh, S. M. (2001). Survival in Academy Award-winning actors and actresses. *Annals of Internal Medicine, 134*(10), 955–962.

Robertson, I. (2012). *The winner effect: How power affects your brain.* London: Bloomsbury.

Roskes, M., et al. (2011). The right side? Under time pressure, approach motivation leads to right-oriented bias. *Psychological Science, 22*(11), 1403–1407.

Russell, B. (1938). *Power: A new social analysis.* London: George Allen & Unwin.

Schultheiss, O. C., Campbell, K. L., & McClelland, D. C. (1999). Implicit power motivation moderates men's testosterone responses to imagined and real dominance success. *Hormones and Behavior, 36*(3), 234–241.

Wacker, J., et al. (2013). Dopamine-D2-receptor blockade reverses the association between trait approach motivation and frontal asymmetry in an approach-motivation context. *Psychological Science, 24*(4), 489–497.

Winter, D. G. (1973). *The Power Motive.* New York: Free Press.

Wirth, M. M., Welsh, K. M., & Schultheiss, O. C. (2006). Salivary cortisol changes in humans after winning or losing a dominance contest depend on implicit power motivation. *Hormones and Behavior, 49*(3), 346–352.

Part II
Culture

4

Management Failure and Derailment

Adrian Furnham

1 Introduction

Some management and leadership careers and roles end in failure. People get sacked or resign or retire early. Management failure, as opposed to success, has only been studied for the last 30 or so years beginning in America. Three things, all of which are surprising and counter-intuitive to many people characterise this growing and important literature. First, there are a surprisingly large number who fail and derail. If you ask people they usually offer a "guesstimate" of between 5 and 10%. The data suggest the number may be more like 50% (Furnham 2010; Hogan 2007). That is, failure is as common as success. It is therefore surprising that the topic has been neglected for so long. Second, failure and derailment comes as a surprise to many because those that do have nearly always been regarded as high flyers and in the

A. Furnham (✉)
University College London, London, UK

© The Author(s) 2018
P. Garrard (ed.), *The Leadership Hubris Epidemic*,
https://doi.org/10.1007/978-3-319-57255-0_4

talent group. Many have had "stellar careers" with considerable early success and a good reputation. It comes, therefore, as a great shock when a supposedly highly successful leader fail and derails. Third, failure is not exclusively due to the personality and pathology. Two other factors play an important role. The first is organisational culture and processes which can allow, even encourage, management failure. The second is employees or followers who are prepared to go along with, and obey the derailing leader.

2   Incompetence vs Derailment

It is important to make the distinction between leadership incompetence and derailment.

2.1   Incompetence

Synonyms include ineptitude, inability, inadequacy, incapacity, ineffectiveness, uselessness, insufficiency, ineptness, incompetency, unfitness, incapability, and skillessness. In essence incompetence means an inability to perform; lacking some ability, capacity or qualification.

Nearly everyone has worked for an incompetent manager. Essentially, the incompetent manager is lacking something: most are simply over-promoted. Others are there because of favouritism or simply bad selection. They do not have the skills, the energy, the courage or perhaps the insight to do that which is required of a good leader. Nepotism, poor selection techniques and complacency often account for the appointment of an incompetent leader. Casciaro and Lobo (2005), in an amusing Harvard Business Review article, distinguished four types based on the dimensions of competence and likeability: competent and incompetent jerk, loveable star, and loveable fool. They caution, quite rightly, against spending too much time with the loveable fool, who is in essence incompetent. In their paper 'The Incompetent CEO', Toney and Brown (1997) noted how these often get appointed through flawed promotional practices: ostracising shining stars, choosing those with a pleasing personality or not examining the nature of their experience. Their advice was to watch out for early warning signs, scrap defective promotional practices, search out and retain really great leaders and train people in the appropriate skills. In their book 'The Peter Principle: Why things always go wrong' (1969), Lawrence J Peter and Raymond Hull state that 'in any hierarchy, individuals tend to rise to their level of incompetence'. Although the book was rejected by 13 publishers, when it was finally published it became an immediate best seller. Indeed Peter made the concept of incompetence popular long before competency or incompetency was on the lips of every manager. In a later book he spelt out a number of corollaries to the Peter Principle:

- The cream rises until it is sour.
- For every job in the world there is someone, somewhere, who can't do it.
- Given enough promotions, that someone will get the job.
- All useful work is done by those who have not yet reached their level of incompetence.
- Competence always contains the seeds of incompetence.
- Incompetence plus incompetence equals incompetence.
- Whenever something is worth doing, it is worth finding someone competent to do it.
- The Peter Principle, like evolution, shows no mercy.
- Once an employee achieves a level of incompetence inertia sets in and the employer settles for incompetence, rather than distress the employee and look for a replacement.
- Lust gets us into trouble more than sloth.

2.2   Derailment

This literally means coming off the tracks and is taken from railroad terminology. It refers to where an otherwise functional train, expectedly "comes off the rails" and is thus left stranded, unable to move, possibly blocking the line and potentially irreparable. The derailed leader is not one lacking in ability: indeed often the opposite. Many are highly talented, well-educated and high flyers. But they come unstuck, often because the dark side to their personality does not fully manifest itself until they acquire significant power.

Incompetence and derailment are sometimes difficult to differentiate because the consequences in the business are often similar. They usually include declining customer service, morale and profits, high turnover and negative media coverage as well as simply things like inadequate quality control and stock flow. In the management literature derailment has come to mean the demise of an otherwise successful business or political leader who seems to have too much of a good thing like self-confidence, boldness or courage. Indeed, it is for those characteristics that they were often chosen. However the strengths became weaknesses, either because of the way they were overused, or because they were initially compensatory.

3   Three Crucial Indicators

The modern literature based on both psychological and psychiatric theory suggests that underlying all leader derailments (and all personality disorders) there are three very fundamental markers. Whilst there are numerous factors that might indicate the possibility of a leader derailing, there are three that are always most important. They concern issues like empathy, intimacy, identity and adaptation.

3.1   Relationships

Can the person establish and maintain healthy, happy, long-term relationships with various sorts of people?

Leadership is accomplished with and through people. It is almost impossible to conceive of a leadership position which does not involve groups and teams. Leaders have to get the trust and loyalty of their team to succeed. They need to build team spirit and understand team dynamics. They must help teams to cope with both triumph and disaster and learn new skills and ways of working together. The ability to form and maintain relationships starts early. People make friends at a very young age for various reasons and some keep them for very long periods. There is vast literature in psychology on the psychological importance of friendship formation and social support. It is essential for mental health to be able to establish relationships. What is clear from the work on the personality disorders and dark-side traits is that for different reasons those with these disorders have difficulty with relationships. It is possible to consider the number of relationship problems that an individual has had including parent-child, sibling, partner, colleague, neighbour etc., over the years. Whilst nearly all researchers have demonstrated that problems with interpersonal relationships are at the heart of the problem for derailed managers it has been suggested that these are often complimented by a whole number of self-defeating features of the Hubris Syndrome. These include being rigid, hostile, defensive, over-committed, suspicious and defensive (Williams et al. 2013). However it seems the case that these self-defeating Hubris symptoms themselves play a big part in derailment because they are related to the inability to establish good relationships.

From the 1960s to the mid-1990s it was common to talk of communication, interpersonal or social 'skills'. These were loosely defined as a set of learned, specific but related skills which allow us to understand and communicate in relation to others by initiating and maintaining social relationships. People who worked in the area maintained that there were various specific assumptions made by social skills researchers. Most would have agreed that social skills are essential. Those who focused on communication concentrated on verbal, vocal and non-verbal abnormalities. They noted that people could be taught to communicate what they felt and thought more accurately and effectively. Hence emphasis on presentation skills and public speaking. Others were more interested in the ability of people to initiate and sustain relationships. These skills concerned being assertive and relationship building. A social skills deficit was thought of as the cause of many problems. Indeed, some adults do tend to be rigid, with poor self-control and social skills and are weak at building bonds. Understanding and using emotions/feelings are at the heart of business and indeed being human.

Often business people prefer to talk about 'emotional competencies' (rather than traits or abilities) which are essentially learned capabilities. Emotional competencies include emotional self-awareness, self-regulation, social-emotional awareness, regulating emotions in others, and understanding emotions. If one is to include older, related concepts like social skills or interpersonal competencies then it is possible to find a literature dating back thirty years showing these skills predict occupational effectiveness and success. Further, there is convincing empirical literature which suggests that these skills can be improved and learnt. One recognized reason for management failure is lack of emotional intelligence. This is most often found in leaders in highly technical areas (finance, engineering) who may have chosen those subjects because of their poor social skills in the first place.

The bottom line, though, is this: all the evidence suggests that derailed managers are unable or unwilling to initiate and maintain healthy, long-term relationships in the workplace. Either because of their lack of social skill or else their egotism and selfishness they tend to have problems with their clients, team and reports.

3.2   Self-awareness

Does the person have insight into themselves? Can they accurately appraise and understand their own abilities and preferences, their impact on others, and the implications of these factors for the risk of Hubris Syndrome. It is essentially reality-testing; a calibration against the facts of life.

Self-awareness is partly knowledge about the self: strengths and weaknesses, vulnerabilities and passions, idiosyncrasies and normalities. It can be derived in many ways. Sometimes self-insight comes from a sudden epiphany in the classroom or on the couch. It can even occur at an appraisal. It comes out of success and failure. What others say and even by receiving feedback from a personality test. There is a pathological form of self-awareness. This is manifest in the hypervigilant, counselling-addicted, self-obsessed individuals who are interested in nothing but themselves. It is a phase most adolescents pass through, and in which some become stuck. It's deeply unattractive and quite counter-productive. It can take years to find out who you are, where you belong (in the family, organization, community), knowing what you can best contribute to others. Some people are lucky: they are given opportunities to test their skills and see their impact. They become more aware of their potential and of how they naturally behave in specific situations: Good in a crisis, or good at provoking them? A good ear for languages? (Real) emotional intelligence? Why certain types of people clearly do not like them? A natural at negotiation and sales? Aware of what stresses them and of their fundamental values. Better self-regulation of emotions and self-management comes with self-consciousness in the sense of having real self-understanding.

Surely, one of the greatest of all faults is to be conscious of having none. So how to improve your self-awareness? Three things help: first *self-testing*, exploration and try-outs. Try new tasks and situations. Adolescents are famous for saying they do not like something that they have never tried. People make discoveries late in life—often through chance discoveries. The second is self-acceptance. This is neither the over- nor under-estimation of your talents. We are not all intelligent, creative or insightful. It is as sad to see people ignoring or underplaying their strengths as their weaknesses. Third, seeking out feedback from others. A good friend, boss, teacher tells it like it is. They help to clarify crucial questions: what is really important to me? Who is the authentic me?

The famous Johari window has four boxes: the *Open Self* is common knowledge, things I know and you know about me; then there is the *Hidden Self* which is the little box of secrets—things I know about me that others do not; the third box is labelled *Blind Self* which is about things other people know about, see in, are sure of, me but which they have not told me. The fourth box is the *Unknown self*—things neither I nor others know about me. Buried, repressed or long forgotten thoughts or even areas of potential. Perhaps they can be mined by therapists interested in, and supposedly able to, drag things from the murky unconscious into the bright light of day.

The bottom line is that most derailed leaders are poorly informed about their strengths and weaknesses. They do not understand how they come across and their effect on others. This is potentially a serious issue.

3.3   Adaptability, Learning and Transitioning

It has frequently been observed that derailed leaders' early career success was often responsible for their later failure because they failed to learn. At various times in a work career people have to learn to let go of old, odd, dysfunctional assumptions and beliefs. Further, they need to acquire new skills and ideas. This often means exposing themselves to learning situations that can be threatening and which may involve failure. Some organizations do a good job in preparing people for senior positions. Through a series of planned experiences and courses they hope to transition them to take on the responsibilities of higher management. All potential leaders need to upgrade and extend their social and technical skills and move from tactical to strategic thinking. Both incompetent and derailed leaders often have too narrow a range of experience and an over-emphasis and reliance on either technical or social skills.

Senior leadership is often about dealing calmly and rationally with ambiguous, threatening and uncertain situations. The inflexible and unadaptable executive seems unable to change his/her mindset and grow to meet changing situations. There are a range of transitions that most people go through. These include promotion to senior and then general management, losing a supportive boss or coherent team, going through a difficult merger or simply experiencing disruptive organisational change. Some are offered coaching, mentoring and other ways to help them over this period. They might be given a mature and functional team. Most importantly they are given feedback on their strengths, limitations and blind spots.

But change happens all the time: technology and law change; internationalisation means new competitors; companies can appear and disappear overnight. People therefore need to be adaptable and able to cope with change. Some are clearly better at this than others.

4 Conditions that Allow for the Emergence of Dark-Side Leaders

There are clearly many factors that account for why potentially derailing leaders make it to the top. Many have pointed out that just as you need three components for fire, namely heat, oxygen and fuel, so you are unlikely to get leadership derailment if you do not have: leaders with a derailment profile; people who are prepared to follow derailing leaders; and environments which allow derailment. Many people have tried to moderate the simple-minded and individualistic trait approach to leadership derailment by stressing the nature of leader-follower dynamics (Clements and Washbush 1999). Ouimet (2010) noted three factors:

4.1 Cultural Factors

There are national and corporate cultural factors that favour the dark-side manager making it to the top. First, individualistic cultures (mainly in the West) more than collectivistic cultures (mainly in the East) value personal achievement over group success. Thus in these cultures it is more natural to look for, and select, people who draw attention to themselves and have significant self-belief.

Further, if the organisation promotes and trumpets values like immediate results, audacity, ambition, individual initiative, financial success, professional prestige and social celebrity they become a breeding ground for dark-side leaders (Ouimet 2010). Thus inevitably dark-side types are drawn to organisations in which they can thrive. This is particularly the case for organisations in sectors which are fast moving and poorly regulated.

4.2 Environmental Factors

There is considerable historical evidence that dark-side leaders emerge in times of political and economic crisis. Where people perceive an imagined or real and significant threat to their well-being and livelihood they are often drawn to the "superman, heroic" leader who promises them he or she can save them. People are drawn to the rhetoric, the self-confidence and the bravado of leaders who can mobilize people and give them confidence. Crises occur for all sorts of reasons. Political crises can trigger economic crises and vice versa. Sudden changes in technology or international law can have an immediate and massive impact on organisations of all sizes who look for immediate solutions. If at this point the bold, mischievous, Machiavellian steps forward the emergence of a dark-side leader is usually guaranteed.

4.3   Organisational Structural Factors

All organisations, for historical but also legal reasons, have processes and procedures which can either facilitate or frustrate the emergence of a dark-side leader. Some place serious restrictions on an individual's power and freedom to make decisions. Some organisations have strict rules and procedures about group decision making and the keeping of records. Others are more relaxed. Furthermore, most organisations have rules about corporate governance. There may be non-executive directors whose explicit task it is to 'keep an eye on' maverick leaders and their decisions. There also may be rules about reports and statements and shareholders meetings which make all sorts of procedures public. In short, the better the corporate governance the less chance a dark-side leader has to emerge. There is a great deal of literature which supports the idea that some environments inhibit and others almost encourage Hubris Syndrome.

5   Dark-Side Traits

Psychologists are interested in personality traits; psychiatrists in personality disorders. Psychologists interested in personality have made great strides in describing, classifying and explaining the mechanisms and processes in normal personality functioning. Psychiatrists also talk about personality functioning. They talk about personality disorders that are typified by early onset (recognisable in children and adolescents), pervasive effects and relatively poor prognosis, and are difficult to cure. Both argue that the personality factors relate to how people think, feel and act. They are where a person's behaviour deviates markedly from the expectations of the culture in which the disorder is manifested. A psychiatric approach makes it very clear that behaviour is not simply an expression of habits, customs, religious or political values professed or shown by a people of particular cultural origin.

Over the years psychiatrists have made great strides in clarifying and specifying diagnostic criteria for personality disorders and these can be found in the various Diagnostic and Statistical Manual of Mental Disorders (DSM). This has changed over the years and it is now in its fifth edition. Some personality disorders (e.g. 'passive aggressive') have been removed. Psychiatrists and psychologists share some simple assumptions with respect to personality. Both argue for the *stability* of personality. The DSM criteria talk of an 'enduring pattern', 'inflexible and pervasive' 'stable and of long duration'. The pattern of behaviour is not a function of drug usage or some other medical condition. The personality pattern furthermore is not a manifestation or consequence of another mental disorder.

The DSM manuals note that personality disorders all have a long history and have an onset no later than early adulthood. Moreover there are some gender differences: thus the anti-social disorder is more likely to be diagnosed in men while the borderline, histrionic and dependent personalities are more likely to be found in women. The manuals go to great lengths to point out that some of the personality disorders look like other disorders, such as anxiety, mood, psychotic, and substance-related states, but have unique features. The essence of the argument is that personality disorders must be distinguished from personality traits that do not reach the threshold for a Personality Disorder. 'Personality traits are diagnosed as a Personality Disorder only when they are inflexible, maladaptive, and persisting and cause significant functional impairment or subjective distress' (p. 633).

One of the most important ways to differentiate personal style from personality disorder is flexibility. There are lots of difficult people at work but relatively few whose rigid, maladaptive behaviours mean they continually have disruptive, troubled lives. It is their inflexible, repetitive, poor stress-coping responses that are marks of a formal disorder.

Personality disorders influence the sense of self—the way people think and feel about themselves and how other people see them. The disorders often also powerfully influence interpersonal relations at work. They reveal themselves in how people "complete tasks, take and/or give orders, make decisions, plan, handle external and internal demands, take or give criticism, obey rules, take and delegate responsibility, and co-operate with people" (Oldham and Morris 1991, p. 24). The anti-social, obsessive compulsive, passive-aggressive and dependent types are particularly problematic in the work place. People with personality disorders have difficulty expressing and understanding emotions. It is the intensity with which they express them and their variability that makes them odd. More importantly they often have serious problems with self-control.

Perhaps the greatest progress in this area occurred when the Hogans developed the Hogan Development Survey, HDS (Hogan and Hogan 1997). Their idea was to use the categories of the Personality Disorders but to conceive of 'dark-side' tendencies rather than disorders. The test now widely used contains 168 true/false items that assess dysfunctional interpersonal themes. These dysfunctional dispositions reflect the distorted beliefs about others, which emerge when people encounter stress or stop considering how their actions affect others. Over time, these dispositions may become associated with a person's reputation and can impede job performance and career success. The HDS is not a medical or clinical assessment. It does not measure personality disorders, which are manifestations of mental disorder. Instead, the HDS assesses self-defeating expressions of normal personality. The DSM V makes this same distinction between behavioral traits and disorders—self-defeating behaviours, such as those predicted by the HDS, come and go depending on the context. In contrast, personality disorders are enduring and pervasive across contexts. The overlap between the terms used in DSM and the Hogan classification, and the categories proposed by Horney, are illustrated in Tables 1 and 2.

There is now a growing research base using the HDS and investigating dark-side factors at work (Furnham and Trickey 2011).

Table 1 The DSM IV and the HDS

DSM labels	Theme	Profile Scale	Theme	HDS Scale	Theme
Borderline	Inappropriate anger; unstable and intense relationships alternating between idealization and devaluation.	Unstable relationships	Flighty; inconsistent; forms intense albeit sudden enthusiasms and disenchantments for people or projects	Excitable	Moody and hard to please; intense, but short-lived enthusiasm for people, projects or things
Paranoid	Distrustful and suspicious of others; motives are interpreted as malevolent.	Argumentative	Suspicious of others; sensitive to criticism; expects to be mistreated	Sceptical	Cynical, distrustful, and doubting other's true intentions
Avoidant	Social inhibition; feelings of inadequacy and hypersensitivity to criticism or rejection	Fear of failure	Dread of being criticized or rejected; tends to be excessively cautious; unable to make decisions	Cautious	Reluctant to take risks for fear of being rejected or negatively evaluated
Schizoid	Emotional coldness and detachment from social relationships; indifferent to praise and criticism	Interpersonal insensitivity	Aloof; cold; imperceptive; ignores social feedback	Reserved	Aloof, detached, and uncommunicative; lacking interest in or awareness of the feelings of others

(continued)

Table 1 (continued)

DSM labels	Theme	Profile Scale	Theme	HDS Scale	Theme
Passive-aggressive	Passive resistance to adequate social and occupational performance; irritated when asked to do something he/she does not want to	Passive-aggressive	Sociable, but resists others through procrastination and stubbornness	Leisurely	Independent; ignoring people's requests and becoming irritated or argumentative if they persist
Narcissistic	Arrogant and haughty behaviours or attitudes; grandiose sense of self-importance and entitlement	Arrogance	Self-absorbed; typically loyal only to himself/herself and his/her own best interests	Bold	Unusually self-confident; feelings of grandiosity and entitlement; overvaluation of one's capabilities
Antisocial	Disregard for the truth; impulsivity and failure to plan ahead; failure to conform with social norms	Untrustworthiness	Impulsive; dishonest; selfish; motivated by pleasure; ignoring the rights of others	Mischievous	Enjoying risk taking and testing limits; needing excitement; manipulative, deceitful, cunning and exploitative

(continued)

Table 1 (continued)

DSM labels	Theme	Profile Scale	Theme	HDS Scale	Theme
Histrionic	Excessive emotionality and attention seeking; self-dramatizing, theatrical, and exaggerated emotional expression	Attention-seeking	Motivated by a need for attention and a desire to be in the spotlight	Colourful	Expressive, animated, and dramatic; wanting to be noticed and needing to be the centre of attention
Schizotypal	Odd beliefs or magical thinking; behaviour or speech that is odd, eccentric, or peculiar	No Common Sense	Unusual or eccentric attitudes; exhibits poor judgement relative to education and intelligence	Imaginative	Acting and thinking in creative and sometimes odd or unusual ways
Obsessive-Compulsive	Preoccupations with orderliness, rules, perfectionism, and control; over conscientious and inflexible	Perfectionism	Methodical; meticulous; attends so closely to details that he/she may have trouble with priorities	Diligent	Meticulous, precise, and perfectionistic; inflexible about rules and procedures; critical of others' performance

(continued)

Table 1 (continued)

DSM labels	Theme	Profile Scale	Theme	HDS Scale	Theme
Dependent	Difficulty making everyday decisions without excessive advise and reassurance; difficulty expressing disagreement out of fear of loss of support or approval	Dependency	Demand for constant reassurance, support, and encouragement from others	Dutiful	Eager to please and reliant on others for support and guidance; reluctant to take independent action or go against popular opinion

Table 2 The higher order classification of the personality disorders

DSM	Horney	Hogan
Cluster A (odd disorders) • **Paranoid personality disorder**: characterised by a pattern of irrational suspicion and mistrust of others, interpreting motivations as malevolent • **Schizoid personality disorder**: lack of interest and detachment from social relationships, apathy and restricted emotional expression • **Schizotypal personality disorder**: a pattern of extreme discomfort interacting socially, distorted cognitions and perceptions	*Moving Away From* People • The need for **self-sufficiency** and independence; while most desire some <u>autonomy</u>, the neurotic may simply wish to discard other individuals entirely • The need for **perfection**; while many are driven to perfect their lives in the form of well-being, the neurotic may display a fear of being slightly flawed • Lastly, the need to **restrict life practices** to within narrow borders; to live as inconspicuous a life as possible	*Moving Away From* People *Excitable*: Moody and hard to please; intense but short-lived enthusiasm for people, projects or things *Sceptical*: Cynical, distrustful and doubting others' true intentions *Cautious*: Reluctant to take risks for fear of being rejected or negatively evaluated *Reserved*: Aloof, detached and uncommunicative; lacking interest in or awareness of the feelings of others *Leisurely*: Independent; ignoring people's requests and becoming irritated or argumentative if they persist
Cluster B (dramatic, emotional or erratic disorders)	*Moving Against* people	*Moving Against* people

(continued)

Table 2 (continued)

DSM	Horney	Hogan
• **Antisocial personality disorder**: a pervasive pattern of disregard for and violation of the rights of others, lack of empathy, bloated self-image, manipulative and impulsive behaviour • **Borderline personality disorder**: pervasive pattern of instability in relationships, self-image, identity, behaviour and affects often leading to self-harm and impulsivity • **Histrionic personality disorder**: pervasive pattern of attention-seeking behaviour and excessive emotions • **Narcissistic personality disorder**: a pervasive pattern of grandiosity, need for admiration, and a lack of empathy	• The need for **power**; the ability to bend <u>wills</u> and achieve control over others—while most persons seek strength, the neurotic may be desperate for it • The need to **exploit others**; to get the better of them. To become <u>manipulative</u>, fostering the belief that people are there simply to be used • The need for **social recognition**; <u>prestige and limelight</u> • The need for **personal admiration**; for both inner and outer qualities—to be valued. • The need for **personal achievement**; though virtually all persons wish to make achievements, as with No. 3, the neurotic may be desperate for achievement	*Bold*: Unusually self-confident; feelings of grandiosity and entitlement; over valuation of one's capabilities *Mischievous*: Enjoying risk taking and testing the limits; needing excitement; manipulative, deceitful, cunning and exploitative *Colourful*: Expressive, animated and dramatic; wanting to be noticed and needing to be the centre of attention *Imaginative*: Acting and thinking in creative and sometimes odd or unusual ways
Cluster C (anxious or fearful disorders)	*Moving Toward* people	*Moving Toward* people

Moving Toward people

(continued)

Table 2 (continued)

DSM	Horney	Hogan
• **Avoidant personality disorder**: pervasive feelings of social inhibition and inadequacy, extreme sensitivity to negative evaluation • **Dependent personality disorder**: pervasive psychological need to be cared for by other people • **Obsessive-Compulsive personality disorder (not the same as obsessive-compulsive disorder)**: characterised by rigid conformity to rules, perfectionism and control	• The need for **affection and approval**; pleasing others and being liked by them • The need for **a partner**; one whom they can <u>love</u> and who will solve all problems	*Diligent*: Meticulous, precise and perfectionistic, inflexible about rules and procedures; critical of others *Dutiful*: Eager to please and reliant on others for support and guidance; reluctant to take independent action or to go against popular opinion

Many note the paradox that whilst dark-side traits may help managers up the greasy pole of management they do, in the end derail people. Thus Furnham et al. (2013) found that Bold, Mischievous and Colourful (Narcissistic, Psychopathic and Histrionic) (*Moving Against*) types tended to get more quickly promoted than others. Another study found those who scored high on Sales Potential scored high on Mischievious, Colourful and Imaginative; while managerial potential was associated with high scores on Bold, Imaginative and Diligent (Furnham et al. 2012).

There is certainly evidence that a person's dark-side profile relates, independently of their skills and values, to the jobs they are attracted to and thrive in. Some studies have looked at those who are attracted to the private vs the public sector (Furnham et al. 2014). The pattern is predictable: those in the public sector tend to score highly on *Moving Away* (Sceptical, Reserved) and *Moving Toward* (Diligent, Dutiful) but lower on *Moving Against* (Bold, Mischievous, Colourful) than those in the private sector.

There have been some interesting, small scale studies, in this area. One of the very first papers in this area was by Moscoso and Salgado (2004) who tested 85 Spanish adults on a Dysfunctional Personality Style questionnaire. They were rated by their supervisors eight months into the job on issues like quality of performance, learning ability, support for colleagues, rules accomplishment, effort, initiative and global performance. These ratings were combined into three scores. Two observations can be made. First, nearly all the correlations were negative indicating the higher one scored on the dark-side factors the lower the performance. Second, the correlations were modest though a third were around $r = 0.30$. Some dark-side factors like Passive-Aggressive and Schizotypal were much more clearly correlated with job performance than others (Borderline and Histrionic). Another study looked at 117 New Zealand CEOs and the relationship between their dark side and leadership. They found a number of significant correlations: those who were rated high on transformational leadership tended to be low of the Cautious and Reserved but high on the Colourful scale; being Bold was associated with Inspirational Motivation, which they argued was the result of dramatisation of issues used by those with charisma.

Another study looked at the dark-side correlates of innovation. Zibarrass et al. (2008) looked at dark-side correlates of motivation to change (persistence and ambition), challenging behaviour (risk-taking and non-conformity); adaptation (evolution not revolution) and consistency of work styles (methodological and systyenatic). They found that Cautious people scored low on everything but that four dark-side traits (Arrogant/Bold; Manipulative/Mischievous; Dramatic/Colourful; Eccentric/Imaginative) were positively associated with the first two measures that were both linked to innovation, but negatively related to the last two which were not. Their conclusion from further analysis was that people who score high on the *Moving Against* cluster tend to be more innovative.

In a much bigger study, Carson et al. (2012) looked at 1796 members of a global retail organisation. They were particularly interested in how two of the higher order dark-side factors, namely *Moving Against* and *Moving Away*, related to such things as job tenure, being fired and leaving the organisation. The results showed, as predicted, that those managers with dysfunctional *Moving Against* tendencies were more likely to leave, after either being fired or quitting.

One central question is when, why and how (or if) Dark Side traits are associated with leadership. Many have made the point that "moderate" scores on the Dark Side Traits tend to be associated with leadership success while extreme scores predict failure and derailment (Kaiser et al. 2014). Thus extremes were related to Enabling, Strategic and Operational leadership. The *Moving Against* leaders are therefore good at making bold moves, setting direction and supporting innovation but weak at monitoring performance, focusing resources and getting the details right. There is a cost benefit analysis with dark-side traits.

In an important meta-analysis Gaddis and Foster (2013) looked at the relationship between the dark-side factors and eight managerial behaviours including trustworthiness, work attitudes, leading others, decision making and problem solving, achievement orientation, dependability, adaptability/flexibility and interpersonal skills.

Spain et al. (2013) did a good job summarising the Dark Side traits at work. These are some of the findings: (Table 3)

Table 3 Summary of Dark Traits at work

Job performance	There is a negative relationship for most traits
Citizenship behaviour	With few exceptions (Dependent Personality) dark-side traits are associated with low communal, citizenship behaviour
Counterproductive behaviour at work	This is positively related to many traits
Creative performance	There is often a positive relationship though the relationship is non-linear
Training	Many dark-side traits are associated with overconfidence but low learning and development
Interviewing	Many dark-side traits are associated with interviewing success
Leadership	They can play a role in both success and failure
Managerial derailment	There are many cases of this
Abusive supervision	This is clearly linked to callous, malicious and destructive traits

Debates over the personality disorders continue. However, what has been most useful is the observation that underlying *all* the personality disorders are a very limited number of issues. The first is the ability to initiate and maintain healthy, happy, productive and long term relationships both inside and outside the workplace. Given that leadership and management is a "contact sport" it seems clear why that is so important. The second issue concerns self-awareness. It is self-evident that people do better if they are aware of their strengths and limitations; how and when they "buckle" under stress, and what sort of situations help and hinder their work.

6   Conclusion

It is not until recently that it has been recognised how many leaders fail and derail. As a consequence there is now an academic literature on the topic. One, but only one, factor that is often implicated in this is hubris. There are perhaps three important "take home messages" from this literature. The first is the paradox that a person's dark-side profile often explains in part how, when and why they climbed the greasy pole of management life but also how they slipped down it so dramatically and (for many people) quite unpredictably. Second, there are four "dark-side" traits called Cluster B or *Moving Against People* that are usually responsible for the failure and derailment. Third, this understanding of the causes of derailment can be used profitably in both selection and coaching.

The views expressed in this paper are those of the author and do not necessarily represent those of the UK Ministry of Defence or any other department of Her Britannic Majesty's Government of the United Kingdom. Furthermore such views should not be considered as constituting an official endorsement of factual accuracy, opinion, conclusion or recommendation of the UK Ministry of Defence or any other department of Her Britannic Majesty's Government of the United Kingdom.

References

Carson, M., Shanock, L., Heggestad, E., Andrew, A., Pugh, S., & Walter, M. (2012). The relationship between dysfunctional interpersonal tendencies, derailment potential behavior, and turnover. *Journal of Business and Psychology, 27*, 291–304.

Casciaro, T., & Lobo, M. S. (2005). Competent jerks, lovable fools, and the formation of social networks. *Harvard Business Review, 83*(6), 92–99.

Clements, C., & Washbush, J. (1999). The two faces of leadership: considering the dark side of leader-follower dimensions. *Journal of Workplace Learning, 11*, 170–175.

Furnham, A., & Trickey, G. (2011). Sex differences and dark side traits. *Personality and Individual Differences, 50*, 517–522.

Furnham, A., Trickey, G., & Hyde, G. (2012). Bright aspects to dark side traits: Personality disorders and work success. *Personality and Individual Differences, 52*, 908–913.

Furnham, A., Crump, J., & Ritchie, W. (2013). What it takes: Ability, demographic, bright and dark side trait correlates of years to promotion. *Personality and Individual Differences*, 55, 952–956.

Furnham, A., Hyde, G., & Trickey, G. (2014). Do your dark side traits fit? Dysfunctional personalities in different work sectors. *Applied Psychology*, 63, 589–606.

Gaddis, B.H. & Foster, J.L. (2013). Meta-analysis of dark side personality characteristics and critical work behaviours among leaders across the globe: Findings and implications for leadership development and executive coaching. *Applied Psychology: An International Review*, 65, 25–54.

Hogan, R. (2007). *Personality and the fate of organizations*. Mahwah, NJ: Lawrence Erlbaum.

Hogan, R., & Hogan, J. (1997). *Hogan personality inventory manual*. Tulsa, OK: HAS.

Kaiser, R., LeBreton, J., & Hogan, J. (2014). The dark side of personality and extreme leader behaviour. *Applied Psychology*, 64, 55–92.

Moscoso, S., & Salgado, J. (2004). "Dark Side" personality scales as predictors of task, contextual, and job performance. *International Journal of Selection and Assessment*, 12, 356–362.

Oldham, J., & Morris, L. (1991). *Personality self-portrait*. New York: Bantam.

Ouimet, G. (2010). Dynamics of narcissistic leadership in organisations. Towards an integrated research model. *Journal of Managerial Psychology*, 25, 713–726.

Peter, L. J., & Hull, R. (1969). *The Peter principle: Why things always go wrong*. New York: Harper Collins.

Spain, S.M., Harms, P., & Lebreton, J.M. (2013). The dark side of personality at work. *Journal of Organisational Behaviour*, 35, S41–S60.

Toney, F., & Brown, S. (1997). The incompetent CRO. *The Journal of Leadership Studies*, 4(3), 84–98.

Williams, F. I., Campbell, C., McCartney, W., & Gooding, C. (2013). Leader derailment: The impact of self-defeating behaviours. *Leadership & Organisation Development Journal*, 34, 85–97.

Zibarras, L., Port, R., & Woods, S. (2008). Innovation and the 'dark side' of personality. *Journal of Creative Behavior*, 42, 201–215.

5

Toxic Leadership in the Military

J.W. Dagless

1 Introduction

In 2011, consternation and concern were expressed in America and more widely when John Steele published his two-year study into Toxic Leadership. The report found that the vast majority, 83% of the 22,000 people surveyed, had worked for an over-controlling and inhibitive leader (Steele 2011). In the same survey, 61% when asked thought that negative and toxic leaders were a serious problem within the American military. At first glance, British Armed Forces do not appear to have the same problem with toxic or negative leadership. Yet a leadership questionnaire conducted amongst 311 newly-promoted Army majors found that 90% of respondents had observed personnel displaying 'toxic leadership' traits in one or more rank (Hart 2015). In the United Kingdom, under the glare of constant media attention and political pressure, we choose to learn from others since the British military prefers to address uncomfortable issues behind closed doors (Knight

J.W. Dagless (✉)
Defence Academy of the United Kingdom, Swindon, UK

© The Author(s) 2018
P. Garrard (ed.), *The Leadership Hubris Epidemic*,
https://doi.org/10.1007/978-3-319-57255-0_5

2014). When asked similar questions, it is a very British and intuitional response to remain silent. The spectre of toxic leadership is one such apparition that the British military acknowledges, but chooses to currently do very little about. Yet, every time there is a scandal, failing or a fault, the military's leadership and culture are brought into question: Royal Marine 'A', Sergeant Alexander Blackman. The British military exists to defend the nation and serve its interests. It expects the highest standards of moral and ethical behaviour. In order to achieve this, the military demands the highest standards of professionalism, individual behaviour and self-discipline, when on operations and whilst off duty. "The expectation is neither fair nor unfair; it is a simple fact of the profession" (Departments of Defense 1988). These qualities underpin the military's values and standards and its ethos, the same values and standards that toxic leadership and other forms of negative and destructive leaders undermine.

Individuals from all sections of society, including the military, are increasingly using the term toxic to define things that are generally negative, poor, underperforming, or unwanted. The misuse of the word toxic often devalues its meaning and divorces it from its origins, pertaining to poison. The same is true for the term 'toxic leader' which, since its inception, has become a label or tag liberally given to those in positions of authority, often without due consideration or thought. The problem with this is that labels are definitive, but the 'phrase' toxic leadership is not. For the purposes of this paper, the term toxic leadership is used in relation to individuals who harm others to enhance themselves and by dint of their destructive behaviour and dysfunctional personal qualities generate a serious poisonous effect (Lipman-Blumen 2005). This paper identifies the two defining characteristics of toxic leadership to be; the poisonous relationship that a toxic leader has with their subordinates; and that the toxic leader's underlying motivation is generated through self-interest. Recognising this, the paper concludes that the concept of toxic leadership will remain poorly defined and open to individual interpretation. This is very similar to the challenge of defining 'good leadership'.

This study does not attempt to distinguish between bad, dysfunctional, negative, destructive, or other malign leadership types or styles. By conducting a comprehensive overview of the literature relating to toxic and other negative leadership theories, facilitated by consultation with staff and faculty from: Army Headquarters; Centre for Defence Management and Leadership; Royal Military Academy Sandhurst; General Dynamics; Northrop Grumman; QinetiQ; and Serco, this paper will start by providing a thorough understanding of the concept of toxic leadership. As bad leadership in itself is not a new phenomenon, this paper will look at the origin and evolution of the term 'toxic leadership' before looking at its three key domains and the interdependencies between the leader, their followers and the environment. Having determined the principal characteristics of toxic leadership this paper will then conduct an analysis of the military's construct to identify how and why toxic leaders can succeed and even be seen to be exonerated or encouraged within the military environment. In doing so the paper will demonstrate that the military has its own unique toxic triangle between the leader, subordinates and the environment. Having identified institutional and structural flaws in this relationship, the paper will then propose that tools such as the 360-degree assessments can improve leadership development. It will finish by concluding that toxic leadership and other negative leadership types can only be addressed by the military's senior leadership, and if this issue is not seen to be addressed, it is highly likely that it will continue to erode and undermine the military's values and standards.

2   Understanding Toxic Leadership

Toxic Leadership is a pejorative term, loaded with negative connotations which are commonly associated with poor, bad, inefficient or destructive leadership traits. The phrase 'toxic leadership' is an oxymoron, since leadership by its own and numerous definitions is regarded as a positive force. For example, in the British Army leadership is seen to "underpin the moral component, the human element of fighting power" (Royal Military Academy Sandhurst (RMAS), 2012). The concept of toxic leadership was first expressed by Marcia Lynn Whicker who identified 3 types of 'toxic leader': The Enforcer (consensus leadership style), who seeks consensus with the leaders to whom they report; The Street Fighter (co-ordination leadership style), often egotistical and charismatic; and The Bully (command leadership style) with a pugnacious approach to others. Ultimately Whicker saw toxic leaders as "leaders that are maladjusted, malcontent and often malevolent, even malicious" (Whicker 1996). The notion of bullying leaders and the concept of the narcissistic or callous boss was not new at this time, but Whicker focussed on explaining the damage that the toxic leader did to an organisation, its culture, its people and ultimately its output or profit. She also recognised toxic leaders as seeking to suppress and exploit those under their control for their own gain. Understating her findings, she described them as "the antithesis of trustworthy leaders" (p. 26). It is important to note that from the term's origin, toxic leadership was seen as a phenomenon that goes beyond a simple failure to apply good leadership, but rather a deliberate act of using leadership negatively.

Since its inception, the term 'toxic leader' has been used loosely, particularly by the business, leadership and management sector. Its use therefore appears to move in and out of fashion, trending with the issues or language of the day. As a result, most commentators have tended to use the term as a general description, failing to grasp the poisonous or corrosive nature of this anti or negative leadership style. This has not been helped by the military's early attempts to understand the concept. Col George Reed, United States Army, was one of the first to write on the phenomenon of toxic leadership within the military, writing in 2004. He saw three key elements of the "toxic leader syndrome" which complemented Whicker's ideas, namely: a lack of concern for subordinates; personality traits that negatively affect the organisation; and a perception that the toxic leader is primarily motivated by self-interest (Reed 2004). Regrettably, some of the reviews and papers that followed misunderstood the subtleties of toxic leadership and sought to add or compile additional negative leadership traits to the term. One

Characteristics		Types
	Dysfunctional	
Incompetence		Absentee
Malfunctioning		Incompetent (Kellerman)
Maladjusted		Co-dependent
Sense of Inadequacy		Passive-aggressive
Malcontent		Busybody
Irresponsible		Paranoid
Amoral		*Rigid* (Kellerman)
Cowardice		Controller
Insatiable ambition		Compulsive
Egotism		*Intemperate* (Kellerman)
Arrogance	Toxic	*Enforcer* (Whicker)
Selfish values		Narcissistic
Avarice and Greed		*Callous* (Kellerman)
Lack of integrity		*Street Fighter* (Whicker)
Deception	Highly	*Corrupt* (Kellerman)
Malevolent	**Dysfunctional**	*Insular* (Kellerman)
Malicious		*Bully* (Whicker)
Malfeasant		*Evil* (Kellerman)
	Highly Toxic	

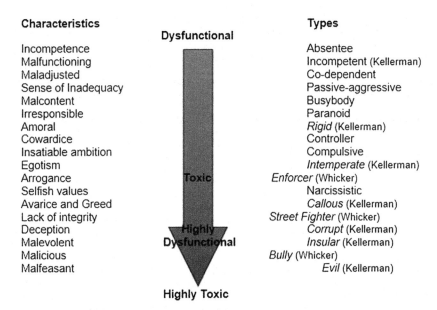

Fig. 1 Colonel Denise Williams' spectrum of leadership characteristics and types

of the most influential was Colonel Denise Williams' 2005 research paper on *Toxic Leadership in the U.S. Army*, which amassed, or rather listed, eighteen characteristics and types of leader and attributed them to a scale of toxic leadership from the subtle to the corrosive. Williams' paper was heavily influenced by Barbara Kellerman's 2004 book on *Bad Leadership*, though Kellerman does not attribute these bad leadership types to toxic leadership as she does not use the term. As a result, this has helped give rise to the notion of a spectrum or continuum of toxicity also espoused by Dr. Alan Goldman (2009) (Fig. 1).

As can be seen from the military's initial attempts to define toxic leadership, like the term leadership in general, it is easier to describe than define and its meaning is often subjective (Reed 2004). Throughout the literature, papers and reports, common descriptions include: bad leadership; bully; tyrant; oppressive; self-interested; unemotional; aggressive; harassing leadership style; closed; uncompromising; ungrateful; and that bastard (or worse). Most descriptions have a propensity to highlight toxic leaders as self-absorbed and self-promoting individuals who put their own personal goals ahead of the organisation, and suppress or undermine their subordinates (Hinds and Steele 2012). Goldman (2009) complements this by defining toxic leaders as "inwardly motivated, inherently destructive, and violate the legitimate interests of the organization". At the time of this paper's original publication, only the US Army had formally sought to define Toxic Leadership in *Army Doctrine Publication 6-22*, recognising it as a type of negative leadership:

> Toxic leadership is a combination of self-centred attitudes, motivations, and behaviours that have adverse effects on subordinates, the organization, and mission performance. This leader lacks concern for others and the climate of the organization, which leads to short- and long-term negative effects. The toxic leader operates with an inflated sense of self-worth and from acute self-interest. Toxic leaders consistently use dysfunctional behaviours to deceive, intimidate, coerce, or unfairly punish others to get what they want for themselves. (Army, U.S., 2012)

Since the paper's original release in 2015, it has helped stimulate debate across the Ministry of Defence and has informed the British Army's 2016 *Army Leadership Doctrine* that describes toxic leadership as:

> a combination of selfish attitudes, motivations, and behaviours that have adverse effects on both subordinates and the organisation. The toxic leader lacks emotional intelligence and has little concern for others, acting only in self-interest. Toxic leaders make maximum use of their positional power and will often employ dysfunctional behaviours to deceive, intimidate and coerce people to work for them. Toxic leaders may achieve the task in the short term, but fail to develop individuals and build strong teams. (Army, 2016)

From these definitions and descriptions it is possible to conceptualise toxic leaders as individuals with a series of psychological character traits rather than just a set leadership style that fits neatly into a preordained list of abnormal or negative leadership behaviours.

Many scholars and psychologists have studied the psychology of leadership, though their findings are often contradictory. For instance, Walter Mischel in *Personality and Assessment* (1968) argues that behaviour is determined by "situational factors" rather than the variables within an individual's basic personality core. This is contrary to Donald Hambrick and Phyllis Mason (1984), who use strategic leadership theory and agency theory to conclude that personality, beliefs and values ultimately shape how leaders react and conduct themselves within a group in any given situation. Whilst most literature focuses on 'good' leadership and seeks the elixir of leadership, there are a growing number of studies into destructive and negative leadership. Noting the self-interest and motivational factors outlined in the definitions above, there is an obvious synergy between toxic leadership and the "dark triad" of narcissism, Machiavellianism and psychopathy (McHoskey et al. 1998). Whilst the three conditions are considered as socially undesirable, depending on the scale of psychosis, some of the character traits exhibited can and are considered as desirable within a military and western business construct.

Narcissistic leaders can be charming, enigmatic and alluring to seniors because they are risk takers; they can be seen to think outside the box and are driven to achieve results (Doty and Fenlason 2013). Yet for those that work for them, they appear vain, manipulative, self-focussed, lack empathy and can be quick to disregard and undermine others (p. 56). Machiavellianism refers to interpersonal behaviour that advocates deception and manipulation for an individual's self-interest (Jakobwitz and Egan 2006). Again, these leaders through their cynical calculations may appear as good leaders to their hierarchy, but they can be considered to be amoral and loathed by their subordinates. Psychopaths, for all their anti-social behaviours, can be selfish and contrived, with superficial charm and exploitative, which again can be hidden from a toxic leader's superiors (Furtner et al. 2011). To a follower they may be emotionally shallow, cold, calculating, lack empathy and fail to take responsibility for their own actions (p. 371). Of the three, particular attention has been paid to the narcissistic leader since it is calculated that an increasing number of "strategic leaders" have this pathological disposition (Maccoby 2004).

It is recognised through historical leadership analysis that leaders can enhance their power, or have power thrust upon them, during times of crisis, upheaval or change (Padilla et al. 2007); and that personality is considered to be around three times more powerful than intelligence in determining leadership emergence (Pendleton and Furnham 2012). Leaders with narcissistic tendencies will naturally appear more appealing given their charisma, self-belief and focussed determination. Historical figures such as Napoleon Bonaparte, Winston Churchill and Franklin D Roosevelt are now considered to have had strong narcissistic tendencies (Maccoby 2004). Military figures such as Generals Montgomery, Patton and MacArthur are also believed to have had strong narcissistic traits (Campbell-Colquhoun 2006). Contemporary examples of highly narcissistic leaders may include Steve Jobs, Bill Gates and Jack Welch (Maccoby 2004). Noting the extraordinary success of these individuals, there is much debate, particularly in the business sector, regarding the positive attributes of narcissistic leaders. A key tenet in much of the literature on these leaders is that they can either be highly constructive or reactive (generally destructive) in relation to their organisations. Sigmund Freud concluded that all humans are a combination of three personal types; erotic, obsessive and narcissistic (Freud 2011). Despite our innermost desires, it is clear from the literature that there is no 'optimum solution' in harnessing the good and alleviating or controlling the negative aspects of narcissists. Whilst covered above in outline, it is worth reiterating some of the narcissists' flaws since they correlate with many of those associated with toxic leaders. Reactive narcissistic leaders are seen as: emotionally cold; self-interested; envious; disdainful to subordinates; volatile; do not listen; bullies and abusive; addicted to control; seek power; distrusts others; risk cavalier; attacks those who question or criticize; prefers unquestioning loyalty; overworks and under praises staff (Boyett 2006). Despite these obvious flaws, many companies are willing to overlook the cost of negative leaders since many of these are either long term or hidden costs as they primarily hit the human or moral component, making them harder to quantify. It has led some observers to speculate that narcissism is virtually a requirement to become the head of a large company in today's economic climate (Weiss 2006).

In order to better understand toxic leadership, consideration should therefore be given to an individual's psychological state and profile. Many companies now use the Five Factor Model[1] to analyse personality and leadership traits during the evaluation and recruitment of senior management and leadership positions (Pendleton and Furnham 2012). Recognition must also be given to the fact that most 'successful' toxic leaders will appear charismatic and have a predisposition and willingness to work long hours with vigour in the pursuit of self-promotion, generated by their need for power (Padilla et al. 2007). These outward characteristics are generally regarded as highly desirable, as will the toxic leader's apparent ability to lead as part of a group, generating positive military or business outcomes over a limited time period. It is however the flawed and poisonous relationship that a toxic leader has with their subordinates that distinguishes them from other negative or destructive leadership types. This has led many writers and commentators to conclude that the toxic leader also lacks emotional intelligence.

Emotional Intelligence is the ability to monitor and understand your own and others' emotions and use this information effectively in personal, social, and survival aspects of intelligence (Sewell 2011). Daniel Goleman in his popular book, *Emotional Intelligence: Why It Can Matter More than IQ* (2006), identified five domains or levels of emotional intelligence: knowing one's own emotions; managing your own emotions appropriately; self-motivation; recognising emotions in others; and handling relations. Goleman through his studies identified the fact that high IQ males tend to be ambitious and productive, but also critical, condescending and fastidious. Whilst high IQ males are not necessarily toxic, they can appear emotionally bland and cold; again a label often associated with toxic leaders. Taking the simplicity of John Adair's leadership model comprising team, task and individual, it is seen that leaders with effective emotional intelligence will recognise and empathise with their people as required and build successful teams around any given task (Adair 1993). In doing so they generally encourage and value diversity, network effectively, and welcome constructive dissent rather than destructive consent (Goleman 2006). Emotional sensitivity and effective understanding between self, people, managers and leaders is now a key tenet within a number of business and industry leadership

Fig. 2 The toxic triangle: Elements in the three domains related to toxic leadership (adapted from Padilla et al. 2007)

models (Serco 2014). The idea of the corporate, hierarchical, manipulative and 'jungle fighting' boss largely disappeared from the business sector in the 1980s, in part due to the pressures of globalisation and information technology as well as changes in the workforce's needs (Goleman 2006). However, the military is still a patriarchal and hierarchical institution that naturally desires strong leadership, particularly at the tactical and operational level (Popper 1996). This wish for strong leadership should not be conflated or confused with the appeal of the toxic leader. It is important to note that whilst the toxic leader might appear strong, they cannot operate unless they are empowered. In order to do this, the culture or environment in which they operate must facilitate or allow toxic leadership to exist, and the leader must have followers, willing or otherwise (Fig. 2).

Whilst most studies tend to focus on the leader, it is recognised that the role of the follower is no less important in the leadership process. Kellerman (2004) distinguishes between two follower types, the "bystander" and the acolyte or "true believer". Lipman-Blumen in her book *The Allure of Toxic Leaders* (2006) identifies three types of follower: the benign follower; the leader's entourage; and the malevolent follower. For the purposes of this paper followers will be referred to as conformers who comply, and colluders that actively participate with the toxic leader. Lipman-Blumen goes on to identify six underlying psychological factors that make conformers seek and accept toxic leaders. These are: the need for an authority figure; the desire for security and certainty; the need to feel special; to be part of a community; a fear of ostracism or isolation; and a fear of powerlessness to challenge (Lipman-Blumen 2005). As Whicker points out in her original book, the toxic leader will fulfil a follower's basic psychological, safety and belonging needs as advocated in Maslow's hierarchy of needs (Whicker 1996). Sigmund Freud would label individuals who blindly conform to authority as psychologically immature as he observed that the prime function of the ego is self-preservation (Storr 1989). Stanley Milgram in his obedience studies found that within a hierarchal structure there is a natural obedience to authority which leads to a level of social conformity (Milgram 2010). This conformity can lead to a homogenisation or acceptance of norms which can influence a person to adopt the behaviour of their peers and can lead some to imitate higher-status individuals (p. 116). Some followers (colluders) will as a result of this willingly comply and accept toxic leadership. Their motivation is most likely self-advancement, though some will associate with the toxic leader's behavioural norms making them more susceptible to become negative leaders themselves in the future, particularly if they also succeed in this guise. If toxic leaders are 'free' to operate, and if they can convince others directly or indirectly that their behaviour is acceptable, it would suggest that there is likely to also be a problem within an organisation's environment and underlying culture.

Culture is "essentially attitudes and values and their expressions or embodiments in performance... which [also] reveals itself in a pattern of social relationship characteristics" (Burke 1987). Organisational culture is a dynamic phenomenon that determines human thinking about behaviour and influences us in a variety of ways (Schein 2010). It is intrinsically linked to the intangible of leadership since it regulates our behaviour, informs and rationalises group or organisational values, and informs our underlying unconscious beliefs that we often take for granted (p. 24). Once set, culture determines the criteria for leadership and inadvertently directs who will and will not be a leader. Yet it is the senior or strategic leader's role to identify dysfunctional or unwanted cultural elements and change them as part of an evolutionary and survivalist process (p. 22). However, it is a logical proposition to assume that all legitimate companies, organisations and institutions have some form of legal, moral and self or business interest in the well-being of their employees. Most companies would therefore consider themselves to be ethical within their own society's socially acceptable norms. It would seem contrary to intuition or common-sense then that many companies continue to employ and promote leaders who are considered as toxic. Goldman observes that most toxic leaders are "embedded in a dysfunctional organisation housing deviance, poor policies, avoidance behaviour, and a negative approach to social intelligence, team building and collaboration" (Goldman 2009). This can be attributed to three environmental and cultural factors. The first, as outlined above, is that a toxic leader can be manipulative and appear highly desirable to senior leadership (Lubit 2003). Secondly, this would indicate that the organisation has failed to apply appropriate checks and balances that can lead to institutionalisation, as a toxic leader may subvert structures and processes for his or her own gain (Lipman-Blumen 2006). Thirdly, this will be as a result of senior leadership failing to understand the cost and potential for toxic leadership to exist within their organisation. At best, this might be due to ignorance, at worst an organisation's senior leadership may suffer from a conspiracy of optimism and denial (Padilla et al. 2007).

Before concluding this section it is worth considering some of the cost disbenefits that can be connected with toxic leadership. Writers such as Lipman-Blumen, Goldman and Wicker conclude that toxic leaders generally come with long-term costs that should be weighed against any perceived short term gains. A toxic leader is seen to affect an employee's loyalty, motivation, health, happiness and productivity (Goldman 2009). If unresolved this will eventually have a negative impact on organisational growth and output, which harms profit and other benefits (Whicker 1996). Toxic leaders therefore undermine the trust agenda between and leader and follower, and the organisation and its employees. Whilst there is no hard statistical evidence about the cost of toxic leadership, the United Kingdom Government's Health and Safety Executive annual report into stress-related disorders provides some macro-level insight. Their 2014 report states that defence, along with education, health and social work, has the highest prevalence of work-related stress with 2030 cases per 100,000 people. From these figures it can be calculated that the Ministry of Defence continues to lose over 110,000 days a year to work-related stress. Whilst there are many variables that contribute towards stress, the data attributes failures in interpersonal relationships as the second highest contributory factor (Health and Safety Executive 2014). This includes causes such as bullying and harassment, attributes commonly associated with, though not exclusive to, toxic leaders. Worse still, some studies in America have identified toxic leadership as a contributing factor in a number of suicides within the military (Zwerdling 2014) and in other areas of employment such as nursing (Roter 2011). In comparison, open-verdict suicides within the British military are currently below the national average, and toxic leadership has yet to be considered as a contributory factor (Ministry of Defence (MoD) 2014). Whilst this highlights a tangible cost, there are many softer costs that can also be attributed to toxic leaders.

The greatest hidden cost that a toxic leader generates is the psychological and mental stress they place their subordinates under (Lipman-Blumen 2006). This, despite the figures for days off due to stress given above, is considered to be just the tip of the iceberg, yet it remains immeasurable (Kusy and Holloway 2009). Factors such as an employee's loyalty to the organisation and their co-workers, their resilience to a toxic leader's demands, and their future employment prospects will affect how they respond (Kirke 2009). In theory, just as good leadership is seen as a positive retention factor, so toxic leadership could be seen to have a negative one. However, there remains insufficient recording within large-scale institutions since companies accept, expect and require an inflow and outflow of personnel from their workforce (Reed 2004). In the case of United Kingdom Armed Forces personnel, the annual Armed Forces Continuous Attitude Survey (2015) continues to highlight that the principal reason for people leaving is the impact of the Service on family and personal life. The survey also states that 72% of personnel believe they are fairly treated, with 13% stating they have been subjected to bullying, harassment or discrimination (MoD 2015a). This additional cost therefore sits within accepted organisational tolerance levels and will only be addressed when retention becomes a critical issue.

Perhaps the most dangerous potential cost associated with toxic leadership is emulation (Reed 2004). Whilst it is widely reported that toxic leaders lack the empathy or patience to mentor others (Maccoby 2004), they are prone to building their own closed groups and networks to avoid external scrutiny (Padilla et al. 2007). This would suggest that toxic leaders are unlikely to promote diversity within their teams, instead preferring to surround themselves with yes-men (Maccoby 2004). Further to this, it is seen that when members of an organisation are made to conform, the need for interaction is reduced and the opportunity for genuine new insights is dramatically decreased (Paparone et al. 2008). Depending on the deliverables, image and reputation of the organisation, this may in turn attract negative press. Whilst the examples of leaders considered to be narcissistic such as Steve Jobs and Bill Gates may imply that leaders who pose characteristics of toxicity can be innovative and pioneering, this is rarely the case. Toxic leaders are generally regarded as poor listeners and authoritarian in nature (Lipman-Blumen 2006). Whilst they may be brilliant in driving a team to deliver set objectives, "organisationally negative they oppress members of a formed body of people, reducing their effectiveness" (Kirke 2007). Ultimately a toxic leader lacks respect for their subordinates which in turn will undermine the cultural ethos of an organisation. It therefore cultivates a selfish and undesirable culture where individuals are more prone to act in their own self-interest rather than those of their followers and the organisation they represent.

In this section on understanding toxic leadership it is possible to see that there are many definitions and attributes associated with the term. Most academics, writers and even the embryonic military definitions agree that the two defining characteristics of toxic leadership are; the poisonous relationship that a toxic leader has with their subordinates; and that the toxic leader's underlying motivation is generated through self-interest. A strong, demanding and decisive leader is not necessary toxic, just as a quiet and considered leader can be. The difficulty as observed by Lipman-Blumen is that "an individual leader may be toxic in some situations and not in others... Moreover, different toxic leaders display varying kinds and degrees of toxicity" (Lipman-Blumen 2005).

This in turn can lead the definition and understanding of toxic leadership to be open to personal interpretation, and has led the term's use to become general, rather than specific. From this it is concluded that the concept of toxic leadership will, for the foreseeable future, remain poorly defined. Whatever definition is used it is true that:

> Toxic leaders generally leave us worse off than they found us. The intent to harm others or to enhance themselves at the expense of others distinguishes serious toxic leaders or unintentional toxic leaders, who may cause significant negative fallout. (Riggio et al. 2008)

It is apparent that an individual's personality, including level of emotional intelligence and psychological predisposition may help explain a toxic leader's behaviour and underlying motives. Ultimately though, toxic leadership is not just about the leader, it is as much about the organisations they operate in, their underlying cultures and values, and the relationship that these leaders have with their subordinates or followers. This dynamic will now be explored in the next section, to better understand why the military is susceptible to toxic leaders.

3 Why Does Toxic Leadership Reside in the Military?

In the military, leaders are responsible for everything that occurs within their command, even tasks that are delegated and undertaken out of sight. "The decisions and actions of leaders resonate and through their behaviours they set the climate and the moral framework for their organisation." (RMAS 2012) The military leader has to be capable of handling volatile, uncertain, complex and ambiguous situations; using inference, improvisation, divergent thinking, creativity and intuition to overcome adversary (Paparone et al. 2008). Many of the personal characteristics or traits that are considered to be essential for success in the most demanding operational environments can be conflated with the attributes of a toxic leader: confidence and arrogance; courage and intimidation; selfless and selfish. The dilemma for the military is that toxic leaders also get results, and they are willing to sacrifice themselves and others to achieve them. As highlighted in the leadership questionnaire conducted by the Army majors, there are still many in the military who agree with the sentiment that toxic leadership is an acceptable price to pay to ensure future mission success (Hart 2015).

Major General Craig Orme of the Australian Army wrote in his findings following a series of embarrassing high-profile incidents that damaged the reputation of the Australian Defence Force that: "the risks of poor or toxic leadership are much greater in the military than they are in civilian organisations" (2011). This section will examine why this is the case and why the military are prone to toxic leaders. In doing so, it will highlight the relationship between the military leader, his or her subordinates, and a number of environmental and cultural factors that make up the military toxic triangle. Many of these elements are not unique to the military. What is different is the military's predisposition to place leadership and behaviours at the centre of everything that it does. This is because the legitimate use of military force "is wholly unlike diplomacy or politics, because it is fought by men whose values and skills are not those of politicians or diplomats" (Keegan 2004). Whilst war is considered to a be part of 'normal human activity' by many academics (Kilcullen 2013) it varies greatly in its nature, scale and task through a spectrum of conflict that is now no longer considered to be linear and is growing in complexity (United Kingdom Developments, Concepts and Doctrine Centre (DCDC), 2010). The need to engage followers to accomplish mission goals is critical for future success. The requirement for clearly understood and enacted military values and standards is also vital, noting the impact that commanders at all levels have on culture, which requires leadership (Northouse 2013). Throughout this chapter it is important to understand that military leaders are a product of their environments (Aubrey 2012). Unlike other governmental departments and the private sector, the military does not hire in senior leaders, as their military responsibilities and duties are mostly, though not exclusively, unique. All militaries cultivate their leaders through the ranks and from officer academies. As such, each military institution takes personal responsibility and accountability for the development and selection of its leaders, up to and including the highest positions. A perceived failure of leadership in any guise, toxic or otherwise, is therefore seen not only as an individual's failing, but also a failure of the organisation that they represent and its values and standards.

The Ministry of Defence advocates numerous leadership methodologies and encourages attributes such as integrity, vision, communication, professional knowledge and humility (MoD 2014). A number of the leadership models such as the Trait Approach, Tannenbaum's and Schmidt's Continuum of Leadership, Belbin's Team Leader Theory, and Bass' Transformational Leadership Theory all stress the importance of values (Defence Academy of the United Kingdom, 2015). In the United Kingdom, these values and standards underpin the ethos and cultural identity of each Service. They, the Royal Navy, Army and Royal Air Force, are given the lead for setting their own values and standards, though there are broad similarities between all three. The Royal Navy's values and standards are formally published in *Book of Reference 3*. It states that individuals must accept and live by their values and that standards must be maintained at all times whether on operations, undertaking peacetime tasking or off duty. These values are encapsulated in the Royal Navy's ethos:

> The enduring spirit derived from our people's loyalty to their ship, unit or team sustained by high professional standards and strong leadership, that gives us courage in adversity and the determination to fight and win. (2014)

The Royal Navy's core values comprise: commitment; courage; discipline; respect for others; integrity and loyalty; all bounded by the Service's history, heritage and reputation (its culture) (p. 21C-3). Recognising the importance of emotional intelligence, the values and standards annex goes on to give specific direction to its leaders and those in positions of authority. At all times it talks of humility, teamwork, morale and the maintenance of good order. The British Army publishes a generic Values and Standards booklet that lists the Army's values as: courage; discipline; respect for others; integrity; loyalty; and selfless commitment (2012). It goes on to stipulate that behaviour must be appropriate, professional and lawful at all times (p. 11–14). This document talks repeatedly of the Army's ethos, but declines to include it, unlike the other Services' publications. The Army's ethos is defined elsewhere as:

> The spirit that inspires soldiers to fight. It derives from, and depends upon, the high degrees of commitment, self-sacrifice and mutual trust which, together, are essential for the maintenance of morale. (2010)

The Royal Air Force also publishes its Ethos, Core Values and Standards in a booklet. Like the Royal Navy, the Royal Air Force provides an ethos statement up front, stating that it aims "to deliver air power no matter the challenge or the environment" (2008). It goes on to encapsulate its values under four headings: respect; integrity; service; and excellence. These are then broken down further into their constituent parts. All three Services highlight the role that an individual plays within his or her own organisation and the importance of teamwork. They all also subscribe to 'the Service Test' in which an individual of any rank or status is judged against:

> Have the actions or behaviour of an individual adversely impacted, or are they likely to impact, on the efficiency or operational effectiveness of the [Naval Service, Army, Royal Air Force]? (Royal Navy 2014)

In return, all three Services promise to value their personnel and to treat them with respect, dignity and compassion, all things which a toxic leader might willingly sacrifice for his or her own self-interest and gain. A toxic leader might appear to adhere to cultural norms and to enact social values and standards as required, but instead of serving to lead, they lead for self (Reed 2004). A toxic leader may also use these values and standards to judge and persecute others, to consolidate his or her control by undermining existing institutions and laws (Padilla et al. 2007). Even within the most altruistic organisations, an organisation's values and standards remain vulnerable to exploitation without credible checks and balances. One of the challenges facing the military is that its values and standards are deliberately aligned to the military's aggrandised history in order to provide context and precedence. In doing so it inflates the role of the strong and heroic leader, which can aid or be seen to justify the actions of a toxic leader (Jacobs 2014).

Heroic leadership is a model that "encourages conformity and adherence rather than one that emphasises how leaders can lead others to lead themselves" (Manz and Sims 1991). It is also a model that many toxic leaders seek to construct for themselves (Padilla et al. 2007). Heroic leadership focuses power and responsibility upon a single accountable leader, empowering the leader to set their own objectives and goals, with only limited consideration for their followers (p. 179). For the model to work effectively it assumes that the leader has the wisdom, ability and integrity to perform in the organisation's and followers' interests (Cohen 2010). Due to the military's hierarchical structure, role and lineage, many within the military accept and even encourage forms of heroic leadership (Chapman 2013). It is not uncommon to hear of hard and uncompromising officers who impose constraints upon their subordinates and deal harshly with those who fail to meet exacting standards. For it is seen that on the battlefield, leaders must have the strength of character and confidence to persevere against adversity, and if required put themselves and others in harm's way. It has been identified many times that under the extremes of battle, "good leaders enable ordinary people to routinely accomplish the extraordinary" (Cohen 1999). But this should not excuse a toxic leader, or allow them to bully and coerce others permanently, or mistakenly equate toxic leaders with strong or heroic leaders. The propensity for the military to tolerate this behaviour was identified by Charles Mosko in what he termed in the 1970s as the "military's genetic self-image as a specialist in violence, ready for combat" (Mosko 1977), and has been described latterly as the "warrior spirit" (Mosko 2001).

Whilst the military's raison d'être is generally focussed on conducting high-intensity war fighting, today's operations are "conducted amongst the people and civilian infrastructure and under the intense scrutiny of the media" (Carter 2013). Contemporary operations also tend to lack temporal parameters (Smith 2005) and the ethical dimension as in Iraq and Afghanistan, together with the increasing application of criminal and human rights legislation, has re-affirmed the need for strong and well understood values and standards, particularly when operating under duress (Benest 2012). Yet toxic leaders can erode the values and standards that the military sees as vital to its success. This warrior or institutional military mindset goes some way towards explaining why 25% of the Army majors surveyed believed that toxic leadership was acceptable if it meant mission success (Hart 2015). It also explains why some leaders who are known to exhibit certain negative leadership traits are allowed to do so, as the system expects a degree of friction. Unsurprisingly, as a hierarchical organisation, most of the military's checks and balances are aligned to the chain of command, making it harder to identify and deal with toxic leaders. This is further compounded by the military's cultural deference to rank, its anti whistleblowing ethos, and the lack of a clear and independent arbitration process, which will be covered in the next section.

There is an old military dictum that states 'rank has its privileges'. This holds true, as in most circumstances rank takes precedence, even where checks and balances are put in place. The rank system forms the backbone of the military's structure since it defines an individual's role and the degree of responsibility that they hold. "The rewards for those who are promoted are great and public… conferring authority, respect, privilege and prestige", (Elliott 2015) not to mention salary and additional benefits. A toxic leader's desire for power and affirmation incentivises him or her to seek higher rank, but it also gives unquestionable authority over subordinates which they can exploit. The requirement for discipline, good order and obedience ironically makes the military more susceptible to toxic leaders. Whilst most modern Western armies have adopted the concept or a notion of 'mission command' that encourages centralised intent and decentralised execution (DCDC 2014) it is still considered an anathema to disobey an order, or deviate from a senior commander's direction. Instructions, operating procedures and orders stipulate what is to be done within set boundaries, and this informs individual and group behaviours across all ranks (Kirke 2010). Most reports and returns as well as the notional military checks and balances that are put in place tend to complement the hierarchical structure, as they primarily flow up and down the chain of command. As such it is seen that "hierarchy and bureaucracy are behavioural artefacts ingrained in the military culture" (Aubrey 2012).

On modelling the relationship between hierarchy and bureaucracy, Jean Tirole observed the deliberate manipulation of information as it passed up the chain of command as details were distorted, concealed, or not reported (1986). Tirole associated this behaviour within large organisations with the psychological desire for rewards and the avoidance of punishment (p. 199). Toxic leaders are skilled at disguising their Hubris Syndrome and appearing to produce results, at least in the short term, whilst hiding their true motives and the cost of their behaviour (Aubrey 2012). With only nominal oversight, toxic leaders within the military environment not only have primacy because of their rank, they also control the passage of information through their respective chain of command. They can manipulate and broadly choose what to send to their seniors, and they can also regulate what comes down within their own group. A toxic leader may also choose to adopt a means of restrictive control, which goes against the tenets of mission command outlined above (Kendall 2007). A toxic leader will therefore exploit the hierarchical structure of the military, aided by a lack of external checks, to remain hidden within the military's bureaucratic, process-laden organisation. In addition to the hierarchical system, the posting or assignment mechanism within the military, which he or she can influence, also aids the toxic leader's survival.

Within the military most, though not all, personnel are posted every two to three years. Depending on the nature of their role and responsibility (aligned with their rank) leaders at every level will be given set freedoms, constraints and deliverables to achieve. Military organisations are almost solely output-focussed; though 'institutional environments' such as Defence often find it difficult to define their outputs (Williamson 1995). This means that many deliverables are esoteric or have some form of historical lineage, for which the organisation is generally structured to produce. Additional tasks are added by situation and circumstance, or more often than not, given by a senior reporting officer who has a particular priority or good idea. This mix of relatively short posting cycles, ambiguity in output, and a focus on results plays to the toxic leader's strengths. As highlighted above, toxic and narcissistic leaders are prone to be more successful in environments where there is uncertainty and change, as an authoritative or driven individual will initially appear to meet organisational and follower needs (Lipman-Blumen 2006). Whilst followership is covered below, it should be noted at this point that the military cyclical posting scheme creates the situation whereby individuals that work for a toxic leader generally only do so for a limited period of time. Whicker noted that proximity and time are key factors that individuals will consider when choosing whether to tolerate a toxic leader (1996). Returning to output, Mark Van Buren and Todd Safferstone identified that those leaders who focussed on achieving some notion of deliverable success tended to score 20% higher than their colleagues who had not (2009). Jeffrey Cohn and Jay complement this in observing that organisations tend to select their leaders on results rather than potential; placing charisma and confidence above integrity, courage and emotional intelligence (2011). It would seem counter-intuitive to place individuals with the core values and standards of an organisation beneath others who prove their worth in some other, potentially more transitory manner. This would imply that there is a limitation or fault within the military's promotion and leadership selection system.

The principal means by which individuals are identified and selected for promotion in the military is the annual reporting system, which is aligned with the chain of command. The current report's format encourages the report-writer to focus on deliverables, considering performance before potential. An individual's ability is measured against a number of criteria. Of the twelve factors for other ranks and ten for officers only two are linked to the military's values and standards (subordinate development; and courage and values), the remainder are performance related (MoD 2015b). The narrative boxes that follow are also in the order of performance, then potential. Whilst it is the 'potential' narrative at the end of the report that is considered in assessing an individual's suitability for promotion and future posts, including leadership positions, it is influenced throughout by 'performance'. It is recognised that, in a competitive environment, be it public, commercial or the armed services, "ambition and promotion are linked and exert a significant influence on behaviour" (Elliot 2015). However, this reporting mechanism favours the output-focussed toxic leader, deviating from the values and standards that the military see as essential to its ethos. Tim Kane in his analysis of the American military reporting system highlights that, despite espousing cultural values such as integrity, teamwork and selflessness, the military's reporting system tends to reward rigid careerism (Kane 2012). Kane goes on to argue that all evaluation systems must continue to evolve in recognition that the skills and leadership values required in the contemporary operating environment are changing (p. 196). Continual review of the British military reporting system is therefore required to ensure that it meets the changing needs of the military and the changing nature and value system of the young people it recruits. The current system fails to take any account of an individual's cultural values and standards, let alone even consider their emotional intelligence or relationship with their subordinates in any meaningful way. This will be reviewed in the next section where the utility and challenges of 360-degree assessments will be considered as a means of combating toxic leadership. The current top-down reporting mechanism can assess a number of leadership traits and criteria, but it is open to manipulation from an effective toxic leader. Largely subjective, the reports are also prone to reflect the reporting officer's and more widely the military's own conscious and unconscious bias; this can also aid the toxic leader.

Due to its heritage and "the unique loyalties and idiosyncrasies within each Service, they create a predisposition, that once formed [are] seldom released" (Elliot 2015). It is these that form the foundations of the military's unconscious bias that allows the toxic leader to manipulate their superior's and follower's perceptions. Binna Kandola observes that prejudice has three components comprising: affective - feeling and emotions; behavioural—actions; and cognitive—thoughts (Kandola 2009). "Implicit prejudice is based on association" and can be used to establish or separate groups (p. 63). A manipulative toxic leader will use this to create closed groups and networks to avoid external scrutiny (Padilla et al. 2007). In the process they will knowingly sideline talented personnel who do not collude, or those who do not conform to the toxic leader's stringent idealised norms (Downs 1977). This in turn can create an environment that revolves around satisfying the needs of the toxic leader who runs the unit, at the expense of their subordinates who take on a supporting role (p. 79). At the same time, the toxic leader will use group identity to associate with his or her senior reporting officer's own predilections (Jones 2003). Whilst much of this sociological interaction can be explained by the military's hierarchical system, Charles Kirke argues that the social and cultural elements within the military go beyond the formal command structure, which makes followership deliberately more robust and tolerant (2009).

The concept or idea of followership is often misunderstood; it is a dynamic relationship between the leader and follower(s) where both have intrinsic powers, roles and responsibilities, relative to one another and their organisation (Chaleff 2009). More importantly, followership is not a passive activity; every leader should also be a follower, and a follower can also lead (RMAS 2012). Looking at this relationship, through the Army's societal construct, Kirke identifies four social structures within the Army that are equally applicable to the Royal Navy and Royal Air Force. They comprise: a formal command structure; an informal structure; a loyalty/identity structure; and a functional structure (Kirke 2009). This wider social environment has evolved over time, is steeped in history and valour, but more importantly it allows formed operational units to function in the chaos and uncertainty of war and other military operations. The construct identified by Kirke helps to explain the strength and resilience of the military follower construct as subordinates follow the formal chain of command, whilst the informal structure allows for/or alleviates deficiencies within the formal chain of command (p. 205). In addition to this, it is seen that a subordinate has a functional duty within an identifiable group to which he or she has a stronger social bond (ibid.). Kirke concludes that these formal, informal and identity systems provide a robust framework that transcends the rank and discipline system (Kirke 2010). In doing so, it ensures that a military unit and many sub-units can continue to function even with deficiencies within their own leadership structures. This is a phenomenon also identified by Nick Jans and David Schmidtchen (2002) in their research that modelled organisational effectiveness against perceived leader performance in which toxic leaders continue not only to survive, but are seen to succeed. This follower resilience and organisational strength, in most cases at unit level, tolerates and inadvertently protects the toxic leader. This principally goes back to one of the military's core values, loyalty. This loyalty is to others rank, position, a unit or organisation and is combined with the sentiment of not telling tales. A common reason why toxic leaders are not identified is the anti-whistle-blowing culture (Lipman-Blumen 2006). In the military, this is compounded further by the hierarchical structure and discipline system that are designed to support the chain of command (Aubrey 2012). This in turn can create a fear of reprisal from peers as well as leaders if a subordinate speaks out against a toxic leader or the chain of command in general (Jacobs 2014). This apparent lack of an effective independent and impartial third-party to enforce external checks and balances will be reviewed in the next section in identifying what can be done to combat toxic leadership.

It can be seen, therefore, that there are a number of environmental and follower traits that the toxic leader is able to exploit, as summarised in Fig. 3. Before the toxic leader does anything, they are by virtue of their senior rank and position given pre-eminence over their followers (Aubrey 2012). It is naturally assumed by 'the system' that military leaders are virtuous, fair, and have their subordinates' interests at heart. If a leader is identified as displaying negative leadership traits this is often excused, or confused with strong or heroic leadership, especially where they are seen to get results. As such, the chain of command, the numerous and often bureaucratic checks and balances, and the discipline system are designed to support, empower and enable military leaders. This hierarchical construct therefore creates what Milgram refers to as a natural obedience mechanism (2010). This is then complemented by the strength and resilience of the military's followership construct, supported by its formal, informal and identity systems. Designed to function under the duress of war, most units will tolerate, even flatter and facilitate the toxic leader as it is generally in their interests and only needs to be endured for a limited period of time. We recall that the two defining characteristics of a toxic leader as having a poisonous relationship towards subordinates and motivation by self-interest. Uncompromising and without thought for their subordinates' needs, the toxic leader will, when in command, seek to deliver some form of

Fig. 3 The military toxic triangle: Elements in the three domains that facilitate toxic leadership

valued success or accomplishment to prove his or her worth (Aubrey 2012). In doing so, the toxic leader will attempt to create a spectre of success. This in turn is likely to satisfy the predisposition of the toxic leader's commander who in turn may reward and promote the toxic leader further. This ability to get results in an output-focussed organisation from a top-down perspective is considered to be a good thing. But is the cost of toxic leadership worth undermining the military's values and standards? This will be examined in the next section which considers what can be done about toxic leadership.

4   What Can Be Done About Toxic Leadership?

As noted, 90% of the respondents to the British Army leadership questionnaire stated they had observed personnel displaying toxic leadership traits in one or more rank (Hart 2015). The first step in dealing with toxic leadership is for the military's top echelon to acknowledge that it exists and to admit that there are organisational failings and individual peccabilities. The second step is to understand the extent and effect that it has across all sections of the military in order to make a 'conscious decision' what to do about it. Given the British military's structures, tasks, people and culture, the responsibility for this sits firmly with the organisation's strategic leadership. There is no single or simple solution. Whicker, Lipman-Blumen, Goldman and others suggest a range of options to deal with toxic leadership including: screening; training and education; coaching and counselling; disciplining; and dismissing. In choosing a combination of treatment, toleration and termination, the military's strategic leadership will have to balance the needs of its future force, noting the range of likely tasks to be placed upon it, whilst considering the time required for delivering cultural and leadership change. "Real cultural change is [only] achieved by selectively applying effort and resources to key pressure points in the institution" (Wong 2014). Understanding how to change is just as important as knowing what to change, and this is likely to require time and restraint in the propagation of any policy. As highlighted in the section above, if the British military wishes to tackle toxic leadership, there are two areas that should be considered as a priority. The first recommendation in identifying and treating toxic and negative leadership traits is the introduction of 360-degree or some form of multi-source assessment feedback. The second is the need for an empowered, independent and accessible body, completely distinct from the chain of command, in order to deal with all complaints, including areas and behaviours resulting from poor or negative leadership. It is the author's opinion that the British military must be seen to do something about toxic leadership if it is to ensure that its selfless leadership principles and cultural ethos are to remain aligned.

The 360-degree or multi-source assessment is a well-known organisational feedback system that continues to be used by business, industry and commerce for leadership development. Whilst the concept can be dated back to the latter part of the nineteenth century, (Coyle and Slater 2014) it was first used in a formal capacity by the German military during the Second World War in order to evaluate selected officers' performances (Smith 2011). Used by the American manufacturing industry throughout 1950–1970 (Coyle and Slater 2014) and propagated globally following continued developments in technology and techniques, it is currently estimated that 90% of all Fortune 500[2] firms use some form of 360-degree or multi-source appraisal systems to develop their workforce and leadership (Maylett 2009). To date, despite its early use by the German military, most Armed Forces have remained broadly sceptical towards the notion of subordinates reporting on, or evaluating their leaders. For many within the military 360-degree assessments are seen as a business sector management tool, used for process and therefore deemed unsuited to combat units (Budihas 2013). It is feared that its introduction would tend to deny the military strong and robust leaders, instead favouring political and less confrontational 'managerial leaders' who are perceived to lack the decisive edge required in battle (Cuevas 2001). Ultimately it is considered that 360-degree assessments could challenge or change the military's leader/follower construct, whilst adding to an already burdensome reporting mechanism.

Despite this, it is recognised among the United Kingdom's senior and strategic military leaders that there are generational differences and an increasing 'culture-gap' between the military's most senior and junior leaders (Carter 2015). It is also acknowledged that junior ranks and officers are more comfortable in talking about the challenges they face in maintaining the military's exacting values and standards, especially when compared to senior officers who are more guarded and reluctant to admit to their own personal failings (Wong and Stephen 2015). This is also reflected in the Army leadership questionnaire's findings, in which 72% of respondents were in favour of introducing 360-degree reporting for themselves, and 75% were in favour of providing confidential, honest feedback to senior officers they had worked with (Hart 2015). Whilst some countries' armed forces such as Canada and Australia have conducted limited trials on 360-degree assessments, or conduct feedback sessions on specific career courses, currently only the American Army has formally embraced the concept. The notion or idea of 'supplementary input' for officer reporting within the United States Army was first proposed in 1970 by General William Westmoreland, after being tasked to conduct a leadership and ethics review, following a perceived decline in standards towards the end of the Vietnam War (Whiteside 2004). Introduced in 2011, the Multi-Source Assessment and Feedback Programme has been designed to inform and enhance leaders through confidential feedback from superiors, peers and subordinates. The programme is open to all ranks, including Army civilians, and encompasses Regular and Reserve components. Its aim is to develop positive leadership growth, maintain standards, and meet the needs of its personnel (Center for Army Leadership 2012). In doing so it is believed that the Multi-Source Assessment and Feedback Programme can combat toxic and other negative leadership traits (Box 2012).

The philosophy or theory underlying 360-degree assessment is that effective leadership begins with 'knowing oneself', as this relatively nascent construct forms the cornerstone of authentic leadership (Avolio and Gardner 2005). It is argued that heightened self-awareness establishes the base upon which positive styles of leadership can rest, such as transformational and ethical leadership (p. 322). Whicker, Lipman-Blumen and Goldman agree that proactive vigilance is required in diagnosing and then treating toxic leadership and that 360-degree reporting, along with other assessment and evaluation methods, is a tool that can help (Goldman 2009). In tackling toxic leadership, Lipman-Blumen distinguishes between deliberate toxic leaders who consciously harm others to enhance themselves, and unintentional toxic leaders who through situation, carelessness or incompetence do not know that their actions are considered toxic (2005). In the context of self-insight and self-development, it is seen that 360-degree feedback is more likely to benefit the unintentional toxic leader, who, through the identification of perception gaps and provided with specific information and help, can adjust his or her behaviour (Center for Army Leadership 2012). For those who do not know that they are considered toxic, and for those that want to change, 360-degree assessments offer the starting mechanism in delivering a solution. As highlighted in the section above, it is possible to deceive one's senior reporting officers, but it is impossible to fool one's subordinates or peers (Hammes 2002). Implemented correctly, the 360-degree assessment can assist in addressing the negative relationship that a toxic leader has with his or her subordinates. For the deliberate and uncompromising toxic leader, 360-degree assessments offer a means of identification. It is however, important to understand that the 360-degree assessment is not a solution by itself, but rather an aid. Whilst it seeks to stabilise leader and subordinate relations and promises longer-term leadership development, it can only help those who are open or want to develop their leadership style. Should the British military or any of its single Services introduce 360-degree assessments, it will represent a significant cultural change. To work, any future implementation must be well-tested, relatively easy to use, and must have the full support of the entire chain of command, from strategic leaders to junior subordinates (ibid.). It can help in providing the needed checks and balances to inhibit the toxic leader, but will still require continual senior leadership engagement and impartial policing. Finally, any technical solution must also be regulated, but completed in confidence, empowering the subordinates to inform and comment free from the fear of persecution.

The requirement for an independent, impartial and empowered third-party, separate from the chain of command, has been well understood across the Ministry of Defence, from The Secretary of State down, for a number of years (House of Commons, Defence Committee 2012). This is why on 26 March 2015, The Armed Forces (Service Complaints and Financial Assistance) Act was passed to improve the complaints system in the Armed Forces. In doing so it created the Armed Forces Ombudsman (House of Commons 2015). This initiative was principally driven by the then Service Complaints Commissioner, Dr Susan Atkins, who continuously acknowledged and reported that she was unable to give "Parliament an assurance that the Service complaints system [was] working efficiently, effectively or fairly" (2014). As the first Commissioner, taking post in January 2008, Atkins sought to protect the rights of all Service personnel, but she found her team had neither the authority nor the resources to investigate complaints (Mcleod 2012). The Service Complaints Commission also lacked the ability to make findings, direct remedial action or impose penalties on the single Service commands (ibid.). The intent of the new Act is to: shorten the complaints process; make it quicker to reach decisions; create and empower the Ombudsman to hold the Services to account; and give the Ombudsman an ability to make future recommendations for change. Whilst this is generally seen as progressive reform, some campaigners believe that the Act does not go far enough. The Ombudsman still lacks the power or resource to conduct its own investigations, making it reliant on the single Services. It is also technically not independent, as The Defence Council retains the final decision, allowing the Ministry of Defence to overrule the Ombudsman's findings (Liberty 2014). The new system is designed to strike a balance between maintaining the authority of the chain of command and providing a strong and independent Service Complaints Ombudsman, but in order to do this, further cultural and procedural change is required.

Early on, during Atkins' tenure as the Service Complaints Commissioner, she identified institutional and cultural resistance, criticising the military for what she termed "'Service focus blindness', an inability to view a case from outside the cultural perceptions of the Service" (2011). The new Service Complaints Ombudsman, Nicola Williams, has also identified the need for cultural as well as procedural change (Williams 2015). As identified in the section above, the military's hierarchical structure and bureaucratic processes are designed to support, not challenge the chain of command. If the new Ombudsman is to be successful, it must act as a counterbalance to the Services' natural predisposition to 'close ranks' and support the chain of command. The Ombudsman must also ensure that due diligence is conducted in all cases, working with the military, but challenging its thinking, and where necessary its procedures. This is made more difficult because cultural change is a leadership responsibility, and leadership is a closely-guarded single Service lead. As such, the Ombudsman is not empowered or responsible for addressing the root causes of many of the complaints it receives, but it can highlight issues, and where necessary make recommendations for change. The Ombudsman will aid the handling and processing of formal complaints, including those that are commonly associated with toxic leadership behaviour, such as bullying, harassment, and victimisation (Whicker 1996). These cases will remain contentious and difficult to handle; as Lipman-Blumen observes, even the most supportive co-workers are likely to turn on 'whistleblowers' and those seen to complain, as there is a natural propensity and self-interest in supporting the organisation you represent (2006).

Currently, even when a complaint is made against an alleged toxic leader, the chance of success is weighted against the complainant. Within the military environment it is common knowledge that the word of a senior rank is considered to have greater credibility, which is unconsciously taken into consideration where evidence is circumstantial. The deceitful toxic leader will, in most cases, be able to justify his or her actions and will rarely leave an evidence trail outlining his or her true intent. Whilst bullying, harassment and victimisation are not tolerated in the Armed Forces, and all allegations are investigated, most cases are dismissed for lack of evidence (Williams 2015). Given the military's cultural predisposition for tolerance, obedience and loyalty, it is also believed that a sizable number of people remain silent either through misplaced loyalty, intimidation, or through fear of direct and indirect reprisals (ibid.). This is despite all three Services' numerous attempts, campaigns and protestations that inappropriate behaviour of any sort is unacceptable, as such Hubris Syndrome goes against military values and standards. Whilst the Ombudsman is tasked with streamlining the complaint's process and now has the power to hold the Services to account, it generally remains the single Services' responsibility to enforce their own checks and balances. Providing advisors, investigators, judge and jury, in most cases with limited oversight, the Services in most instances continue to operate from within their own cultural boundaries. The challenge now facing the single Services is that of balancing the military's traditional values and standards against society's changing cultural norms, whilst being seen to remain fair, just and proportionate in its actions. However, any perceived tolerance of Hubris Syndrome that draws 'the Service Test' and the military's ethos into question, including the actions of a toxic leader, must be dealt with appropriately. If not it risks inadvertently being seen to support such conduct.

If the British military wishes to retain its values-based leadership system, it must understand what tenets it holds central to its leadership, and reinforce them through education and action. In America, the chairman of the Joint Chiefs of Staff, General Martin E. Dempsey, publicly worked to reform the United States military's leadership, which started in 2013 with an overhaul of ethics training. Between 2003 and 2015, 18 flag officers and 255 officers holding the rank of lieutenant colonel and above were removed from command for personal misconduct for offences including: adultery; harassment; sexual assault; financial irregularity; bullying; and negative (toxic) leadership attributes

(Stone 2015). Whilst most of these officers were considered to be outstanding professionals, it was recognised that they were flawed leaders, with many found to be too self-focussed (ibid.). The Australia Defence Force has also sought to address similar issues through the reassertion of its values and standards in the 2012 publication, *Pathway to Change: Evolving Defence* Culture. This was later reinforced by the Australian Chief of Army, Lieutenant General David Morrison, following allegations of unacceptable behaviour by Army personnel (Morrison 2013). Despite a number of recent single Service reviews and initiatives, the British military has yet to reassert its position on values and standards. Until this action is taken, personnel who are known to bully, harass and victimise their subordinates, but who get results, will continue to operate. Worse still, the toxic leader's selfish deeds, if excused, may increasingly become the norm and influence otherwise "good people to become bad" (Zimbardo 2007).

In order to identify and remove toxic behaviour from within the military there has to be appropriate checks, balances and safeguards. The implementation of these should be suitably prioritised and wherever possible facilitated by appropriate cultural behaviours and attitudes. Like any organisation or institution, these checks must strike a balance between the military's unique requirements, whilst ensuring that its personnel, both military and civilian, are led and administered correctly. The formal introduction of 360-degree assessments would represent an opportunity to deliver real and tangible culture change. The tools to deliver it are continuing to grow in credibility, aided by improvements in technology and techniques. There are also a growing number of Service personnel who believe that they would benefit from receiving and giving this information, free of persecution. It is acknowledged that the demand for change is principally 'bottom-up' and represents part of the generational culture gap between junior and senior leaders. In order to implement any change the problem of cultural resistance by the single Service 'top brass' must also be overcome. Whilst 360-degree assessments are not a panacea, feedback from the United States Army's implementation is generally positive across all ranks (Army, U.S., 2015), with only a few deriding it as an administrative nuisance (Wong and Stephen 2015). It is known that real culture change to transform underlying values and standards is only delivered through the actions of leadership (Wong 2014), not through computer software. As a tool, 360-degree assessments have been proved to provide a means of identifying and delivering help to Lipman-Blumen's 'unconscious' toxic leader, but only to those who want to change. For the toxic leader who persists in selfish and poisonous behaviour, with the appropriate processes in place, and the right evidence trail, it remains a chain of command responsibility to decide how it will treat, tolerate or terminate an individual's behaviour, regardless of the individual's perceived talent. Before any of this can happen, the British military must first acknowledge the problem and make a conscious decision what to do about it and where to draw the line before any corrective action can be taken.

5   Conclusions

It is evident that the British military has an issue with toxic leadership and, despite numerous incidents, reviews and investigations, it remains broadly silent on the subject. Despite priding itself on its 'selfless leadership' principles and style, those at the very top are aware that this exemplar is rarely fully instilled in today's military leaders (Richards 2014). Despite this, the military continues to inculcate its personnel with the selfless values and standards that are required to govern its soldiers, sailors and airman (Paparone et al. 2008). Understandably, it is through the values of courage, discipline, respect for others, integrity, loyalty, and selfless commitment that we expect to be led, since they underpin the military's culture. Because the British military is simultaneously a department of State and a cluster of practising professions, it will take extraordinary courage for a strategic military leader to publically acknowledge the shortcomings and frailties of their Service in order to better the military profession as a whole.

This paper has demonstrated that, since the concept of toxic leadership was first introduced by Whicker, the term 'toxic leader' has become a label commonly associated with nearly all negative leadership traits. Most academics and writers agree, amongst other contested theories that the two defining characteristics of toxic leadership are; the poison-ous relationship that a toxic leader has with his or her subordinates; and that the toxic leader's underlying motivation is primarily generated through self-interest. As these characteristics are generic rather than pre-scriptive, and as they are closely associated with other negative leader-ship models and traits, the paper concludes that the concept of toxic leadership will remain poorly defined and open to individual inter-pretation. This will result in good, as well as bad leaders continuing to be branded as toxic by subordinates who may question their leader's actions and motives.

In order to identify the subtleties of toxic leadership, it is important to understand the relationship between the leader, the environment and his or her followers. Having examined the most likely psychological profiles of the toxic leader, the nuances of culture, and reviewed a num-ber of followership models, it has been possible to analyse the military's construct and susceptibility to toxic leadership. Like Major General Craig Orme, this paper concludes that "the risks of poor or toxic lead-ership are much greater in the military than they are in [many] civil-ian organisations" (Orme 2011). The military is a proud institution that celebrates its past and in doing so often defines itself through its lead-ers. It is the military's overriding desire for strong, heroic, and vision-ary leaders that makes it particularly susceptible to the allure of the toxic leader. Visionaries tend to be narcissistic and are therefore more likely to be considered toxic, as are those with Machiavellian tenden-cies for whom "the ends, no matter how treacherous, justify the means" (McAlpine 2000). The dichotomy for the military is that it wishes to retain those considered to have the best minds for war, whilst at the same time being seen to uphold its own values and standards. The mili-tary does not want to suffer from having part of what it considers to be its 'fighting edge' removed, especially when it sees other capabilities being reduced or withdrawn in comparison to its allies and potential future adversaries. Yet crucially, on closer inspection, it is possible to see that strong, demanding and decisive leaders are not necessary always toxic. The paper shows that due to the military's leader, environment and follower construct, the quiet, considered and calculating toxic leader also prospers, remaining concealed from the senior leadership above. Hierarchical and output focussed, the British military is observed to suffer from a mix of deliberate ignorance and institutional ambivalence towards toxic leaders as they get results.

Finally, the paper has demonstrated that the military already has many of the policies and procedures in place to combat toxic leaders, should the military's strategic hierarchy choose to implement them. The paper proposes that the introduction of 360-degree assessments would represent an opportunity to assist in the development of its leaders at every rank, noting that it is an aid and not the solution to toxic or other negative leadership traits. Real change can only be delivered through sustained engagement from the military's 'top brass' and their leadership. The military remains a noble profession, considered more than a vocation as it is filled with skilled and dedicated servants who believe in the organisation's values and standards. Yet the profession's foundations of trust and integrity are at risk of being eroded by negative leaders who are considered to be toxic. The military has to make a choice, whether it chooses to continue to appear to turn a blind eye, or be seen to actively enforce its policies in order to protect its ethos. If it does not, the notion that toxic leaders are not appropriately dealt with will persist, and at worst could signal to others that such negative behaviour is acceptable.

Notes

1. The Five Factor Model considers the five personality traits comprising: openness; conscientiousness; extraversion; agreeableness; and neuroticism.
2. The Fortune 500 is an annual list compiled and published by Fortune magazine that ranks the top 500 public corporations according to their gross revenue in the United States.

References

Adair, J. E. (1993). *Effective leadership: How to develop leadership skills.* London: Gower.

Army, U.S. (2012). *Army Doctrine Publication 6-22, Army Leadership.* Washington: Department of the Army.

Army, U.S. (2015). *Multi-source assessment and feedback: Testimonials.* http://msaf2.army.mil/Home/Testimonials.aspx.

Atkins, S. R. E. (2011). *Service complaints commissioner for the armed forces: Annual report 2010.* London: Ministry of Defence.

Atkins, S. R. E. (2014). *Service complaints commissioner for the armed forces: Annual report 2013.* London: Ministry of Defence.

Aubrey, D. W. (2012). *The effect of toxic leadership.* US Army War College Strategic Research Project, Pennsylvania.

Australian Defence Committee, Department of Defence. (2012). *Pathway to change: Evolving defence culture.* Commonwealth of Australia.

Avolio, B. J., & Gardner, W. L. (2005). Authentic leadership development: getting to the root of positive forms of leadership. *The Leadership Quarterly, 16*(3), 315–338.

Benest, D. (2012). A liberal democratic state and COIN: The case of Britain, or why atrocities can still happen. *Civil Wars, 14*(1), 29–48.

Box, J. E. (2012). *Toxic leadership in the military profession.* Carlisle: U.S. Army War College.

Boyett, J. H. (2006). *Surviving the destructive narcissistic leader.* Alpharetta, GA: Boyett & Associates.

Budihas, C. (2013). Evaluating leaders. *Marine Corps Gazette, 97*(3), March 13.

Burke, P. (1987). *The Italian renaissance: Culture and society in Italy.* Cambridge: Polity Press.

Campbell-Colquhoun, B. H. G. (2006). *Toxic leadership: A necessary evil?* Defence Research Paper, Defence Academy of the United Kingdom, Shrivenham.

Carter, N. P. (2013). The divisional level of command. *British Army Review, 157,* 7–16.

Carter N. P. (2015). *The future of the British Army: How the army must change to serve Britain in a volatile world.* London: Chatham House Transcript.

Center for Army Leadership. (2012). Leader development through the multi-source assessment and feedback programme. Official U.S. Army site.

Chaleff, I. (2009). *The courageous follower: Standing up to and for our leaders* (3rd ed.). San Francisco: Berrett-Koehler.

Chapman, C. (2013). *Notes from a small military.* London: Blake Publishing.

Cohen, W. A. (1999). Battle leadership examples from the field. *Military Review, 79*(3), 82–87.

Cohen, W. A. (2010). *Heroic leadership: Leading with integrity and honor.* San Francisco: Jossey-Bass.

Cohn, J., & Moran, J. (2011). *Why are we bad at picking good leaders a better way to evaluate leadership potential?* Hoboken: Wiley.

Coyle, A., & Slater, R. (2014). The governing of the self/the self-governing self: Multi-rater/source feedback and practices 1940–2011. *Theory & Psychology, 24*(2), 233–255.

Cuevas, E. E. (2001). *Evaluating feedback systems by civil service employees.* Fort Bliss: Webster University.

Defence Academy of the United Kingdom. (2015). *Leader theory overview.* Shrivenham.

Departments of Defense. (1988). Army, Navy, Air Force, and Marine Corps, Department of the Army Pamphlet 600-2, The Armed Forces Officer. Washington, DC: Government Printing Office.

Doty, J., & Fenlason, J. (2013). Narcissism and toxic leaders. *Military Review,* 55–60.

Downs, A. (1977). *Beyond the looking glass: Overcoming the seductive culture of corporate narcissism.* New York: AMACOM.

Elliott, C. L. (2015). *High command: British military leadership in the Iraq and Afghanistan wars.* Oxford: Oxford University Press.

Freud, S. (2011). *The Ego and the Id.* LaVergne, TN: Pacific Publishing Studio.

Furtner, M. R., Rauthmann, J. F., & Sachse, P. (2011). The self-loving self-leader: An examination of the relationship between self-leadership and the Dark Triad. *Social Behaviour and Personality: An International Journal, 39*(3), 369–379.

Goldman, A. (2009). *Transforming toxic leaders.* Palo Alto: Stanford Business Books, Stanford University Press.

Goleman, D. (2006). *Emotional intelligence: Why it can matter more than IQ.* London: Bloomsbury.

Great Britain. Health and Safety Executive. (2014). *Stress-related and psychological disorders in Great Britain 2014.* London: HMSO.

Great Britain, MoD. (2014). *Suicide and open verdict deaths in the UK Regular Armed Forces 1984-2013.* Bristol: Defence Statistics.

Great Britain, MoD. (2015a). *Armed forces continuous attitude survey 2015.* London: Defence Statistics.

Great Britain, MoD. (2015b). *Joint Service Publication 757: Tri-Service Appraisal Reporting Instructions, Version 1.3.*

Hambrick, D. C., & Mason, P. A. (1984). Upper echelons: The organization as a reflection of its top managers. *Academy of Management Review, 9*(2), 193–206.

Hammes, T. (2002). Time for a 360. *Marine Corps Gazette, 86*(4), 49–51.

Hart, S. J. E. (2015). *Army leadership review: Army division response.* Shrivenham: Defence Academy of the United Kingdom.

Hinds, R. M., & Steele, J. P. (2012). Army leader development and leadership: Views from the field. *Military Review, 92*(1), 39–44.

House of Commons. (2015). *Armed Forces (Service Complaints and Financial Assistance) Act 2015: CHAPTER 19.* London: The Stationary Office Limited.

House of Commons, Defence Committee. (2012). *The work of the Service Complaints Commissioner for the Armed Forces: Eighth Report of Session 2012–13.* HC 720. London: The Stationary Office Limited.

Jacobs, C. (2014). *Poor, negative and ineffective leadership behaviours.* Shrivenham: Centre for Defence Leadership and Management.

Jakobwitz, S., & Egan, V. (2006). The dark triad and normal personality traits. *Personality and Individual Differences, 40*(2), 331–339.

Jans, N. A., & Schmidtchen, D. (2002). *The real C-cubed: Culture, careers, and climate.* Canberra: Strategic Defence, Studies Center, Australian National University.

Jones, S. M. (2003). Improving accountability for effective command climate. *A strategic imperative.* Carlisle: U.S. Army War College.

Kandola, B. (2009). *The value of difference: Eliminating bias in organisations.* Oxford: Pearn Kandola Publishing.

Kane, T. (2012). *Bleeding talent: How the US military mismanages great leaders and why it's time for a revolution.* Basingstoke: Palgrave Macmillan.

Keegan, J. (2004). *A history of warfare* 2nd ed. London: Pimlico.

Kellerman, B. (2004). *Bad leadership: What it is, how it happens, why it matters.* Boston: Harvard Business School Press.

Kendall, P. A. (2007). *The rogue commander: The double-edged sword of narcissistic leaders.* Defence Research Paper, Defence Academy of the United Kingdom, Shrivenham.

Kilcullen, D. (2013). *Out of the mountains: The coming age of the urban guerrilla.* London: Hurst & Company.

Kirke, C. (2007). *Bullying, or what?: A Framework for addressing constructions of 'bullying' in the British Army.* Shrivenham: Defence Academy of the United Kingdom.

Kirke, C. (2009). *Red coat, green machine: Continuity in change in the British Army 1700 to 2000.* London: Continuum.

Kirke, C. (2010). Orders is orders… aren't they? Rule bending and rule breaking in the British Army. *Ethnography, 11*(3), 359–380.

Knight, J. (2014). *Sexual harassment and assault in the armed forces both violate military ethics and are a consequence of culturally contingent interpretations of military values in practice.* Defence Research Paper, Defence Academy of the United Kingdom, Shrivenham.

Kusy, M., & Holloway, E. (2009). *Toxic workplace!: Managing toxic personalities and their systems of power.* San Francisco: Jossey-Bass.

Liberty. (2014). *Plans for a new Armed Forces Ombudsman fatally flawed.* https://www.liberty-human-rights.org.uk.

Lipman-Blumen, J. (2005). Toxic leadership: When grand illusions masquerade as noble visions. *Leader to Leader, 2005*(36), 29–36.

Lipman-Blumen, J. (2006). *The allure of toxic leaders: Why we follow destructive bosses and corrupt politicians-and how we can survive them.* Oxford: Oxford University Press.

Lubit, R. H. (2003). Coping with toxic managers, subordinates… and other difficult people: Using emotional intelligence to survive and prosper. Financial Times, Prentice Hall Books.

Maccoby, M. (2004). Narcissistic leaders: The incredible pros, the inevitable cons. *Harvard Business Review, 82*(1), 92–101.

Manz, C., & Sims, H. P., Jr. (1991). Superleadership: Beyond the myth of heroic leadership. *Organizational Dynamics, 19*(4), 18–35.

Maylett, T. (2009). 360-Degree feedback revisited: The transition from development to appraisal. *Compensation and Benefits Review, 41*(5), 52–59.

McAlpine, A. (2000). *The ruthless leader, three classics of strategy and power.* New York: Wiley.

McHoskey, J. W., Worzel, W., & Szyarto, C. (1998). Machiavellianism and psychopathy. *Journal of Personality and Social Psychology, 74*(1), 192–210.

McLeod, R. A. (2012). Defence Committee Written Evidence from R A McLeod LLB MA JP (SCC 004).

Milgram, S. (2010). *Obedience to authority: An experimental view.* London: Pinter & Martin.

Mischel, W. (1968). *Personality and assessment* (1st ed.). New York, 1995.

Morrison, D. L. (2013). *Message from the chief of army*. The Australian Army Website.

Mosko, C. C. (1977). The all-volunteer military: Calling, profession, or occupation? *Parameters, 7*(1).

Mosko, C. C. (2001). What ailas the all-volunteer force: An institutional perspective. *Parameters, 31*(2).

Northouse, P. G. (2013). *Leadership: Theory and practice* (6th ed.). California: Sage.

Orme, C. W. (2011). *Beyond compliance: Professionalism, trust and capability in the Australian Profession of Arms Report of the Australian Defence Force Personal Conduct Review*. Australian Defence Department, Commonwealth of Australia.

Padilla, A., Hogan, R., & Kaiser, R. B. (2007). The toxic triangle: Destructive leaders, susceptible followers, and conducive environments. *The Leadership Quarterly, 18*(3), 176–194.

Paparone, C. R., Anderson, R. A., & McDaniel, R. R. (2008). Where military professionalism meets complexity science. *Armed Forces & Society, 34*(3), 433–449.

Pendleton, D., & Furnham, A. (2012). *Leadership: All you need to know*. Palgrave Macmillan: Houndmills.

Popper, M. (1996). Leadership in military combat units and business organizations: A comparative psychological analysis. *Journal of Managerial Psychology, 11*(1), 15–23.

Reed, G. E. (2004). Toxic leadership. *Military Review, 84*(4), 67–71.

Richards, D. J. (2014). *General David Richards the autobiography: Taking command*. London: Headline Publishing Group.

Riggio, R. E., Chaleff, I., & Lipman-Blumen, J. (Eds.). (2008). *The Art of followership: How great followers create great leaders and organizations*. San-Francisco: Jossey-Bass Publishing.

Roter, A. B., (2011). *The lived experiences of registered nurses exposed to toxic leadership behaviours*. Doctoral dissertation, Capella University, Minneapolis.

Royal Military Academy Sandhurst. (2012). *Developing leaders: A Sandhurst guide*. Camberley: Ministry of Defence.

Schein, E. H. (2010). *Organizational culture and leadership* (4th ed.). San Francisco: Jossey-Bass.

Serco. (2014). *Leadership guide: Leader of managers*.

Sewell, G. F. (2011). How emotional intelligence can make a difference. *Military Review, 91*(2), 79–83.

Smith, J. (2011). *Conducting a performance appraisal—What you need to know: definitions, best practices, benefits and practical solutions.* Tebbo Publishing.

Smith, R. A. (2005). *The utility of force: The art of war in the modern world.* London: Allen Lane.

Steele, J. P. (2011). *Antecedents and consequences of toxic leadership in the U.S. Army: A two year review and recommended solutions.* Kansas: Center for Army Leadership Fort Leavenworth.

Stone, F. (2015). Why the military's solution to bad leadership isn't going to fix anything. *Take and Purpose.*

Storr, A. (1989). *Freud.* Oxford: Oxford University Press.

Tirole, J. (1986). Hierarchies and bureaucracies: On the role of collusion in organizations. *Journal of Law Economics and Organization, 2*(2), 181–214.

United Kingdom Army. (2010). *British Army: An introduction.* Ministry of Defence.

United Kingdom Army. (2012). *Values and standards of the British Army.* Andover: AC 63813, PS2(A).

United Kingdom Army. (2016). *Army leadership doctrine.* Camberley: Ministry of Defence.

United Kingdom, Developments, Concepts and Doctrine Centre. (2010). *Future character of conflict.* Shrivenham: DCDC.

United Kingdom, Developments, Concepts and Doctrine Centre. (2014). *Joint Doctrine Publication 01: UK Joint Operations Doctrine.* Shrivenham: DCDC.

United Kingdom Royal Air Force, (2008). *Ethos, core values and standards.* Air Publication 1, 2nd Edition.

United Kingdom Royal Navy. (2014). *Book of Reference 3*, Part 5 - Life Management, Annex 21c Ethos, Values and Standards.

Weiss, T. (2006, August 29). The Narcissistic CEO. *Forbes.com.*

Whicker, M. L. (1996). *Toxic leaders: When organizations go bad.* Westport, CT: Quorum Books.

Whiteside, C. (2004). From one to three sixty: Assessing leaders. *Military Review, 84*(5), 86–88.

Williams, D. F. (2005). *Toxic leadership in the US Army.* Carlisle: U.S. Army War College.

Williams, N. (2015). *Service complaints commissioner for the armed forces: Annual report 2014.* London: Ministry of Defence.

Williamson, O. E. (1995). *Organization theory: From Chester Barnard to the present and beyond.* Oxford: Oxford University Press.

Wong, L. (2014). *Changing the army's culture of cultural change.* Strategic Studies Institute.

Wong, L., & Gerras, S. J. (2015). *Lying to ourselves: Dishonesty in the army profession.* Strategic Studies Institute and US Army War College Press.

Zimbardo, P. G. (2007). *The Lucifer effect: How good people turn evil.* London: Rider.

Zwerdling, D. (2014). *Army takes on its own toxic leaders.* NPR News Investigation.

6

Dysfunctional Leadership in Corporations

Dennis Tourish

1 Introduction

Dysfunctional leadership in corporations is all too common. Given the enormous size of many modern corporations the toxic effects of such leadership may be felt more keenly by more people than ever before. There is nothing intrinsically new in power warping people's sense of perspective and sense of entitlement, diminishing their ability to empathise with the needs of others and fomenting hubris. These are age old problems. However, part of the problem in reflecting on these issues today is that most studies of leadership are overwhelmingly positive in nature.

Burns's (1978) seminal text, largely responsible for popularising the idea of 'transformational leadership,' was highly influential in this regard. It differentiated between 'leaders' (who successfully engage and

D. Tourish (✉)
University of Sussex, Brighton, UK

© The Author(s) 2018
P. Garrard (ed.), *The Leadership Hubris Epidemic*,
https://doi.org/10.1007/978-3-319-57255-0_6

satisfy followers' motives) and 'power holders' (who use followers for their own purposes, and utilize 'naked' and 'brute' power to achieve their ends). Burns asserted that 'power-wielders' were not leaders. For example, he argued that Hitler was not a leader but a tyrant, 'an absolute wielder of brutal power' who crushed all opposition: 'A leader and a tyrant are polar opposites' (1978: 3). This approach sanitizes the concept of leadership to such an extent that brutal dictators and autocrats are no longer considered to be leaders at all. The tendency to 'purify' leadership of questions related to power has become increasingly embedded in mainstream business school teaching and research on leadership (Collinson and Tourish 2015). In my view, this is a mistake. It prevents serious engagement with a problem that is only too evident and which affects us all—that which forms the title of this chapter.

In what follows, I seek to redress the balance. Accordingly, I challenge the fixation on what I see as those myths of heroic leadership that have informed much management thinking and practice. In doing so, I offer examples of where they lead us astray, and relate these to the research on the effects of having power. Lastly, in articulating a way forward, I look at the much neglected but invaluable role of critical upward communication from followers to leaders, and discuss how we can get more of it. In my view, this is essential to minimise the prevalence of hubris and produce much more effective models of leadership.

2   A Fixation with Heroic Myths of Leadership

We are encouraged to become fixated with leadership. To be more precise, we are encouraged to become fixated on myths of leadership, in which leaders only ever do good, and are the main or even only factor in determining an organization's fortunes. Leaders are supposed to solve climate change, eliminate Ebola, resolve the problems in the Middle East, restore the American economy to health, deliver Scandinavian levels of public services alongside US levels of personal taxation, and end deforestation in the Amazon—ideally, during their first week in office. Paradoxically, these high expectations help to explain our disillusionment with the leaders that we habitually encounter in the real world.

The more grandiose the ambitions that we have for leaders the less possible it is for any human being to deliver on them, and the more likely it is that disillusionment will take root.

One measure of the fixation we have with the subject is the number of books published dealing with it. At the time of writing, there are a staggering 176,964 listed on Amazon with the word 'leadership' in their title. Typical of many is a text by Kouzes and Posner (2012). Its main title is *The Leadership Challenge,* while its sub-title promises to show you *'How to Make Extraordinary Things Happen in Organizations.'* Evidently, the oeuvre lends itself to hyperbole. The appeal of this approach is shown in the fact that the book in question is now in its fifth edition. In this world, success is passé. Rather, something 'extraordinary' lies in prospect, in which powerful leaders will deliver results that go far beyond what most mere mortals can achieve or sustain. There are few, if any, limits on what they are expected to accomplish. When leaders themselves take such expectations seriously it is no wonder that they fall victim to hubris.

It is instructive to contrast this with the number of books available on followership—a total of 372. Yet without followers there are no leaders, since the effectiveness of leaders depends entirely on their ability to influence others. Less often discussed but of equal importance, followers exercise a profound influence on leaders. In particular, most feedback that followers give their leaders is far too flattering in nature, a contributory source to the gargantuan egos that so many leaders seem to develop, and which becomes a mighty wellspring of hubris. I return to this important issue later in this chapter.

These views of leadership have been framed, to a large extent, by a great deal of writing about transformational leadership in the last 30 years (Bass and Riggio 2006).[1] This proposes that leaders must be charismatic in order to be effective. Clearly, there are examples of charismatic individuals who exercise a profoundly positive effect on organisations and society. We think of people like Mandela, Martin Luther King and President Kennedy. In business, whatever his defects, Steve Jobs seems to have had some degree of charisma as well. But there are also plentiful examples of charismatic leaders who inflict enormous damage on people, organizations and society. This is sometimes referred to as the Hitler problem. Was Hitler a charismatic leader, and was he even a leader? As I noted above, some scholars emphatically say no. In expressing my dissent, I challenge the assumption that charisma is invariably a good thing, or that we should become less sceptical towards those who appear to possess it. Rather, we need to understand the importance of context, and acknowledge that when charismatic individuals have too much power there is a heightened risk of them using their charisma to achieve ends that may be in their own interests rather than anyone else's.

In business as well there are many people who think of themselves as charismatic leaders and yet have a negative effect on people and the organizations that they lead. One particularly memorable individual, the head of Sunbeam-Oster, an American manufacturing company famous for its kitchen Mixmaster, was known as 'Chainsaw Al Dunlap'. He was also known as 'Rambo in Stripes' and actually posed for the cover of a book written about him dressed as Rambo and brandishing what I assume were imitation firearms. His tenuous grip on reality is shown by his assumption that this conveyed a positive image. Dunlap's abusive, hubristic and ultimately dysfunctional management style is thoroughly documented by Byrne (1999), in a book that remains well worth reading today. Writing of his time at Sunbeam, Byrne (p.5) gives this far too typical example: 'Though some had spent hours preparing elaborate presentations, most were forced to keep their remarks short. It was rare for anyone to get more than fifteen or twenty words out before Dunlap broke in with a pointed question. When anyone hesitated, even momentarily, Dunlap would snap: 'I expect you to know these things.' 'It was like a dog barking at you for hours,' Boynton later said. 'He just yelled, ranted and raved. He was condescending, belligerent, and disrespectful.' Such an approach may help explain why Dunlap felt the need to purchase a handgun and a bulletproof vest, both of which he naturally claimed on expenses.

While we have come some way from those macho views of leadership and charisma, organizations still often license destructive practices by leaders (Tourish 2013). I suggest that the more we accept the idea that all fundamental decision making authority should be vested in the leader, the more likely it is that these dysfunctional power dynamics will take effect. Moreover, the more we uncritically promote the idea of charisma, the more likely we are to encounter lots of people who think they are charismatic visionaries while other people just see boring men in suits. The danger here is what might be termed the 'David Brent Syndrome.'[2]

Transformational leadership theorists have also promoted the idea that leaders must have a compelling vision and the bolder that vision the better it is likely to be for the organisations that they lead. The problem here is that while the vision they come up with might well be perfectly sensible it might equally well be berserk, self-serving or impossible to achieve. In an environment where improving shareholder value is often held to be the primary or even only aim of business, it is also very difficult to construct a vision that genuinely captures the real best interests of all organizational stakeholders. Consider the current problems of the retail giant Tesco in the UK. While its ills have many sources, Hutton (2015) describes it as 'a company whose focus transmuted from serving customers and building a company to serving shareholders and driving up directors' pay.' There is truth in this. I pose what is surely an obvious question. How can a leadership team whose primary focus is its own financial well-being and that of other shareholders possibly articulate a vision that will capture the support of low paid employees, many on zero hours contracts, and who sense in the marrow of their bones that they are viewed as, say, 'contingent units of cost intensive units of productive capacity', rather than human beings?

But if we become convinced that developing 'a vision' and getting support for it is a top priority, it is also very easy to embrace another common assumption that underpins much leadership practice. This is the idea that we must have a 'common culture'—one, moreover, that will be designed by its most senior managers, with minimal if any input from others (see Willmott 1993; 2013, for an incisive critique of such views). We all know that we need certain agreed norms if any organisation is to function. People need to know that when the fire bell rings we get out, that there are in many instances set hours of work, that there are constraints on what we can claim on expenses and so on. But when we take the idea of a common culture to an extreme, as many business leaders do, it simply becomes a synonym for saying that there must be no dissent from whatever decisions are proclaimed by top managers. Conformity is prized above critical thinking. I believe that these ideas are at the root of much of the dysfunctional leadership that we find within organisations. A book published a few years ago and scarily called *Corporate Religion* (Kunde 1999) was particularly enthusiastic in advocating this view. The dust jacket of the book argued that in the organisation of the future there would be no space for dissenters. As it put it, disbelievers must look elsewhere. Or, in the words of one management scholar, being a CEO today is the nearest thing you can become to being king of your own country (Finkelstein 2003). This is not a formula for success in countries, societies or business organisations.

Typical of the resulting approach is an article in the *Harvard Business Review* which attempts to identify the best performing CEOs in the world (Ignatius 2014). I do not want to simplify the arguments in this particular paper. On the other hand, there are no arguments in it to simplify. It is simply *assumed* that the only thing that determines whether an organisation will succeed or fail is the person who is the CEO. The irony of this is that while much management thinking (if that is the right word) routinely credits responsibility for all organisational success to the wisdom of the leader, it is also quick to apportion all blame for failure to the self-same leaders (e.g. Amar et al. 2012). This is an equally pernicious mistake, and a mirror version of the first. So you often have the paradoxical situation that certain management behaviours, such as decisiveness, are singled out and praised when an organisation and a CEO is on the up. But when something in the environment changes and performance is adversely affected this 'decisiveness' is relabelled as 'impulsiveness' or 'recklessness.' Oddly enough, the behaviour of the person concerned remains fundamentally what it was in the earlier period of success (Rosenzweig 2014). As I will now argue, rather than challenge these notions business schools have in general been complicit in their development.

3   Business Schools as Incubators of Hubris

The two attendant dangers with the approaches I have been criticising are hype and hubris. Unfortunately, these dangers are often promoted by business schools. Consider a book written by a former *Daily Telegraph* journalist who for some reason decided that it was a good idea to do an MBA at Harvard Business School (Delves Broughton 2010). This documents what I would describe as an endless stream of 'heroic' propaganda that the institution aims at students even before they arrive. They are constantly assured that they are an elite, that they are exceptional human beings, that they will transform the world. It is scarcely surprising that so many of them develop hubris.

Nor is Harvard alone in this. With two colleagues, I have studied the marketing materials and pedagogic approaches of most of the leading business schools. We reached the conclusion that these are often little more than primers in hubris (Tourish et al. 2010). The incessant message from many of them is that their students have to possess truly extraordinary reserves of ability, determination, intelligence and judgement to succeed. But it is also suggested that by virtue of the fact that they have been admitted to the school they already have the qualities in question. Students are promised that not only will they will study transformational leadership, they will become such leaders themselves, and are already well on the road to perfection.

I am also critical of how leadership is depicted by some of the journals that we encourage our students to read. Consider a special issue of the *Harvard Business Review* in January 2007 devoted to 'the tests of a leader'. Alongside this strapline, the image that adorns the cover of the magazine is that of a shirt-sleeved male executive performing push-ups on a boardroom table. This extraordinarily macho image seems to imply that a leader must in some way become a Superman figure. Women, presumably, merit scarcely any consideration.

This is pernicious guff. While it does nothing to promote a sense of modesty it is easy to see how it promotes hubris. Do we really need more leaders burdened with an excessive sense of self confidence and entitlement at the helm of our corporations?

Such approaches also assume that people will agree with whatever a given leader argues or decides. As a result, too few leaders recognise the need to patiently explain their ideas to other people, and actively seek a dialogue with them on their merits in place of a monologue. Rather, they assume that their visions, strategies and decisions are so self-evidently wise and for the common good that no-one with any sense could conceivably challenge them. Dissent is viewed as resistance to be overcome rather than useful feedback. This is particularly evident when we look at the management of change. For example, some theorists write about opposition to change in terms of a lack of psychological resilience, preference for low levels of stimulation and novelty, cognitive rigidity and reluctance to give up old habits (Oreg 2003). In this view, if you don't like change it reflects a personal weakness on your part. There is undoubtedly an element of this in at least some cases. It is also entirely possible that resistance to change sometimes makes sense. As an illustration, many leaders remain infatuated by downsizing as a solution to each and every problem. While this may be sometimes inevitable (less often than is commonly assumed), research has long shown that it generally has more negative than positive effects on organizational performance, including profitability (e.g. Luan et al. 2013). Nor is it hard to understand why those directly affected might have legitimate points of opposition to make! As I now suggest, these effects are amplified by the fact that merely having power tends to change our behaviour, and to do so for the worse.

4   The Harmful Effects of Power

There are many good things from having power and none of us want to be powerless, either in our private lives or in our work lives. But there are also downsides. These are considered far too infrequently in the leadership literature. Too often, acquiring even a modest degree of power unleashes our inner Führer. Look at the evidence. Lammers et al. (2010) designed an ingenious set of experiments with 61 subjects designed to manipulate how powerful people felt. They were asked to recall a time when they felt either powerful or powerless. Levels of hypocrisy instantly increased in those who felt more powerful: they were more inclined to condemn cheating—but only in others; when given the chance to decide how many lottery tickets they would receive by privately rolling dice they were more inclined to lie about their scores in order to obtain extra tickets. The same subjects were also more likely to condemn tax dodging, speeding or holding onto stolen goods, but thought it less heinous if they did it themselves. Power, it seems, breeds a sense of entitlement and an inclination to hold others to standards of behaviour that we cannot live up to ourselves.

In another experiment, people were given maths problems to solve as individuals (Langer and Benevento 1978). They were then given similar tasks in pairs. Some subjects were supplied with stopwatches and given the job of timing how long this took. In some groups, they received neutral labels, such as 'timer.' But in other two person groups the person with a stopwatch was called 'the boss,' while some subjects were given the label 'assistant.' Lastly, everyone once more solved problems on an individual basis. I find the results astonishing: those who had been given the label 'boss' showed a marked improvement in their performance. 'Timers' or 'solvers' showed no change in performance. But those who had been 'assistants' showed a decrease in performance.

There are, I believe, important implications for leadership. It seems that we are by nature highly sensitive to either the presence or absence of power, and fine tune our behaviours accordingly. When people have a label applied to them such as 'boss' they seem to feel more responsible for the task at hand, and intensify their efforts accordingly. But when given a label such as 'assistant' their competence goes down, possibly because they conclude that they are less responsible for the task. After all, there is a 'boss' to assume ultimate responsibility. Regardless, most organisations seem to stress status differentials, and many managers long for large offices and imposing titles to describe their role. Organisations typically have 'Directors' of every function under the sun, crowding out everyone else. Such titles may be unwittingly adding to the burden of expectation carried by their holders, while ensuring that their ability to do their jobs goes down in conjunction with others assuming less and less responsibility.

Keltner et al. (2003) illustrate this very well. They had three person student teams engage in a joint writing exercise together. More precisely, two people engaged in the task while one had the job of evaluation—in essence, they were allocated the role of a boss. When at a certain point a plate of cookies was provided the evaluators were more inclined to take a second one, while also chewing with their mouths open and spraying crumbs in all directions. Sutton (2010: 28) sums up the leadership implications as follows: 'When people (regardless of personality) wield power, their ability to lord it over others causes them to (1) become more focused on their own needs and wants; (2) become less focused on others' needs, wants and actions; and (3) act as if written and unwritten rules others are expected to follow don't apply to them.' Hubris ensues.

Other studies have found that the more power people have, the less concerned they are to seek out advice from others, and the less likely they are to listen to it when it appears (See et al. 2011). These are things that we tend to forget, instead joining in the widespread assumption that somebody having powerful people make decisions for us is a good thing. I think we need to remind ourselves that that is not necessarily the case.

5   The Example of Enron—What Not to Do

To give some specific examples we can do worse than start with Enron. This was the biggest bankruptcy in US corporate history, until that of Lehman Brothers in 2008. One indication of the hubris that ensnared it was that barely a year before its demise Enron had declared its intention to become 'the world's leading company,' moving on from its ambition to be its 'leading energy company.' A banner proclaiming this goal was unfurled outside its headquarters. How far the mighty subsequently fell.

George Bush called one of its leaders, Ken Lay, "Kenny Boy"—such was the intimacy of their relationship. Lay only managed to escape prison by dying before he could be sentenced. The organization's other main figure, Jeffrey Skilling is set to be released from prison early, in 2019. Enron had a number of systems that illustrate the dysfunctional habits that I am highlighting in this chapter, and have discussed in detail elsewhere (Tourish and Vatcha 2005). Here, I focus on their system of 'differentiation'—or 'Rank and Yank' as it was known internally.

An internal Performance Review Committee (PRC) rated employees twice a year. They were graded on a scale of 1 to 5, on ten separate criteria, and then divided into one of three groups—'A's, who were to be challenged and given large rewards; 'B's, who were to be encouraged and affirmed, and 'C's, who were told to shape up or ship out. Those in the top category were referred to as 'water walkers'. Those in the bottom category were given until their next review to improve. In practice, however, with another 15% category emerging within six months sufficient improvement was almost impossible, and they tended to leave quickly. Furthermore, those in category two were also now in a position where they too faced the strong possibility of being 'yanked' within the next year. A cutthroat culture was created. The overall impact is well summarised by Fusaro and Miller (2002: 52):

> It is clear that Enron's management regarded kindness as a show of weakness. The same rigors that Enron faced in the marketplace were brought into the company in a way that destroyed morale and internal cohesion. In the process of trying to quickly and efficiently separate from the company those employees who were not carrying their weight, Enron created an environment where employees were afraid to express their opinions or to question unethical and potentially illegal business practices. Because the rank-and-yank system was both arbitrary and subjective, it was easily used by managers to reward blind loyalty and quash brewing dissent.

Anyone who queried accountancy practices was likely, at best, to be reassigned or lose a bonus. A 1995 survey of employees found that many were uncomfortable about voicing their feelings and 'telling it like it is at Enron' (Swartz and Watkins 2003: 76). The example of Sherron Watkins illustrates the mind-set. Watkins was a senior employee who worked with Enron's Chief Financial Officer, Andy Fastow. When she realised that the company's losses would become apparent sometime in 2003 or 2004, she drew her concerns to the attention of Ken Lay, who had stepped back into the role of CEO. Support was not forthcoming from other senior executives, who evidently feared that to acknowledge the problems would damage their careers at Enron. Lay's own response suggests these fears were well founded. Within days of meeting with Watkins, he contacted the organization's lawyers to inquire if grounds could be found for firing her.

It is hard to imagine more fertile grounds for hubris. Enron's leaders perched atop a pyramid of mendacity that they themselves had created. Employees became fearful of each other, since it was in everyone's interest to make someone else look bad rather than face being 'yanked.'

Cut adrift from corrective feedback, Lay, Skilling and others could easily convince themselves that they were superior beings, and that their corrupt methods of doing business would escape detection indefinitely.

But they are not alone in having adopted such practices. The Royal Bank of Scotland introduced the same system of differentiation as Enron in the years before it too went bankrupt. To their embarrassment, one of the people who did very well under it and was named their star performer of the year three times in a row turned out to be embezzling the bank of £21 million. Part of his defence in court was that he was under huge stress from the sales targets that RBS were putting upon him (Fraser 2014). We need to pay attention to the institutional mechanisms that have emerged in organisations whereby hubris, narcissism and the excessive concentration of power in the hands of a leader are amplified and made common.

We should know by now that every management practice has unintended, as well intended, consequences. But when leadership is viewed as non-contested top down influence, it follows that openness to feedback ranks low on the leader's list of priorities. It is this issue that I now want to consider in more detail.

6 The Role of Critical Upward Feedback

Let's take an example from General Motors. Steve Rattner was appointed by President Obama to rescue the organisation after it filed for bankruptcy. He wrote a very interesting article in *Fortune* magazine about his experiences (Rattner 2009). One vignette says much: 'At GM's Renaissance Center headquarters, the top brass were sequestered on the uppermost floor, behind locked and guarded glass doors. Executives housed on that floor had elevator cards that allowed them to descend to their private garage without stopping at any of the intervening floors (no mixing with the drones).' Such was their disconnect from reality that when General Motors and the other companies needed bailout money from Washington they hired private jets to go and tell the politicians that they needed state support. Not surprisingly, this did not go down well.

I am currently undertaking a project, financed by the Daedalus Trust, on hubris within the banking sector. This builds on a longstanding interest in how bankers often exonerate themselves from mistakes but are quick to claim credit for success (Tourish and Hargie 2012). One woman I interviewed worked in a senior position within a financial services organisation. In a dreary echo of General Motors, her female CEO also had a key that meant that the lifts did not have to stop on the way down to the basement where her car was parked. My interviewee added that she had met her CEO at a Marks and Spencer's check-out till and dared to exchange a few pleasantries. The following day she was reprimanded by her boss for speaking to the CEO. Hubris could hardly assume a starker form.

These examples demonstrate an insufficiently theorised aspect of life in organisations: that is, the role of critical upward communication between leaders and followers. Winston Churchill (1941: 653) sums it up very well. Writing about a major disaster in the First World War, he observed that 'The temptation to tell a Chief in a great position the things he most likes to hear is one of the commonest explanations of mistaken policy. Thus the outlook of the leader on whose decision fateful events depend is usually far more sanguine than the brutal facts admit.' To put it less grandly, most of us know this as 'sucking up to the boss.' The well-known philosopher, Homer Simpson, expressed this very clearly in an episode of *The Simpsons* where he was giving Bart some career advice. His key point was that Bart should always remember to say 'good idea boss.' Academics inevitably have a grander name for the process - ingratiation theory (Rosenfeld et al. 1995; Tourish and Robson 2006). This expresses the well-worn finding that when we have a power differential between two people, the person with the less power typically exaggerates how much they agree with the person of greater power in order to acquire influence over them. We are quite skilled at this. Thus, people tend to identify an issue of little significance where we express disagreement, in order to make it even more credible when we agree with the boss on the big picture messages that are important to her or him. This runs rife in leader/follower relations. It is worth reflecting on the effects of such dynamics, and in particular on how it can encourage hubris.

One major consequence is that it becomes more and more difficult for leaders to really know what is going on inside their companies. Good news floats to the top, while bad news sinks *en route*. Consider TV programmes like *Back to the Floor* or *Undercover Boss* where the top managers spend some time with lower level employees, often doing their jobs alongside them. In every single episode the leader is flabbergasted at the reality of life on the ground. This is not necessarily a reflection of bad behaviour in the leader. But I suggest that it is a reflection of the ingratiation dynamic I am highlighting here. If they are at the receiving end only or even mainly of positive feedback, leaders of corporations can become like a rock star with a sycophantic entourage. Inevitably, they will fall victim to hubris, and make increasingly poor decisions that threaten the sustainability of their organisations.

It is of course very human to prefer positive feedback rather than that which is critical. Most of us would prefer to view a movie entitled 'A Reassuring Lie' rather than one called 'An Inconvenient Truth.' By the same token we are all highly sensitive to critical feedback. We react instinctively against it—what is known as the automatic vigilance effect (Pratto and John 1991). But this incentivises people to offer us more and more praise and less and less critique, even when it is the latter that we really need. Critical feedback becomes paralysed by hesitation. This produces a dynamic where leaders drift more and more out of touch with what is happening around them, and become more likely to develop hubris.

President George W Bush on one occasion accidently said something profoundly correct on this issue: 'You know a lot of time in politics you have people who look you in the eye and they tell you what's not on their mind.' People tell those who have power over them what they would like them to think is on their minds. They reflect back to the leader what they think the leader is thinking, and then pretend that they are in agreement with it. These might be the only wise words George Bush has ever spoken but I believe that they are very useful in this context.

It is clear that that possessing extraordinary power does not necessarily have a good effect on leaders either. The more narcissistic leaders are, and the more unwarrantedly optimistic their view is of those organisations they lead, the more likely it is that the leader in question will eventually be fired (Park et al. 2011).

What do we need to do about it? I think we need a different model of leadership. We need to recognise that leadership is not about having all the answers. It is sometimes, and very often, about asking the right questions. It is recognising that the more difficult the situation we face, the more important that task is. Faced with what can be termed 'wicked problems'—that is, issues that have not been encountered often or at all before, and where it is far from obvious what to do—Grint (2005) argues that effective leaders must seek a more collective view on how to determine a way forward. This does not mean consensus management or decision by the lowest common denominator. But it does mean that we cannot rely on the wisdom of a solitary genius surrounded by a multitude of marvelling minions. This is a recipe for disaster in politics or in organisations. We need to recognise that in companies, as well as in countries, we need an active engaged citizenry. Total power in the hands of one person does not produce desirable outcomes in North Korea. Nor did it leave an impressive legacy in Iraq, Libya, Nazi Germany or Stalinist Russia. Why should it be any different in business organisations?

7   An Agenda for Change

Some years ago I proposed what I called 'ten commandments' to secure more critical upward feedback in organizations (Tourish 2005). These were:

7.1   Experiment with Both Upward and 360-Degree Appraisal

Such practices are no longer regarded as revolutionary, and are commonly employed in many leading corporations, including AT&T, the Bank of America, Caterpillar, GTE and General Electric. They are a powerful means of institutionalising useful feedback. It is of course vital that the feedback obtained is utilised to shape changes in behaviour.

7.2   Managers Should Familiarise Themselves with the Basics of Ingratiation Theory

I have found that most top teams readily accept the notion of ingratiation. During workshops I have conducted with senior managers, many have swapped amusing anecdotes that vividly describe the process in action. But, in line with the great deal that is now known of self-efficacy biases, they then mostly go on to assume that they themselves are immune to its effects. Typical phrase: 'Of course, this doesn't happen with me.' In reality, it always does. I sometimes illustrate the point by showering the group concerned with obviously exaggerated praise and positive feedback at an early stage of our discussion. When, later, I ask them to identify the last time someone engaged in ingratiation with them they struggle to provide an example, even though they have just received precisely that from me a few minutes earlier. Since ingratiation feels intuitively more valid than criticism it is difficult to recognise that someone is offering it to us even when it is at its most blatant. Senior managers, in particular, should recognise that they will be on the receiving end of too much feedback that is positive and too little that is critical, whatever their intentions. Moreover, they are just as susceptible to the effects of flattery ('Good idea, boss') as anyone else. While increased awareness never solves a problem by itself, it is an essential first step. Managers at all levels need to become more aware of ingratiation dynamics, of their own susceptibility to their effects and of the most effective responses to adopt in dealing with it. Such awareness forms part of the ABC of emotional literacy. Managers without it risk building catastrophically imbalanced relationships with their people, and of developing both narcissism and hubris.

7.3   Positive Feedback Should Be Subject to the Same, or Greater Scrutiny, Than Negative Feedback

Without such scrutiny, positive feedback will come to predominate, managers will give it undue attention, and they will then go on to develop a dangerously rose-tinted view of the climate within their own organisations. In turn, this means that key problems remain off the agenda, and will therefore grow worse. Managers should adopt a thoroughly questioning attitude to all feedback from those with a lower status, and treat feedback that is unremittingly positive in tone with considerable scepticism. Perhaps Jonathan Swift, author of Gulliver's Travels, offered the most instructive advice on how to react: 'The only benefit of flattery is that by hearing what we are not, we may be instructed what we ought to be.' Management meetings should combat the tendency to bask in positive feedback, and instead focus on a regular agenda of questions such as the following:

- What problems have come to our attention recently?
- What criticisms have we received about the decisions we are taking?
- Are the criticisms valid, partially or completely? What should we change in response to them?
- How can we get more critical feedback into our decision-making processes?

As in all things, balance is critical. A focus *only* on critical feedback would be as detrimental as its opposite, even though, in the present climate, there is little danger of this occurring. That is not the intention here. Rather, the suggestion is that both positive and critical feedback should be probed to ascertain how accurate it is. In particular, the motivation of the person or persons engaged in flattery should be considered. Flattery is best thought of as a non-monetary bribe. It preys on similar weaknesses. Managers should therefore ask themselves: What does this person have to gain by flattering me? And also: What they have to lose by disagreeing with me?

7.4 Managers Should Seek Out Opportunities for Regular Formal and Informal Contact with Staff at All Levels

This should replace reliance on official reports, written communiqués or communication mediated through various management layers. Informal interaction is more likely to facilitate honest, two-way communication, provide managers with a more accurate impression of life and opinions at all levels of their organisation, and open up new opportunities for both managers and staff to influence each other. 'Back to the Floor' initiatives are increasingly recognised as a useful means of achieving this. A key focus during such contact should be the search for critical feedback. By contrast, Royal Tours and flying visits yield nothing in the way of useful feedback. There are many other means by which managers can put more distance between themselves and head office, and less distance between themselves and non-managerial employees. The opposite happens too often. I know of one University Vice Chancellor who wrote to all his staff complaining that they were emailing him directly to raise issues, rather than go through their Heads of School and Deans of Faculty. He insisted that this practice should stop. It is not a coincidence that this same VC offended so many people in even more powerful positions that he was eventually dismissed. As a rule of thumb, the more reliant a manager is on official channels of communication and established chains of command the more likely it is that s/he will be out of touch with the mood of his or her people. In turn, the more likely it is that they will develop hubris.

7.5   Promote Systems for Greater Participation in Decision-Making

Participation involves the creation of structures that empower people, and which enables them to collaborate in activities that go beyond the minimum co-ordination efforts characteristic of much work practice. In general, people should be encouraged to take more decisions on their own. Lessons can be drawn from General Electric's famous 'Work Out' Programme, where people from a large cross section of business units were brought together to identify ways they could dismantle bureaucratic obstacles to action (Sull 2003). These techniques could usefully be adapted to address the feedback issues identified in this chapter.

7.6 Create 'Red Flag' Mechanisms for the Upward Transmission of Information that Cannot Be Ignored

Organisations rarely fail because they have inadequate information. But they will fail if vital information either does not reach the top, or is ignored when it gets there. Mechanisms need to be created whereby problems rather than flattery get to the top, where people feel safe to speak truth to power, where decisions are scrutinised for their weaknesses as well as their strengths, and where candour prevails over conformity. This is not rocket science. It is a matter of paying attention. Help is available if we ask for it. Harford (2011: 62) recounts the following example from the career of the renowned General Petraeus: '(in 1981) as a lowly captain he was offered a job as an aide to Major General Jack Galvin. Galvin told Petraeus that the most important part of the job was to criticise his boss: 'It's my job to run the division, and it's your job to critique me.' Petraeus protested but Galvin insisted, so each month the young captain would leave a report card on his boss's in-tray.' Can measures like this be more widely applied?[3]

7.7 Existing Communication Processes Should Be Reviewed to Ensure that They Include Requirements to Produce Critical Feedback

With few exceptions, team briefings emphasise the transmission of information from the top to the bottom. This is akin to installing an elevator capable of travelling only in one direction—downwards. Team briefings should also include a specific requirement that problems and criticisms be reported up. Again, balance is vital. As already noted, exclusively critical feedback may end up being as damaging as exclusively positive feedback, and create a fearful climate dominated by the expectation of imminent catastrophe. No one can innovate, or work with even minimal effectiveness, if they confidently expect the imminent arrival of the four horsemen of the apocalypse. Nevertheless, with that proviso in mind, most organisations are a long way from having to worry about the risk of too much critical feedback disturbing the tranquillity of those in top positions. Targets should be set for critical feedback, and closely monitored. A culture change is required. In particular, managers who tell their people 'Don't bring me problems, bring me solutions' need to re-engineer their vocabulary—they are generating blackouts rather than illumination.

7.8   Train Managers to Be Open, Receptive and Responsive to Employee Dissent

When managers behave in such a manner they are signalling receptiveness to entire workgroups. However, training in the appropriate skills is often lacking. As with many other vital communication skills, it is frequently just assumed that managers will have access to the right tool kit. This optimistic assumption is unwarranted. Even if people have some notion of which tools are available to them, training is required so that they select the right one for each task. In improving skill levels in this area, we can make serious inroads on the perils of hubris.

7.9   Power and Status Differentials Should Be Eliminated or, Where that Is Impossible, at Least Reduced

The example given earlier of Enron's 'rank and yank' system was designed among other things to instil fear and uncertainty into employees; similar approaches are employed in many companies. I believe that such appraisal systems give managers far too much power over employees, and make open communication virtually impossible. They should be eliminated—at warp speed. More broadly, status differentials can be reduced by blitzing some of the most visible symbols of privilege, such as reserved parking, executive dining rooms and percentage salary increases far in excess of those obtained by other employees. A growing body of research suggests that excessive and highly visible signs of executive privilege undermine organisational cohesion and effectiveness. In particular, it promotes an 'us versus them' mentality rather than one of 'us against the competition.' The risks with addressing this question are few, but the potential gains are immense.

7.10 The CEO, in Particular, Needs to Openly Model a Different Approach to the Receipt of Critical Communication, and Ensure that Senior Colleagues Emulate This Openness

Many studies have shown that when people are asked to gauge the efficacy of communication in general and the role of senior managers in particular they personalise the issue into the role of the CEO. Organisations that take communication seriously are generally led by CEOs who take communication seriously. CEOs that are defensive, uncertain, closed to feedback and dismissive of contrary opinions may indeed get their way—in the short term. At the very least, they will be gratified by effusive public statements of compliance. But coerced compliance is usually combined with private defiance. Ultimately, it produces a fractious relationship between senior managers and their staff, and organisations where managers and employees are at war with each other, rather than with the competition, cannot conquer new markets. Without a clear lead on communication at the level of the CEO, and his or her immediate colleagues, it is unlikely that progress on the issues discussed in this chapter will be made.

At the time, I thought these were radical suggestions. In the aftermath of the 'Great Recession', I feel they are far too timid. Winston Churchill famously remarked that 'democracy is the worst form of government except all the others that have been tried.' True. I would urge the extension of the elective principle in our business organizations. It is remarkable how little influence most people exercise in the places where they work. Outside of work, they choose governments, participate in their communities and raise children—the latter a much more challenging assignment than anything we face at work. But in work it is assumed that, for the most part, they must just do more or less what they have been told. It is sometimes argued that if leaders are elected people will choose those who are more likely to give them an easy time, rather than prioritise the interests of the organization. This might be a convincing argument—if we were able to accept that existing CEOs and their colleagues are much more motivated by a wider collective interest than the evidence indicates is the case. Why are we encouraged to be so sceptical about real, meaningful participation in decision making by people at work more than in any other environment?

I visited a creative industries company recently where everyone was very proud of a radical new innovation. It had been decided that a new meeting room required a name. Staff voted to determine what it should be called. Surprisingly, the organization did not disintegrate under the strain of this bold experiment in participative decision making. It is now attempting to identify other issues where people can vote on decisions. I hope that these are even more important than the naming of a room. Here, I offer one example of just how far this can go. In reading it, I invite you to think of how such an approach can help to curtail hubris.

Ricardo Semler is President of a hugely successful Brazilian company, Semco. Delivering a presentation to business students at MIT, he recounted how his company makes appointments to senior roles, such as Chief Finance Officer.[4] We all know how this is done in most businesses. In Semco, when such a position is identified employees are notified of a meeting to determine what the role will involve and what kind of a person is required to fill it. Anyone can attend. If you do not, it is assumed that you lend authority to take decisions to those who do. Shortlisting then depends on whether applicants meet the criteria, above all whether they can actually perform the core tasks identified as vital for the job. Those shortlisted are invited to face a grilling by anyone in the company who attended the first meeting. This group then votes on how many of the short listed candidates they want to invite back for extended meetings with anyone in the company they wish to see. When this is complete, the original group reconvenes and decides who to appoint. Everyone, including Semler, has only one vote. As he pointedly remarks, why not? Once you know that they can do the job the only question remaining is whether they like you and you like them.

What a marvellous opportunity this approach is to engage people in real decision making, take some of the load from those at the top, and institutionalise people's involvement in the companies for which they work. What makes it so rare is that we remain trapped in hierarchical decision making, and are blind to the potential that surrounds all of us in the form of the people with whom we work. Our intellects and imaginations are imprisoned by heroic models of leadership. Yet if leaders want employees to behave like responsible adults, rather than as delinquent children or fawning sycophants, they have to be *treated* as responsible adults. Naturally, this is not a panacea. But I would suggest that we are likely to face fewer problems when we go down this road than what we now experience with the *status quo*. We need to shift our management practices in a more participatory direction and so really put limits on the frequency of hubris. Challenging as this is, imperfect as it is, maddening as it is—what exactly is the alternative?

While leadership matters, we need to recognise that it is only one ingredient from a long list of what makes organisations soar and prosper, or crash and burn. In trying to do it better, we need to do it with more humility, more input from other people and much more awareness of the danger of hubris.

Notes

1. An article by van Knippenberg and Sitkin (2013) delivers a comprehensive demolition of much of this theory. See also my book *The Dark Side of Transformational Leadership: A Critical Perspective* (2013), for a discussion of its effects.
2. David Brent's misguided belief that he excelled at motivating his staff in the hit BBC comedy series *The Office* is replicated by many managers around the world.
3. Petraeus's eventual fall from grace in 2012, over an extramarital affair and the associated mishandling of classified information, does not invalidate the point.
4. His presentation can be seen on Youtube at the following link: https://www.youtube.com/watch?v=JJ0FQR2gXe0. Last accessed 1 May 2015.

References

Amar, A., Hentrich, C., Bastani, B., & Hlupic, V. (2012). How managers succeed by letting employees lead. *Organizational Dynamics, 41,* 62–71.

Bass, B., & Riggio, R. (2006). *Transformational leadership* (2nd ed.). New Jersey: Lawrence Erlbaum.

Byrne, H. (1999). *Chainsaw: The notorious career of Al Dunlap in the Era of profit-at-any-price.* New York: Harper Collins.

Burns, J. M. (1978). *Leadership.* New York: Harper Row.

Churchill, W. (1941). *The world crisis 1916-1918.* Abridged ed. London: Macmillan.

Collinson, D., & Tourish, D. (2015). Teaching leadership critically: New directions for leadership pedagogy. *Academy of Management Learning and Education, 14,* 576–594.

Delves Broughton, P. (2010). *What they teach you at Harvard Business School: My two years inside the cauldron of capitalism.* London: Penguin.

Finkelstein, S. (2003). Seven habits of spectacularly unsuccessful people. *Business Strategy Review, 14,* 39–50.

Fraser, I. (2014). *Shredded: Inside RBS, the bank that broke Britain.* Edinburgh: Birlinn.

Fusaro, P., & Miller, R. (2002). *What went wrong at Enron: Everyone's guide to the largest bankruptcy in US history.* Hoboken, NJ: Wiley.

Grint, K. (2005). Problems, problems, problems: The social construction of 'leadership'. *Human Relations, 58,* 1467–1494.

Harford, T. (2011). *Adapt: Why success always starts with failure.* London: Little Brown.

Hutton, W. (2015, April 26). Tesco's fall tells a wider story about our failing capitalism, *The Observer,* Available online at http://www.theguardian.com/commentisfree/2015/apr/26/capitalism-woes-tesco-meltdown, Last accessed 1 May 2015.

Ignatius, A. (2014, November). Leaders for the long term. *Harvard Business Review,* 47–56.

Keltner, D., Gruenfeld, D., & Anderson, C. (2003). Power, approach and inhibition. *Psychological Review, 1,* 265–284.

Kouzes, J., & Posner, B. (2012). *The leadership challenge: How to make extraordinary things happen in organizations* (5th ed.). New Jersey: Jossey-Bass.

Kunde, J. (1999). *Corporate religion.* London: FT Prentice Hall.

Lammers, J., Stapel, D., & Galinsky, A. (2010). Power increases hypocrisy: Moralizing in reasoning, immorality in behavior. *Psychological Science, 21,* 737–744.

Langer, E., & Benevento, A. (1978). Self-induced dependence. *Journal of Personality and Social Psychology, 36,* 886–893.

Luan, C., Tien, C., & Chi, Y. (2013). Downsizing to the wrong size? A study of the impact of downsizing on firm performance during an economic downturn. *The International Journal of Human Resource Management, 24,* 1519–1535.

Oreg, S. (2003). Resistance to change: Developing an individual differences measure. *Journal of Applied Psychology, 88,* 680–693.

Park, S., Westphal, J., & Stern, I. (2011). Set up for a fall: The insidious effects of flattery and opinion conformity toward corporate leaders. *Administrative Science Quarterly, 56,* 257–302.

Pratto, F., & John, O. (1991). Automatic vigilance: The attention grabbing power of negative social information. *Journal of Personality and Social Psychology, 51,* 380–391.

Rattner, S. (2009, October 21). The auto bailout: How we did it. *Fortune,* http://archive.fortune.com/2009/10/21/autos/auto_bailout_rattner.fortune/ index.htm, Last accessed 30 April 2015.

Rosenfeld, P., Giacalone, R., & Riordan, C. (1995). *Impression management in organizations.* London: Routledge.

Rosenzweig, P. (2014). *The halo effect: How managers let themselves be deceived* (2nd ed.). New York: Simon & Schuster.

See, K., Morrison, E., Rothman, N., & Soll, J. (2011). The detrimental effects of power on confidence, advice taking, and accuracy. *Organizational Behavior and Human Decision Processes, 116,* 272–285.

Sull, D. (2003). *Revival of the fittest: Why good companies go bad and how great managers remake them.* Boston: Harvard Business School Press.

Sutton, R. (2010). *Good boss, bad boss: How to be the best… and learn from the worst.* London: Piatkus.

Swartz, M., & Watkins, S. (2003). *Power failure: The rise and fall of Enron.* London: Aurum Press.

Tourish, D. (2013). *The dark side of transformational leadership: A critical perspective.* London: Routledge.

Tourish, D. (2005). Critical upward communication: Ten commandments for improving strategy and decision making. *Long Range Planning, 38,* 485–503.

Tourish, D., Craig, R., & Amernic, J. (2010). Transformational leadership education and agency perspectives in business school pedagogy: A marriage of inconvenience? *British Journal of Management, 21,* S40–S59.

Tourish, D., & Hargie, O. (2012). Metaphors of failure and the failures of metaphor: A critical study of metaphors used by bankers in explaining the banking crisis. *Organization Studies, 33,* 1044–1069.

Tourish, D., & Robson, P. (2006). Sensemaking and the distortion of critical upward communication in organizations. *Journal of Management Studies, 43,* 711–730.

Tourish, D., & Vatcha, N. (2005). Charismatic leadership and corporate cultism at Enron: The elimination of dissent, the promotion of conformity and organizational collapse. *Leadership, 1,* 455–480.

Van Knippenberg, D., & Sitkin, S. (2013). A critical assessment of charismatic-transformational leadership research: Back to the drawing board? *Academy of Management Annals, 7,* 1–60.

Willmott, H. (1993). Strength is ignorance; slavery is freedom: Managing culture in modern organizations. *Journal of Management Studies, 30,* 515–552.

Willmott, H. (2013). 'The substitution of one piece of nonsense for another': Reflections on resistance, gaming, and subjugation. *Journal of Management Studies, 50,* 443–473.

Part III

Hygiene and Antidotes

7

Heads of Government, 'Toe-Holders' and Time Limits

Lord David Owen

1   Introduction

The most charismatic politician of the twentieth century was Franklin D Roosevelt. Nobody denied his charisma, even his opponents. But he was not a consensual figure; he knew how to handle hate. In his second Presidential election in the latter stages of the 1936 campaign he made a self-confident, hard-hitting and highly partisan speech mocking those Republican speakers who had attacked him. "They are unanimous in their hate for me—and I welcome their hatred." Roosevelt was hubristic in the sense that many politicians are hubristic, and many leaders in other walks of life are hubristic. I personally do not think he did acquire Hubris Syndrome. We could go into many aspects of his character to find out why he did not acquire it, but one important aspect worth drawing attention to was he had a cynical sense of humour. Humour

L.D. Owen (✉)
House of Lords, London SW1A 0PW, UK

© The Author(s) 2018
P. Garrard (ed.), *The Leadership Hubris Epidemic*,
https://doi.org/10.1007/978-3-319-57255-0_7

is one of the things that sometimes inhibits or stops people developing hubris. Roosevelt was America's only four-term president. He took his country through the long economic depression in the 1930s, and then war after Pearl Harbour from 1941 to 1945.

On 11 July 1944, four months after having been diagnosed as suffering from left ventricular cardiac failure he was put on digitalis by a young naval cardiologist (defying the Surgeon Admiral who served as the President's physician). At a press conference, he read from a letter to the Chairman of the Democratic National Committee saying he would run again as President. "All that is within me cries out to go back to my home on the Hudson River… reluctantly but as a good soldier I repeat that I will accept and serve in the office if I am so ordered by the Commander in Chief of us all, the sovereign people of the United States."

The moment that he came closest to developing Hubris Syndrome was in February 1937, when he tabled proposals to increase the size of the Supreme Court up from nine to fifteen. Jeff Shesol, the author of Supreme Power (2010) wrote that after the second inauguration in November 1936 the United States "was now closer to one-party rule than it had been since Reconstruction" (i.e. after the Civil War). There was no attempt to deny that Roosevelt's deliberate intention, if he got it through Congress, was to pack the Supreme Court with more liberal-leaning Democrat Justices. The Court had been putting down a whole raft of reservations and judgments, effectively neutering and sometimes disabling New Deal provisions on which, in fairness, Roosevelt had just won a thumping election victory.

When the proposals were announced the press kept on asking how Roosevelt could do such a thing, and why he would ignore people's advice. Their answer was 'hubris', and certainly that was the moment when, if he was going to develop Hubris Syndrome, he would have done so. It is worth remembering the Senate then had 76 Democrats (the Senate was smaller back then) but on 22 July it rejected his Court Bill by 70 votes to 20. In less than six months he had been defeated by Democrats switching in a massive vote against him. In terms of what went wrong Shesol writes: "… it was not a choice that Roosevelt made impulsively. It may have been driven—to a dangerous degree—by ego and emotion, but it was also the product of reason. It may have been wrong but it was not rash. Neither was it made in a vacuum. By the time of Roosevelt's second inauguration, there was a growing national consensus that something had to be done about the Court…" (pp. 249–250). When he lost he told the Cabinet it was time to laugh again and he intended to have fun. In August he nominated for a vacancy of the nine a Senator who had voted for the Court Bill knowing they would not vote down one of their own. So much for any continued hostility from Democrats who had voted against Roosevelt.

An important fact to recognise about Roosevelt is that he chose people to be close to him whom he encouraged to argue with him; he wanted them to dissent, and they were given a licence to dissent. These people were 'toe-holders' and in fact the person who invented the word toe-holder, was a very interesting figure called Lewis Howe. He was in Roosevelt's life from 1911. He used to live wherever Roosevelt was. If he was in Albany, as the Governor of New York, he would use a room in the mansion in Albany. If he was in the White House he would live in the White House. He was the only person of the paid staff who called him Franklin when he was President and he would say, "You damned fool" or "Goddammit Franklin, you can't do that" or even "Mein Gotte! That is the stupidest idea I've ever heard of." He was constantly there, always an independent voice. He died, tragically, in the spring of 1936 and was given a state funeral. Some people say Roosevelt would never have tried to pack the Supreme Court if Lewis Howe had still been alive in 1937.

His earliest toe-holder, and a very important one, was Eleanor, his wife. Eleanor was a formidable woman in her own right and many people, in my view, underestimate her crucial contribution. After Roosevelt died, President Truman very wisely appointed her to be the US representative on the UN Human Rights Commission. She became a very effective chairman of that body and an astute observer said about her, "never have I seen naiveté and cunning so carefully blended." (Rowley 2010) She was a New Dealer, at times when her husband was often wavering. She was always there in his mind, though more rarely there as a presence.

Another classical case of a woman holding back her husband from developing Hubris Syndrome is Clementine Churchill, who in June 1940 wrote a very touching letter. If there was ever a time when Hubris Syndrome loomed it was probably then for Churchill. She spotted a change in his behaviour and said, in effect, that he was not like he used to be; she reminded him that he would previously have welcomed and engaged with new ideas, particularly from young people, who now knew that he would just snap at them and therefore stopped providing ideas. The text of her letter (originally published in Soames (1979)) is worth quoting in full:

I hope you will forgive me if I tell you something I feel you ought to know.

One of the men in your entourage (a devoted friend) has been to me & told me that there is a danger of your being generally disliked by your colleagues and subordinates because of your rough sarcastic & overbearing manner – It seems your Private Secretaries have agreed to behave like school boys & 'take what's coming to them' & then escape out of your presence shrugging their shoulders – Higher up, if an idea is suggested (say at a conference) you are supposed to be so contemptuous that presently no ideas, good or bad, will be forthcoming. I was astonished & upset because in all these years I have been accustomed to all those who have worked with & under you, loving you – I said this & I was told 'No doubt it's the strain'–

My Darling Winston. I must confess that I have noticed a deterioration in your manner; & you are not as kind as you used to be.

It is for you to give the Orders & if they are bungled – except for the King, the Archbishop of Canterbury & the Speaker, you can sack anyone & everyone. Therefore with this terrific power you must combine urbanity, kindness and if possible Olympic calm. You used to quote: - 'On ne règne sur les âmes que par le calme –' I cannot bear that those who serve the Country & yourself should not love you as well as admire and respect you–

Besides you won't get the best results by irascibility & rudeness. They will breed either dislike or a slave mentality. (Rebellion in War time being out of the question!)

Please forgive your loving devoted & watchful

Clemmie

Returning to Roosevelt—after 1936 there was a short gap, in which there was no obvious replacement for Howe. Then in 1938, and for all the war years, the key figure was Harry Hopkins. For a long time I thought that Harry Hopkins was a great international expert, a strategic figure, who had been brought in by Roosevelt to advise him and fill a gap in his knowledge of international affairs. Not a bit of it. He was a social worker from the Corn Belt, who knew nothing about international politics when he came into Roosevelt's orbit. What he did know was how to handle Roosevelt and learn from him. He was an extraordinarily clever man and had a very organised mind that went to the root of the matter. Judge Rosenman (another toe-holder) said he "had only one loyalty in life—and it was kind of religion—Franklin D Roosevelt." From the basis of utter loyalty Hopkins could afford to be critical, and his advice was often accepted. He had a huge influence, and General Marshall, later Secretary of State under Truman, said he rendered a service to his country which will never be even vaguely appreciated. When Roosevelt sent him to see Stalin in 1941 he had no written instruction. Roosevelt just wrote to Stalin '...treat him as if it was myself in the room; say to him anything as if I was there'. It was an extraordinary relationship, and he could talk—and did talk—frankly to the President. Like Howe, he too came and lived in the White House. In fact, he got married in the White House and brought his new wife there to live with him.

The other toe-holder, like Howe and Eleanor, there right from the start, during the making of Roosevelt after he developed polio on the Canadian island of Campobello, was Missy LeHand. Starting as a secretary she was always called just Missy. She was an extraordinary influence on him. Somebody said she was his real wife. It was disputed between his children whether there was physically a sexual relationship; although Roosevelt was paralysed from the waist down he was not impotent. But she was always there when Eleanor was frequently not there. She would play poker and mix his beloved cocktails. She would even help him to arrange his stamp collection. But she knew how to say no to him and how to be frank with him, particularly in private. Judge Rosenman said of her, "Missy was the one person he would always listen to." When Missy had to leave the White House in March 1942 after a stroke, as level headed a man as Rosenman told Justice Felix Frankfurter her stroke had been "a calamity of world dimension." Rosenman also told Frankfurter she was "one of the very, very few people who was not a yes man, who crossed the President in the sense that she told him not what she knew to be his view or what he wanted to hear, but what were in fact her true views and convictions." This is the best description of what a 'toe-holder' is.

Judge Rosenman was a more emotionally detached toe-holder. A judge in New York City; he was from 1928 a steadying influence. Roosevelt was always aware of the need to stay within the law, but ready to go quite close. He used Rosenman often the phone, pushing ideas up against him, to ask in effect whether he was going too far; basically asking 'Am I stretching the truth?' Roosevelt needed this type of advice more and more in war time when he was living in Washington, and in 1942 Rosenman reluctantly moved down and became a Presidential adviser.

By discussing toe-holders first I do not want to underestimate the valuable role of mentors. People who are prone to hubris need professional help to grapple with incipient Hubris Syndrome as it develops. Such people are skilled in helping to pull back the person they are mentoring but are not as closely involved as a toe-holder. Mentors have an extremely difficult role to play, and in business they are now increasingly used on a professional basis. They are often part of a very private arrangement and few know they are involved. In good companies that process starts 20 years before they might become chief executive. One arrangement I know of was in a company singling out young people to be possible future chief executives. They sometimes spot people who they thought had elements of hubris developing (though they did not call it hubris but difficulties with human relationships). The ideal mentor would be an older person; from discussions with the person to be mentored they might choose someone he or she admired, often in the same industry but not necessarily from the same company. All that was required of this type of mentor was to build trust between them, to go out to supper or lunch two to four times a year and hopefully they would build a relationship such that the person being mentored could seek advice and particularly discuss general management issues such as how to handle people, on a broader base. It was felt this was much more effective than coming from the person's own management or HR department.

Hubris Syndrome, judging by the list of identified signs and symptoms, more often found together than apart, is a narrow concept, whereas hubris itself is a vast concept. Though rooted in Greek mythology it has in modern times many different aspects. It is part of a spectrum of human behaviour and character, and it is a personality change in people who exercise power. People exercise power at every level in our society; we should not always think of presidents and prime ministers or even chief executives of large companies. Power is relative: the head of a school, even a primary school, exerts significant power in relation to other teachers. We all encounter these power holders in all walks of life and the public is well aware of the syndrome. I sometimes wish that important decision makers were as aware of it as the public. Many business schools are as yet remarkably resistant to analysing behaviour. Perhaps this is because in a way they are feeding the hubristic view of leadership. What is very important to remember is that excluded from Hubris Syndrome is anyone with a psychiatric illness, whether a depressive illness or, in particular of course, a bipolar disorder. Again, that is a spectrum illness in diagnostic terms today, much more so than when it was referred to as manic depression. Unless you are one on one, treating them as a patient, or working closely with them as a colleague, it is very difficult to be sure that there is no underlying mania. Hubris Syndrome was ruled out, for example, in the case of President Lyndon Johnson, one of the most hubristic presidents there has ever been, though he hid it in all levels. He was diagnosed by a Duke University study (Davidson et al. 2006) of US Presidents, as having been bipolar, and where that exists it is better to leave it as diagnosed and not couple it with Hubris Syndrome.

The other aspect of Hubris Syndrome, which fascinates me is that it is acquired. It is much easier to argue for acquired personality change now, after the 20–25-year-old debate on post traumatic stress disorder, PTSD. The medical profession resisted labelling PTSD as an illness, mainly because they did not think that you could acquire personality change. That reluctance goes back to Freud, Jung, and Adler and runs through a lot of American psychiatry, though to a lesser extent in Europe. Now that PTSD has been accepted, and I think rightly so, as being acquired it is time to convince professional opinion today that Hubris Syndrome is also acquired. What fascinates me on this issue is that if power is removed, what happens? If it is acquired, it should phase down, maybe go completely when the individual who has acquired it no longer exercises power.

In 2007 I wrote a small paperback The Hubris Syndrome about Bush and Blair and the Iraq war and in 2009 an article in *Brain* with Jonathan Davidson (Owen and Davidson 2009). I had supper, with our wives, in Downing Street—once in December 1999 and then in the summer of 2002. The issues were the same: Saddam Hussein's Iraq, and my belief that the UK should not join the Euro against Blair's passionate wish that we should adopt the currency and give up the pound sterling. What was revealing was the difference in Blair's personality over the two and a half year gap. In my wife's words after the second evening he was 'messianic'—a term now frequently used to describe him but previously much less so.

I have never met George W Bush, and I was therefore less certain about the diagnosis. But I will never forget watching him on television in a children's classroom in Florida being told by an aide that a second plane had flown into the other tower of the World Trade Centre in New York. You can see the shock of the news on his face. Increasingly after that he began to show signs and symptoms of Hubris Syndrome: taking the loudspeaker from the fireman at the still smouldering site; later, in May 2003 when the war was literally years from being over, theatrically landing on board USS Abraham Lincoln with the backdrop banner "Mission Accomplished" on it. Hubris was ever present in the first three and a half years of his Presidency, but after winning a second term he seemed to be listening more and hubris began to subside after he replaced Rumsfeld as his Secretary of State for Defence with the level headed and experienced Republican, Robert Gates. Gates later went on to serve President Obama in the same role, for longer than many expected. Gates was a great help to Bush over implementing the 'surge' in extra troops at the end of 2006. Senior military leaders were opposed right up to the sending of five brigades to Baghdad and two further battalions of marines. The surge lasted until September 2007 and it undoubtedly helped settle the situation. Had it been done in early May 2003 the story of the Iraq war would have been very different. Gates described in his book (2014) the reaction to the new policy:

All hell broke loose. In a span of forty-five years, serving eight presidents, I can recall only three instances in which in my opinion a president risked reputation, public esteem, credibility, political ruin and the judgement of history on a single decision he believed was the right thing for our country: Gerald Ford's pardon of Nixon, George H. W. Bush's assent to the 1992 budget deal [against his previous stance, 'Read my lips: no new taxes'], and George W Bush's decision to surge in Iraq. In the first two cases, I think one can credibly suggest the decisions were good for the country but cost these two presidents reelection; in the latter case, the decision averted a potentially disastrous military defeat for the United States.

When he retired, Bush seemed in a very noticeable way to revert in his behaviour and attitudes, losing much of his hubris. He did not seem to want to go on television, he was very honourable and friendly to Obama. To some of those who knew George W Bush in those earlier days he changed while in the presidency, and was now back as the old George again. This is only one man's exposure to the stress following an undoubtedly traumatic experience. And there is a need to be very careful in this whole area when you are studying people's behaviour in some depth, not to draw too many conclusions from one or two cases. I am very, very conscious of that, so I try to remain wary on all those scores.

What, if anything, can be done about those who acquire Hubris Syndrome? It is not an accident that Franklin Roosevelt has featured in this chapter. After dying only a few months into his fourth term in 1945, it became the majority view in the United States that four terms was too long a period for any president to serve. The Twenty-Second Amendment to the US Constitution was passed by Congress in 1947 and ratified in 1951 limiting an elected president to two terms in office, a total of eight years. The Amendment does, however, specify that if a Vice President, or other successor, takes over from a President—who, for whatever reason, cannot fulfil the term—and serves two years or less of the former President's term, the new President may serve for a further two full terms. Truman and Lyndon Johnson, both of whom assumed office after the death of a President, could have argued they were eligible for a third term, but neither did and both served for less than eight years.

In Addis-Ababa, Ethiopia on 28 July 2015 President Obama addressed fellow Presidents in the African Union and spoke forcefully about the region's history of Presidents hanging on to power with little if any time limit constraints. He was speaking when only that month the President of Burundi had chosen to go ahead with elections for a third term. Speaking with the authority of America's first American president with roots in the African continent and well into his second and last term he said "I think if I ran, I could win. There's a lot that I'd like to do to keep America moving, but the law is the law and no person is above the law, not even the President." Earlier visiting Ghana he had said "Africa doesn't need strongmen. It needs strong institutions."

The record of Presidents or monarchs staying on in office in Africa is a troubling one. About half of the 54 countries in the AU have already been in power longer than Obama. Teodoro Obiang Nguema Mbsango has ruled Equatorial Guinea since 1979. Robert Mugabe Zimbabwe since 1980, Paul Biya Cameroon since 1982, Yoweri Musevini Uganda since 1986 and Omar Hassan Al-Bashir Sudan since 1989. Last year the President of Burkino Faso tried to extend his 27 years in power but rioting caused the collapse of his government. In Rwanda President Paul Kagame, close to Bill Clinton and Tony Blair, has just made a constitutional change to allow a third term.

Speaking in Nelson Mandela Plenary Hall, according to a long, detailed report in the New York Times, President Obama reminded his audience that neither China nor Russia were model democracies and that Mandela, like George Washington, had understood that voluntarily leaving office and handing over control peacefully was a powerful legacy. In the UK we have never had a serious debate about limiting the term of office of our Prime Ministers. Yet the UK under successive governments has played a prominent role for the last 30–40 years, in trying to persuade new presidents in independent countries, particularly in Africa, and particularly Commonwealth countries, to accept a two-term limitation on the period in which a president should exercise office. Why can that be the UK position overseas but not at home? We argue for it for everybody else but ourselves. The more one looks at the issues involved the more one needs to grapple with this issue soon.

In November 2014 I tabled a Private Member's Bill in the House of Lords to effectively limit to two terms the period one can be Prime Minister in the UK. Under the 2010 legislation introducing for the first time a five-year fixed term parliament this would mean 10 years (two terms of five years). Then to some surprise and a little consternation from fellow Conservatives at the start of the General Election the Prime Minister David Cameron announced on 24 March that he would not serve a third term if re-elected. "I'll stand for a full second term, but I think after that it will be time for new leadership. Terms are like Shredded Wheat—two are wonderful but three might just be too many." This was without precedent and constitutionally a very important statement that just might pave the way for legislation. In fact, Cameron left office the morning after the UK voted to leave the EU, despite promising to remain whatever the result.

The legislation I introduced in the Prime Minister (Limitation of Period of Office) Bill provided for a maximum limitation to the period during which a Prime Minister ("PM") can hold office of two terms of Parliament under the Fixed-term Parliaments Act 2011, in effect a 10 year maximum period (subject to Section 2 of that Act). I assumed that the fixed term limit of five years for the Parliament starting in 2015 would remain and this looks likely to be the case under Theresa May. Personally I would prefer a four year fixed term as was initially proposed by the Liberal Democrats in the 2010 coalition talks after that election. It was the Chancellor of the Exchequer, George Osborne, who proposed five years: perhaps anticipating a long haul before the British economy recovered from the Global Crisis of 2009. If that legislation were ever to be changed then my legislative proposal would automatically limit the Prime Minister maximum period of office to 8 years.

There are important lessons to learn from the Spanish experience with their existing Prime Minister Aznar running through a general election campaign, when three days before voting a coordinated series of bombings hit Madrid as commuters travelled into work on the morning of 11 March 2004—a tragedy that is referred to in Spain as 11-M. The dead totalled 191 and 1800 were injured. Later the Spanish judiciary found that the attacks were directed by an Al-Qaeda inspired terrorist cell, though no direct Al-Qaeda participation was established.

Political analysts have criticised Aznar's leadership during the crisis in that the impression was given that the Basque separatist movement ETA was responsible, when many felt at the time that the bombings were far more likely to have come from a terrorist grouping retaliation to the Aznar government's high profile support for the Iraq War. A consequence of this incident is that politicians in Spain and elsewhere are wary of having a "caretaker" Prime Minister during an election, one who is time expired and has to retire as soon as the votes are counted. Instead a view has emerged that it is better for a Prime Minister to step down well before an election is called and a successor chosen who is responsible for the campaign and intends to stay in office after the election.

In the UK, therefore, it is likely parties would ensure their leader goes earlier than the maximum term. In effect, with a five-year fixed term it would involve, in reality, a Prime Minister leaving office after nine years continuous or broken service and with a four-year fixed term, would mean a Prime Minister leaving in his seventh year of office. That, I think, would be the best limitation period but I doubt it would win support in the House of Commons.

British reluctance to fix a term for a Prime Minister has many roots. The most important is a feeling that MPs know what is going on in a Prime Minister's mind well before others outside the House of Commons do. Though they have accepted pressures for a more democratic process to modify the mechanisms for choosing the leader and future Prime Minister they do not want any further weakening of their capacity to remove their leader whether because of incompetence, impending dementia, alcoholism, depression or hubris: to name but a few factors. In recent years the toll of leaders removed, apart from as a result of electoral defeat, is a long one: Asquith in 1916 when alcoholism played a part; Lloyd George in 1922 when his acquired Hubris Syndrome featured; Lansbury in 1935 over pacifism; Chamberlain in 1940 when Hubris Syndrome contributed to Munich two years earlier as well as failure in Norway; Churchill ageing and cerebrovascular disease in 1954; Eden hepatitic fevers after a surgical mistake cutting his bile duct 1957; Thorpe ousted because of scandal; Thatcher acquiring Hubris Syndrome after the 1987 general election which resulted in her being forced out following a leadership election against Michael Heseltine in 1990; Duncan Smith for incompetence; Blair for acquired Hubris Syndrome beginning in 2002, after being forced by Labour MPs in 2006 to give a public commitment to leave office; Charles Kennedy due to alcoholism; David Cameron referendum hubris.

In the case of Prime Ministers Thatcher and Blair, had there been in place legislative time limits of the sort discussed here the anguish and psychological trauma of their forced removal would have been avoided. Also they were pursuing policies in the latter part of their terms of office which were by any standard of objectivity against British interests: in the case of Thatcher towards German reunification in 1989 and in the case of Blair toward Lebanon in 2006. It would be wise to anticipate that this pattern of Prime Ministers wedded to retaining power is likely to happen again.

What about time limitations in business? For the last 20 years I have been a businessman, sitting on four boards of international public companies. The best mechanism is that after five years any public company board should automatically have to consider as part of company law the record of the chief executive. That assessment must be a process which is not entirely internal and guidance must stipulate that a measure of external assessment be introduced. If all companies comply it ensures it is not a criticism of the chief executive who may be doing very well for shareholders and by other standards of corporate governance. If you make no exceptions then it does not raise much 'angst' or trigger unrest within the company. If the CEO is found wanting in important particulars that is the moment when the board decides whether they are going to go out to look for a new CEO and not renew the present CEO's contract.

I have no doubt if the British Parliament were to legislate it would require the overt support of the Prime Minister of the day, and that David Cameron might have been tempted. Such an act would ensure a praiseworthy legacy that would impact on the British Commonwealth in particular. That would be reinforced if international companies were also seen to be establishing time limits and best procedures. This is no minor matter: the abysmal record of bad governance worldwide both in politics and in companies is very frequently accompanied by extensive corruption. We are not short of words we are desperately short of action.

References

Davidson, J. R. T., Connor, K. M., & Swartz, M. (2006). Mental illness in US presidents between 1776 and 1974: A review of biographical sources. *Journal of Nervous and Mental Disease, 194,* 47–51.

Gates, R. (2014). *Duty: Memoirs of a secretary at war* (p. 48). New York: Alfred A Knopf.

Owen, D., & Davidson, J. (2009). Hubris syndrome: An acquired personality disorder? A study of US presidents and UK prime ministers over the last 100 years. *Brain, 132,* 1396–1406.

Rowley, Hazel. (2010). *Franklin and Eleanor. An extraordinary marriage* (pp. 294–295). New York: Farrar, Straus and Giroux.

Shesol, J. (2010). *Supreme power: Franklin Roosevelt vs The Supreme Court.* New York: W.W. Norton.

Soames, M. (1979). *Clementine Churchill* (p. 291). London: Cassell.

8

Influential Partnerships—A Possible Role for a Modern-day Court Jester

Gillian Hyde

1   Overview

Derailing tendencies, or extremes of personality that can become dysfunctional or counterproductive, are almost inevitable among business leaders. As leaders move up the career ladder and increase their sphere of influence the impact of these counterproductive behaviours becomes more widespread. At the same time, the behaviours are likely to become more extreme and unfettered as the potential for a counterbalancing influence decreases. In most modern corporate structures there is no opportunity for, or power invested in, colleagues to contradict or candidly advise successful leaders who continue to rise through the hierarchy. So the challenge is to create a model for influential partnerships in organisations by drawing on historical references—from monarchs to politicians and business leaders—to inform future directions.

G. Hyde (✉)
Psychological Consultancy Ltd, Royal Tunbridge Wells, UK

© The Author(s) 2018   **179**
P. Garrard (ed.), *The Leadership Hubris Epidemic*,
https://doi.org/10.1007/978-3-319-57255-0_8

2   The Nature of the Problem

2.1   Psychology Only Goes so Far

The field of applied business psychology, and personality assessment in particular, provides a rich source of information to explain and describe derailing characteristics. Robert Hogan, a world expert on personality assessment and personality research (Hogan 1976, 1987, 1988, 2006), has devised a number of personality assessment instruments. One of these assessments, the Hogan Development Survey (Hogan and Hogan 1997), measures derailers through a taxonomy that is aligned with personality disorders. This instrument enables psychologists to assess individuals and identify and interpret their derailer profiles. Psychologists also know how to give good, pertinent feedback and advice to increase the self-awareness of leaders and managers about these potential derailers. But psychologists give advice from a distance; they are not present in the workplace and therefore cannot monitor whether the leader actually implements any strategies to manage, restrain and constrain these behaviours on a daily basis, over a prolonged period of time. It may be that there are lessons to be learned and inspiration to be found from the study of influential partnerships in the past.

2.2   Derailers are Inevitable

For almost every strong character in a leadership or managerial position there will be some downside aspects to their personality. Derailers are commonplace behaviours that are, essentially, overplayed strengths. It is unlikely, for instance, that a creative spark, someone who is truly imaginative and innovative and who has a completely different view of the world to most people, wouldn't also have a sprinkling of eccentricity, a degree of self-absorption and perhaps a touch of vagueness at times. Similarly, a dynamic, optimistic, can-do leader probably also displays some arrogance at times, is perhaps a little overbearing or dominant, or even too forceful. A final example here would be the passionate, intense risk-taking entrepreneur who dares to create a totally new business venture that others would not be so brave to try. But alongside these qualities might also be some anguished self-doubt, an edginess, perhaps an irritability and even a degree of anxiety.

2.3 Counterbalancing Influences Decline with Success

While it is almost inevitable that successful individuals will possess extreme counterproductive characteristics, the potential impact these have on their behaviour is amplified by the declining influence of peers and colleagues. Those individuals surrounding the leader have less and less ability to act as a counterbalance through debate, argument, contradiction, criticism or advice as leaders rise through an organisation.

In a survey of American CEOs by RHR International (2014), 50% of respondents reported experiencing loneliness in their role. Perhaps this should come as no surprise. The corporate world is competitive, political and game-playing; it is likely that friends will be lost and enemies made on the way to becoming the CEO. For some, this is a price worth paying but it will likely lead to isolation and a lack of opportunity for them to critically evaluate their performance. The resulting lack of self-awareness and critical evaluation of their strengths and weaknesses will ultimately damage their own career, their colleagues' careers and the organisation as a whole.

Continuing this theme, Chamarro-Premuzic (2014) has identified what he calls the 'Feedback Bubble'. He argues that as individuals acquire more power they are less likely to ask for feedback, fewer people are prepared to give them feedback and, on the rare occasion they do receive feedback, they may not be able to handle the truth.

People in power often grow more pleased with themselves, feel invulnerable and prefer to receive only the kind of feedback that reinforces their own positive image of themselves. In a study of more than 1000 New Zealand business leaders, Winsborough (2012) discovered the main complaint against poorly performing leaders was that they did not seek or accept feedback. "With every move up the ladder, you're more impressed with yourself as you impress other people," says Geoff Trickey, Managing Director at Psychological Consultancy Ltd (2014).

"When you are massively successful you no longer feel you need to make any concessions to anybody because you're now top of the heap. You're admired, successful, powerful, and wealthy, so why should you bother with what anyone thinks?"

People surrounding the leader are fearful; few dare to risk criticising the boss. In order to fit in, they may praise or even over praise the leader, and of course this exacerbates the problem. "You're on your own at the top," says Trickey. "Nobody is speaking truth to power. No one's telling you you're a fool or that's a stupid idea. Everyone's saying how great it was. You're beginning to feel indestructible so, at that point, the dark side is just lurking around the corner. It's been creeping up on you as you've moved up the building."

Finally, if leaders are ever actually given some honest feedback they may not handle it well. "When most people are confronted with the fact that they have made the wrong decision, they are unwilling to admit it," says Chamorro-Premuzic (2014). "In order to save face and avoid feeling stupid, they engage in a range of unconscious tactics that help them distort reality in their favour."

3   The Scale of the Problem

Turning to the scale of the problem, the published estimates of failure rates among leaders or managers are quite sizeable. They range from between 33% to as many as 67% (Sorcher 1985; Hogan and Hogan 2001; Riddle 2009). In 2009 my colleagues and I published a research paper called 'A Decade of the Dark Side' (Trickey and Hyde 2009) that examined our archival database of people who had completed the Hogan Development Survey. This personality questionnaire characterises people along 11 different potentially dysfunctional styles of behaviour—overplayed strengths that could derail a career. In our sample of over 18,000 people, only 15% did not get a very high score on any one of the scales, suggesting that 85% of the population had at least one potentially derailing style of behaviour. In fact, 22% of the sample had one high scoring derailer, 21% had two, and 16% had three, with the remaining 26% possessing four or more.

4 Who Dares Speak Truth to Power?

Exploring influential partnerships as a potential mechanism to rein in some of these behaviours brings us to a number of historical, literary, political and business world examples. Analysis of these cases suggests two main groupings of people who have, in the past, dared to speak truth to power. One is the jester, or fool, and the other is the trusted aide, who may be a long-standing colleague, spouse or partner.

4.1 The Court Jester

Beatrice Otto, in her book *Fools are Everywhere* (Otto 2007), describes the history and global provenance of the jester. She has created a list of specific characteristics that apply to jesters; these characteristics may provide the key to explain how the jester is able to speak truth to power.

- First, the jester used humour strategically to advise or criticise the monarch, clearly distinguishing him from other court entertainers. Secondly, jesters were not devious or calculating; rather they spoke their mind when the mood took them. Thirdly, they did not pose a power threat to the monarch or to those they were advising. Next, they had little to gain by caution and everything to gain by honesty; their role was to advise and to speak plainly to the monarch with no artifice. They were required to be candid and open. Jesters were peripheral to the game of politics, so there was no self-interest in the advice that they were giving. Their advice was not geared to their own personal ambition or advancement.
- Jesters were not noted for flattery or fawning, they spoke plainly. They were somewhat isolated from the intrigues of the court which made them a good confidante for the monarch. Finally, their ability to use humour helped them to soften critical comments and advice, to make the advice more acceptable and palatable to the monarch.

One of the most famous examples of a jester was Will Sommers, jester to Henry VIII. There is a delightful description of him, written in 1676, which clearly illustrates his ability to find favour with those in power, at the same time as speaking very plainly to the leaders (Anon 1676, 1794). For instance, he is described as having an "easie nature". He gained grace and favour not just from the monarch but also from the nobility. He "was no carry-tale, nor whisperer nor flattering insinuator". He did not deceive. He was not trying "to breed any discord and dissension". Then there is this charming descriptive phrase that he was: "an honest, plain, down-right that would speak home without halting". His popularity enabled him to speak plainly and for people to accept his criticism. Of course, Henry VIII was not the easiest of monarchs to find favour with.

In the world of literature there are numerous examples of the jester or fool, with perhaps the most famous one being King Lear's fool. The fool is key to the play and tells Lear uncomfortable truths about his plans to abdicate and divide up his kingdom between his daughters. Although he criticises and reminds Lear of the negative consequences of making these ill-advised decisions, at the same time he endears us to Lear. He engages the audience with Lear and Lear's plight through his care and concern for his monarch (Rosenberg 1972, 1993).

What about modern-day parallels of the jester or the fool? Are there any people who use humour these days to criticise people in power? In the western world, today's equivalent would be with politicians, rather than with monarchs, and there are several examples. For instance, the political cartoonists who draw and write new cartoons daily to criticise, mock and sometimes ridicule politicians. We also have alternative comedians who poke fun and criticise politicians and, of course, political comedy television and radio programmes such as Have I Got News for You, Mock the Week and, in the 1980s, Spitting Image.

Here are a couple of examples, from the US comedian Jay Leno, of jokes targeted at politicians:

> Sarah Palin has admitted she tried marijuana several years ago, but she did not like it. She said it distorted her perceptions, impaired her thinking, and she's hoping that the effects will eventually wear off.

> In an interview that was taped yesterday, President Bush said that the biggest disappointment of his presidency was the people who expressed bitterness about his leadership. And that was just at the Christmas dinner with his family.

So politicians are routinely exposed to criticism and knocked down to size on a fairly regular basis, often through the use of humour, so there is, perhaps, an analogy with the jester or fool. However, these modern-day examples of critics have more of an agenda. They often have something to sell, whether it be newspapers, a comedy show or television programme. Also, this type of criticism differs from that Will Sommers gave to Henry VIII, or Lear's fool gave to King Lear because it is delivered, for the most part, without sympathy for the characters involved. These days, humour is more likely to be used to simply mock those in power rather than employed as a device by those who care for the leaders and want to give them constructive advice.

4.2   The Trusted Aide

What about the other type of influential partnership that has been identified, the trusted aide? This person could be a spouse or partner, or they could be a work colleague. Whoever they are, the relationship between them and the leader will undoubtedly have evolved over some time, and of critical importance is the lack of competition or any power struggle between the two.

One modern-day political example of this type of trusted bond is the relationship between Willie Whitelaw and Margaret Thatcher. Malcolm Rifkind wrote of Whitelaw (2002) that it would be "highly desirable to have at least one Whitelaw in every British cabinet", and continues, "consider the advantage of a senior minister no longer with personal ambition able to tell the Prime Minister, without fear or favour, when he was acting foolishly, improperly or in a manner that would do the government serious damage". While Whitelaw clearly fulfilled this role of honest adviser, he was also alert to the potentially negative impact of Thatcher's Hubris Syndrome and her more insensitive moments. He played a key role in appeasing those who might be offended and in rescuing Thatcher from the consequences of such insensitivity.

Another example is the relationship between Winston Churchill and his wife, Clemmie. It is beautifully illustrated in a letter from Clemmie to Churchill five days after the French had signed an armistice with Germany, leaving Britain alone to face the threat of invasion. Clemmie prefaces the letter by begging Churchill's forgiveness, but she feels she needs to address him because one of his entourage has spoken to her about a seeming change in Churchill's behaviour. She says, "there is a danger of your being generally disliked by your colleagues and subordinates because of your rough, sarcastic and overbearing manner...... You won't get the best results by irascibility and rudeness. They will breed either dislike or a slave mentality." (Soames 1999). This is an excellent example of good, constructive, honest advice from a trusted aide to a leader. Clemmie does not mince her words, but her position of trust and status outside of the power hierarchy means she can speak truth to power and the advice can be accepted and acted upon rather than shunned or scrutinised.

There are a couple of examples from the modern corporate world that illustrate advice that comes from a trusted aide who has been a long-standing work colleague. First, the relationship between Larry Page, the founder of Google, and Eric Schmidt, his former CEO seems to fall into this camp. Larry Page is described as being rather insensitive, critical, probably a suspicious, hostile kind of a person with a distinct lack of social grace (Carlson 2014). He is apparently very socially awkward, avoids making eye contact and has a need for control. For instance, if colleagues are giving a product demonstration and the software is slow to load he is known to start counting out loud, no doubt distracting and de-motivating the presenters. So Schmidt, his former CEO, controlled Page's input in group situations. Schmidt and Page would go into meetings together but Page stayed to one side while Schmidt led the proceedings, asking Page to contribute his expertise and knowledge only when needed.

Another example is the relationship between Richard Branson and his former Special Adviser and President of Virgin Galactic, Will Whitehorn. Whitehorn gets a special mention on the Virgin corporate website, even though he is no longer with Virgin. Branson describes him as being his 'right-hand man' for a long time, and he praises his knowledge and understanding of the brand and his enthusiasm. However, it is clear from descriptions of Branson and Whitehorn that they are very different characters who overcame their differences by recognizing and admiring their individual unique contributions. Branson's strengths are on the people side, in building relationships and having great ideas while Whitehorn is more into the detail, providing the logic and the reasoning behind Branson's ideas. Whitehorn (2007) has been quoted as saying "Richard is highly intelligent but educationally dyslexic, it has freed him to live by his gut reaction to things, and that has served him well. I was brought up in a more academic environment—to find there was always a reason why something can't happen. Richard hates it when people tell him that. He isn't hamstrung by academic disputes. He finds them tedious." Whitehorn has been described as a key tactician, with an intense personality that is in sharp contrast to the bubbly outgoing persona of Branson. Former City diarist and PR consultant Damien McCrystal, who has known him for 30 years, says: "He has an amazing mind that retains every fact he hears." (McCrystal 2009).

But a successful organisation needs diversity of personality as illustrated by the partnerships of Page and Schmidt and Branson and Whitehorn; in both examples there is one person who has the energy to found the company, who has the overarching vision, but one of them lacks the necessary people skills to keep everyone motivated and engaged and happy and the other lacks the attention to detail to keep everything on track. They both need a counterpart advising them and moderating and mediating those behaviours that could, potentially, be counterproductive for relationships with their staff and for their organisation.

4.3   The Everyday

It is worth contrasting these examples of people speaking truth to power with the more commonplace every-day experiences in organisations. Most of the examples given above are unusual because the people in power could have been lampooned or criticised whilst still in power. Mostly, leaders who fail in the corporate world are not criticised at all. If their fall from grace is part of a newsworthy scandal, the media criticism will probably happen after the event when it's all too late. Fred Goodwin at RBS and his disastrous leadership style would be an example of this. However, in most organisations leaders and managers are routinely left to their own devices. There is no restraining influence, so those who engage in counterproductive behaviours continue to have a negative impact on those who work with them and around them. Unless there is an influential partnership in place between the leader and someone whose advice they trust there is no positive source of day-to-day restraint.

5   Breaking Through the Taboo

Perhaps, though, we have the leaders we deserve. In western corporate society we tend to revere and promote leaders who are dynamic, energetic, confident, decisive, bold; but these characteristics that we value highly, that enable people to play politics and climb to the top of the tree, have a downside. It's unlikely that these types of leaders would be natural listeners. Intriguingly, monarchs in the past must have been aware of the need for a plain-speaking adviser and specifically created the role of the jester. These days, however, it is becoming almost taboo to criticise our leaders or our managers. People are fearful of losing their jobs if they speak up or criticise their leaders. Whistleblowers have had a rough time. Fred Goodwin at RBS is alleged to have sacked people who did not agree with him (Martin 2013). We need to try to find a way to break through this taboo, both at the individual level, but also at the organisational level to work towards creating what Bennis has called a culture of candour (Bennis et al. 2008).

6   From Hubris to Humility

The big challenge, then, is to apply this information to help leaders bridge the gap from hubris to humility. Could it be possible to apply strategies from any of the above examples of influential partnerships to relationships between leaders and a trusted adviser? Clearly, there are benefits to the restraining influences of those influential partnerships. Could there be a mechanism to help leaders and organisations create influential partnerships.

There are many interventions and sources of advice available to leaders these days. For example, psychologists assess leaders' extreme personality characteristics and provide feedback to increase self-awareness of their potentially counterproductive behaviours. 360° surveys tell leaders what other people think about them and what they could do better. Employee engagement surveys give leaders an idea of how engaged their employees are, what they think about the organisational culture, the policies and the procedures. But, on a daily basis, how much impact do these have on leaders? Is it possible to go a step further? Is there a way that influential partnerships in business could be created so that there is a more regular feedback cycle?

Starting with the example of the trusted aide type of influential partnership, there is a sense that this kind of role could only ever evolve naturally. The examples given previously of Whitelaw and Thatcher, Churchill and his wife, Larry Page and Richard Branson and their significant advisers, are all relationships that have been built up over a number of years and that are based on high levels of trust and respect and no obvious power struggle. However, when making critical significant appointments there could be scope to consider recruiting a leader along with their existing adviser or partner, if they have one. Certainly this happens within the sporting world, within football, for instance, when coaches and managers are sometimes recruited together as a team.

Next is the jester. Would it be feasible to create a modern-day role for a jester or fool? It might be possible to give somebody permission to criticise the leader, but this would be very difficult to implement. The exception would be situations where the leader in question is an entrepreneur or a founder/owner of the organisation; somebody who is very secure in their power base and therefore doesn't see the jester as a competitor. These types of leader are unlikely to feel threatened by receiving criticism from a 'jester', and it would probably be their idea to appoint someone to the position. So competition for power and status cannot be an issue for this type of influential partnership to work. There would need to be very clearly defined boundaries for that relationship and the leader would need to trust and respect the person chosen for the role, otherwise it could become something of a poisoned chalice.

But what about those leaders and managers who do not have a trusted aide or adviser, or who are not entrepreneurs or founder/owners? What sources of influential partnerships or restraints are available to them? Perhaps the time is ripe for a new breed of executive coach. While many people work as executive coaches, encouraging leaders to increase their self-awareness and reflect on their behaviour, this relationship has its limitations. Certainly, it is limited when we compare it to the type of advice given by the jester or the fool. It seems there may be scope for a more tough-talking coach, one who is integrated with the business.

Such a coach would need to be acutely aware of the issues arising from any negative impact the leader was having on colleagues. They would need to have an ear to the ground, elicit feedback from others and become aware of the sensitivities. At the same time, this new breed of coach would need to be given free rein to speak very plainly and honestly, to give candid feedback to the leader. They would need to involve themselves at times with the business or organisation, or at least have other key informants who could monitor the situation.

Looking back at the examples of different types of influential partnerships illustrated here, both modern day and historical, there are some clear common themes that emerge. Listed below are a number of these themes that could help to define the key qualities that influential partners need to possess in order to have a successful relationship with the leader.

1. The leader must have faith in and trust the influential partner.
2. The partner must not compete for power or resources.
3. The partner must have the leader's best interests at heart, and this must be evident.
4. The partner must also have their ear to the ground. They need to know what is going on, to have an understanding of the concerns of the people around, within the organisation, and they must have a sensitivity to the counterproductive effect that the leader is having on their colleagues.
5. They must be present as much as possible so that their influence is regular and frequent.

6. The partner must be protected; they must be given permission or licence to give criticism, to tell uncomfortable truths to the leader or manager without fear of losing their job or status.

7   Conclusion

In conclusion, the impact of hubris is far-reaching; it doesn't just take its toll on the leader and their advancement, it impacts on all the people who work around them, and, ultimately, on the organisation they are all a part of.

We are only human and we tend to revert to our natural style of behaviour if we don't have someone constantly tapping us on our shoulder and reminding us of when we are tipping over into our more self-destructive, counterproductive behaviours. It is an effort to present ourselves to the world in a socially acceptable way all of the time. It is demanding. While we might be very self-aware about our faults, inevitably there will still be times when we let the mask slip and our less acceptable behaviours will be exposed.

Influential partnerships, we have seen, can undoubtedly have a positive impact on restraining and constraining leaders' more extreme dysfunctional tendencies. If we could find a mechanism to help leaders create sustainable influential partnerships this would clearly benefit leaders, their colleagues and the organisation.

References

Anonymous. (1676, reprinted 1794). *A Pleasant Historie of the Life and Death of Will Sommers.*

Bennis, W., Goleman, D., & O'Toole, J. (2008). *Transparency: How leaders create a culture of candor.* San Francisco: Jossey-Bass.

Carlson, N. (2014). *The untold story of Larry Page's incredible comeback.* UK: Business Insider.

Chamarro-Premuzic, T. (2014). *Avoiding the feedback bubble.* Tulsa, OK: Hogan Assessment Systems.

Hogan, R. (1976). *Personality theory: The personological tradition*. Englewood Cliffs, NJ: Prentice-Hall.

Hogan, R. (1987). Personality psychology: Back to basics. In J. Aronoff, A. I. Rabin, & R. A. Zucker (Eds.), *The emergence of personality* (pp. 79–104). New York: Springer.

Hogan, R. (1988). The meaning of personality test scores. *American Psychologist, 43,* 621–626.

Hogan, R. (2006). *Personality and the fate of organisations*. New York: Lawrence Erlbaum.

Hogan, R., & Hogan, J. (2001). Assessing leadership: A view of the dark side. *International Journal of Selection and Assessment, 9,* 40–51.

Hogan, R., Johnson, J., & Briggs, S. (Eds.). (1997). *Handbook of personality psychology*. Academic Press.

Martin, I. (2013). *Making it happen: Fred Goodwin, RBS and the men who blew up the British economy*. Simon & Schuster.

McCrystal, D. (2009). Quoted in http://www.prweek.com/article/913962/profile-will-whitehorn-special-adviser-sir-richard-branson-president-virgin-galactic#dK6JsiEGOidcyEVY.99.

Otto, B. (2007). *Fools are everywhere: The court jester around the world*. Chicago: The University of Chicago Press.

RHR International. (2014). *CEO Snapshot Survey*.

Riddle, D. (2009). *Executive integration white paper*. Centre for Creative Leadership.

Rifkind, M. (2002). Everyone needs a Willie. Margaret Thatcher's trusted deputy may have appeared an amiable old buffer, but he was also irascible and "infinitely cunning". *New Statesman*.

Rosenberg, M. (1972, 1993). *The masks of King Lear*. Newark: University of Delaware Press.

Soames, M. (Ed.). (1999). *Speaking for themselves: The private letters of Sir Winston and Lady Churchill*. London: Black Swan.

Sorcher, M. (1985). *Predicting executive success*. Wiley.

Trickey, G. (2014). *In avoiding the feedback bubble*. Tulsa, OK: Hogan Assessment Systems.

Trickey, G., & Hyde, G. (2009). *A decade of the dark side*. Tunbridge Wells: Psychological Consultancy Ltd.

Whitehorn, in Specter, M. (2007, May 14). Branson's luck. *The New Yorker*.

Winsborough, D. (2012, February). Bad managers. *Employment Today*.

9

Preventing and Curing Hubris in Leaders

Karen Otazo

1   Introduction

Every part of the world has had its history of abuse of power, often by emperors, dictators and royalty. The Greeks named the phenomenon Hubris, and it is central to their myth of Daedalus and Icarus—a father and son who attempted to imitate the gods. That, in a nutshell, is the essence of hubris. If you are caught in it, you feel that you have a divine right. If you have power, money and success, over time you start to think of yourself as invulnerable and entitled. No wonder kings thought that they had a divine, god given right to their positions. What happens to leaders who have power, wealth and credentials is that they start to think that they have a right to all of it and other people don't.

Their excessive pride and extravagant self-confidence make them look like powerful leaders. When that happens, hubristic leaders lose touch

K. Otazo (✉)
Karen Otazo Global Leadership Network, Midvale, UT, USA

© The Author(s) 2018
P. Garrard (ed.), *The Leadership Hubris Epidemic*,
https://doi.org/10.1007/978-3-319-57255-0_9

with reality and forget about the people they are leading. Many political leaders have moved in and out of the Hubris Syndrome. Usually it takes years of power to push them into it. According to the research done by Lord Owen, George W. Bush moved into full-blown Hubris Syndrome after 9/11. This was characterized by a lack of interest in follow-through and details. For Margaret Thatcher, that did not happen for nine years after her win in the Falklands. With the Hubris Syndrome the hubristic leader imagines that their view is reality and everything else is untrue. That happened to both Tony Blair and George W. Bush (Owen 2012).

Leaders with Hubris Syndrome often take action first, especially those actions that make them look good, then think about the consequences later. Their restless and reckless way of acting along with their messianic way of talking makes them look action oriented like Donald Trump. Women like Hillary Clinton or Theresa May are more likely to carefully consider all of the variables, and this may make them look overly cautious. However, hubristic leaders have an overwhelming arrogance—a feeling that they are entitled to bully and intimidate anyone less powerful, verbally and physically, especially women and those in lower positions. They think that they are always entitled to more and don't even need to listen to others, even those who are serving their needs.

2   Avoiding Hubris

Two well-known leaders, Angela Merkel and Abraham Lincoln, were able to avoid being pulled into the Hubris Syndrome as a result of the deprivation and trauma of their childhoods. It is ideal if someone can develop empathy and compassion early in their lives and carry those into their leadership experience. Otherwise, it is almost inevitable that leadership hubris will happen over time with power and success.

Whatever helps you swallow your pride helps you lead without hubris: a leader's self-knowledge and awareness can do that. The power of position puts leaders into a manic state that gets the leader energized. Rude, selfish, behaviour develops, such as interrupting others, abusing them and treating them with rudeness and intolerance. They feel as if they can get away with anything. It is much easier to stop these behaviours before they start. Leaders gain power from their positions the more time they put in. Many, if not most, politicians have turned hubristic.

So, to avoid this, it is essential for a leader to maintain the following nine qualities. If a person reminds themselves to always show these qualities and practice these acts, not only will the person become "nicer" for the sake of personality, but it will actually help his/her business life in securing their career. They will have a noticeable change in outcome and in the quality of their decisions.

2.1   Generosity

Generosity is a quality that is the opposite of selfishness. Generosity in action means giving time, money, food, and kindness. You might give away things or money or put others before yourself. Generosity of spirit is more powerful yet vital for leaders. When you are forgiving and gentle to people, you show generosity. When you give others help, credit, and respect, regardless of social status, you are being generous. The world would be a better place if more people showed generosity of spirit. Generosity of Spirit connects with St. Augustine and his concept of Caritas, or neighborly love as well as the Jewish term *mensch*, a good human being. Buddhism maintains that no spiritual life is possible without a generous heart.

A person who is generous is generally considered a magnanimous person. Generosity and magnanimity are valuable in leaders, as they indicate a commitment to be high-minded and honourable. People who have generosity of spirit take complete responsibility for their lives. They do not blame others or circumstances for their problems. They do the best possible things for all concerned.

I have encountered a couple of situations where lack of generosity can end a person's career and honourability, but they then use generosity to turn everything back around. Here is one example. A highly successful entrepreneur was vigilant about competitors. When companies dared to challenge his company's hegemony in his field he bought them or crushed them. Then the EU sanctioned his company for being a monopoly. He turned away from his former ways and started looking at the world with new eyes. With a realization that his money might rid the world of terrible diseases like malaria and polio he generously devoted part of his fortune to do the right thing, unlike other entrepreneurs who have used money, power, and position to bully others. This entrepreneur has encouraged many like him around the world to join him with their generosity. All of his hard work and new generous endeavours have allowed him to be once again respected in the business community, especially among his peers.

To prevent the beginning of that story, creating a special group to encourage generosity has worked to raise money. Connecting with peers is one of the best ways to encourage individuals be part of a group that is generous. Here are some easy ways in which busy leaders, who need to stay grounded could be generous:

1. Giving donations to reputable causes you support. Give enough so that the amount is meaningful and useful.
2. Volunteer for the nonexecutive boards of the groups you support.
3. Offer a coaching session in your area of expertise.
4. Celebrate the successes of others.
5. Give time or money without expecting anything in return.
6. Stay positive to help others be optimistic.
7. Offer your time and expertise to support and facilitate an organization or group—not to control it.
8. Use your energy to energize others and get them going.
9. When needed, be willing to step in and lead, if only for an interim period.
10. Go out of your way to promote and publicize worthy people, organizations and causes.

2.2   Graciousness

Graciousness is a demonstration of tact, kindness, warmth, elegance, or courtesy to others. Since it is often a hallmark of wealth and good upbringing it may refer to indulgence towards people who are lower in the social ladder. Graciousness is used in reference to a merciful and compassionate God in both Christianity and Islam.

The British national anthem starts: *God save our gracious Queen.* The queen, a queen's mother, or a dowager queen may be called "Her Most Gracious Majesty." The only change for a king would be to change Her to His. Royalty are expected to be the embodiment of graciousness in all they do. The term "good upbringing" usually refers to those who have been taught to behave politely and properly to everyone in all circumstances, which sometimes is associated with wealth, but not always. Their family and friends are often role models.

Graciousness is an essential trait for any leader, even those not in royalty. Possession of this extra trait, this form of being, allows for one to understand so much more and to have many more doors open, just like my client Shigeki. Shigeki had just been appointed to the leadership position of Managing Director in the Tokyo office of a multinational company. As a rite of passage, he had gone to a management programme in London, part of which required him to attend a performance of a Shakespeare play in London. The other training programme participants were all native English speakers. Although Shigeki spoke English at work, the archaic language of the play was not easy for him to understand. Then the programme facilitator gave a lecture on the characters and the meaning of the play. He was unsure how the play and the lectures would help him be a better leader. When he got back to Tokyo he asked for executive coaching help to get the most out of his leadership training experience. The executive coach acted as an interpreter for his experience so that Shigeki could find the courage to practice what he been exposed to in order to become a better leader. Once he learned how a gracious leader should act he started practicing. We found an acting company in Tokyo for him to join so he could practice. We kept in close touch by email for the next year while he took on as many leadership roles as he could handle, acting at night while he worked at his day job. That year was a life changing experience for Shigeki. He grew in his leadership ability and in his family relationships. To his amazement, the theatre experience practicing graciousness helped him improve his group's work performance enormously and rewarded him with a promotion.

To practice graciousness, the following were effective:

1. Carefully thinking out and practising (the way he memorized his lines for plays) everything he said to others at work. He spent a lot of time practising at home so that his children learned how to do the same.
2. Meditating each day at home and for short periods during the day for focus and relaxation.
3. Ensuring that he was pleasant and kind to everyone.
4. Making sure to introduce visitors.
5. Paying attention to each employee for some time each day.
6. Making sure to thank others, for even the smallest gestures.
7. Making sure to never put anyone down.
8. Paying attention when others talked.
9. Making sure to recognize and praise others in little ways.
10. Always being courteous.

2.3   Respect

Respect for people is acknowledging and showing that they have value in themselves. Respect in action includes using good manners with everyone from the least significant person to the most powerful. Einstein said that he spoke to everyone in the same way '...whether he is the garbage man or the president of the University'. A lack of respect can create many enemies, people who would not mind seeing you in ruins. Disrespectfulness is extremely powerful, as my client proved to everyone around him.

Peter was in his dream job as the Managing Director of a top Fortune Global 500 company. He had risen up the ranks by taking on the most difficult projects around the world and making them work. From Africa to Malaysia he developed excellent relations with every country's political and industry elites. Peter had a reputation for ensuring that his projects were on time and on budget. He did this by pushing his company's employees to work around the clock. He was so driven that he begrudged taking the time to listen to employee presentations. Peter pushed his way forward so that he reached his goals.

He didn't sleep easily or wake easily and he looked sallow and sick most of the time. When anyone came to talk with him he would say, "This meeting has a hard finish. You must stick to the time limits." If the presenters were lower level employees, he would interrupt them and make deprecating comments as they spoke. He would even do that with his direct reports. Once he left remote locations and came back to head-quarters, his reputation really deteriorated.

At the same time, his head of finance was so irritated that he searched for a way to retaliate against Peter to make him look bad. When he found an ambiguous accounting discrepancy and reported it to the board, Peter became aware of his treachery. In astonishment, he wondered what had happened to make a colleague of long standing turn against him. When he eventually took the time to have a discussion his CFO the situation became clear. He saw that it was time for a change in attitude, for an 'injection of respect'. He needed help to get along with those who could sabotage him. One of his fatal flaws was about to sink him. That was when he acquiesced to working with an experienced executive coach and thinking partner.

In effect, he needed to find a way to get the people he dealt with to feel easy meeting with him instead of shaking in their shoes at the very thought of him. There had been many complaints over the years that he had ignored, because he was successful. He could not ignore them now.

Our work together started with a comprehensive structured interview looking at his entire career. In the process he revealed that he had always felt inferior since he had grown up in an impoverished working class family a long way from his country's capital. Having gone to state schools, he wasn't one of the top candidates for special executive track programs at top companies. He clawed his way to the top with his skills.

He was able to admit his fears and feelings of inferiority, even crying in the process. One big fear was that if he was too nice to subordinates he would be subordinating himself to them. Peter was taught that if he treated others with dignity they would kick him around. He would get into a manic state that helped propel him into action. When he pushed others he would feel more powerful. He especially did not know how to work with executive women. Peter didn't want female executives to think that he was flirting with them. He would sarcastically say that he couldn't listen to a female executive with 'that hair', if her hair was frizzy or messy.

After interviewing a variety of coworkers whom had met with, or who had presented to him, his behaviours became clear. The coworkers included not only Peter's subordinates but their subordinates as well, plus his entire team and the board. His lack of respect for all but board members played out in many ways. After working on what he learned, he could more effectively personify respect. Specifically, Peter:

1. Learned to lower the stress of subordinates at meetings by letting them know how he would like his information. He preferred short, to the point presentations with no more than three to five uncluttered slides.
2. Did not put down any employee in public or private.
3. The lower the level of the employee, the more time he allocated for a relaxed give and take at their presentations to allow for follow up.
4. Stopped working on his computer or smart phone during presentations (his Respect App cutting the devices off during meetings).
5. Spent short periods several times a day in meditation for stress management and serenity.
6. Said part of an Anglican prayer that he loved whenever he became irritated or wound up.
7. Stopped worrying about looking the part of the senior company executive and how others looked.
8. Thanked all presenters and meeting participants.
9. Realized that not respecting himself was a choice that messed up his thinking in his childhood, while his respect for others would not bring back the bullies but vanquish them.
10. Learned that giving respect eradicated his shame about lack of a high-end university education. The act of giving freed him.

To consolidate his personification of respect Peter worked to ensure that his team did the same. One of his subordinates, Wally, was treating every low level employee without respect. Worse than Peter, Wally was contemptuous of the company drivers who had to drive him to the airport; it was so gruesome that they took turns, driving him only when necessary. Some of them paid the others to take their turn just because of Wally's attitude. One older driver with slightly darker skin was slow to pick up suitcases. He was always there to do his job and felt that he deserved to be treated with care considering his many years of service. He was very respectful to all the executives. He simply couldn't jump and run for them.

Wally expected that he would have his own driver, like Peter. He felt that since he deserved Peter's job, he should get the perks as well. His assistants typically lasted 3–4 months and moved on since it was a big, respected company. One of the tests of Peter's personification of respect was being able to put up with his subordinate's lack of respect. As Peter developed his sensitivity for respect, he was able to somewhat put up with Wally's lack of it, but started working with him to improve.

2.4   Limits

Limits can include adhering to all laws, rules and regulations to ensure that people coexist with an assurance of health, safety and confidence. Yet adhering to limits is not solely complying with rules, regulations, and laws. At its core, not doing something because you can get away with it, or ignoring the limits can destroy civil society. Without limits we have tyranny and chaos. Having lived in China for many years, I was able to observe the arbitrary lack of limits in rules, regulations, and laws that included care for regulations of maintenance and care for machinery. With scant history of nothing more mechanical than bicycles, attention to machine safety was something not widely present in the culture of even the companies there.

It was shocking when a well-known energy company acted like a third world country, with a series of avoidable and deadly mishaps. These included a deadly refinery explosion with 15 employees dead and many more ill, and the Alyeska Pipeline leaks. The well-known company had acquired two American energy companies, both of which had superb safety records. As I was an employee of one of them I saw some of the problems first hand. For instance, a company I had formerly worked for had run a mechanical pig through the Trans Alaska Pipeline (TAPS) to check for leaks every six months. The whole company cheered when the Pipeline got a clean bill of health. The acquiring company only ran the mechanical pig through TAPS once leaks were discovered, ten years after the acquisition.

The head of the well-known energy company had been rewarded for his business success. Nicknamed by employees the "Sun King" for his management style, he pressed employees for quick returns with relatively low investment. His lack of limits, his lack of concern for safety and need to cut corners everywhere caused him to go on trial for negligence. Even during this it was claimed that this member of the House of Lords had bragged that safety didn't matter since it cost too much and reduced profits. An employee death would only "cost about ten million dollars;" that didn't significantly reduce the energy company profits.

Breaking the limits, legal and regulatory, forced this hubristic leader to resign. Regardless of this experience, he was replaced by another hubristic leader, which meant that the company made no real changes in the way it operated. About three years later the company managed to have one of the worst industrial accidents in US history, with eleven dead and millions affected in the short and long term. The effects may last in perpetuity.

As a classical hubristic, the head of the company ignored the needs of the employees and of those affected and complained that he wanted his life back because dealing with the new accident was difficult for him to handle. The difficulties included internal, external, governmental, and community issues. The lack of attention to the limits to save time and money resulted in gross negligence and reckless conduct that are typical of the Hubris Syndrome.

The details of the cause of the whole thing are the following: the three Blow Out Protectors (BOP) were designed to prevent explosions, but the company gamed the BOP permitting system by obtaining a new permit every day, even though it was supposed to plan ahead. One BOP was redesigned, one was missing and one was replaced, and all were improperly maintained. These vital safety protectors were treated as a cost to be eliminated even though they were part of the basics of doing business safely. They were examples of "penny wise, pound foolish" mistakes that hubristic leaders often make to ensure getting bonuses and looking good on the balance sheet. The original Lord was the role model.

There were many vital changes to be made to ensure a viable and successful future for this well-known company. In addition to general cost cutting measures, to pay for the record-setting government fines and penalties for breaking the legal and regulatory limits the company restructured its business portfolio. It became obvious that the replacement CEO of the well-known energy company could not handle their latest mishap. It was time for a new CEO and new thinking.

The new American CEO brought in an American thinking partner for all executives and the organization to work together. The move opened up options for individual and group coaching support. The following were some organizational and leadership adjustments that made a big difference in adhering to the limits:

1. Health Safety and Environmental concerns and actions take precedence in meetings.
2. Regulatory colleagues should be invited into meetings to encourage open communication with them.
3. All leaders are responsible for assessing and supporting employee morale regularly in small ways and occasionally in larger ways.
4. Community Relations are every leader's responsibilities. Regular meetings and connections are important.
5. It was time to discard some of the constraints of hierarchy to ensure that the opinions of Operations are elevated.
6. Clarify the lines and frequency of communications with weekly checkups.
7. Restructure the Washington office to keep in touch with regulators.
8. Identify some employees as connectors who are responsible for connecting across the white space on the organization chart.

2.5   Trust and Loyalty

You need people you can trust, but how do you get them? While it might seem ideal to surround yourself with people you have known for years, they may not be the best choices for new leaders and for candidates in business and politics. As comforting as that option may appear, it can be dangerous to cut yourself off from new ideas and points of view. It pays to put in the time and effort to build mutual trust with experts, as well as old and new colleagues who will support you in your leadership position. This reciprocity is essential; however efficient and knowledgeable you may think you are, you will not be able to do your job in isolation in spite of what your personal hubris convinces you that you can do.

There is no formula for generating trust: trust is a gut feeling, something that evolves through shared experiences. However, in building effective trust in your leadership position, it can be helpful to consider what kind of trust you need, and in whom. That is vital for your success. And you regularly test everyone you work with. There are four major types of trust to think about and test as you work with new and known people:

2.5.1 Get-it-Done Trust

Get-it-done trust involves knowing that others, like your team, will meet commitments on time and within budget and will alert you to any potential delay or problems. This is vital with anyone to whom you delegate tasks. You test this kind of trust by making small requests and noting how and when people get them done. Then you'll know whom you can trust when a crucial project with an inflexible and vital deadline comes along. You can nurture a climate of get-it-done trust by making it clear that people should come to you with any concerns about meeting deadlines as soon as they have them. Even if you get staff assigned from previous leaders or from the civil/ government service system, you must make sure that they have doable deadlines with consistent clarity of expectations. Deadlines are magic. Treat them with respect and follow up with them so that they matter.

Note that your experience with trusted staff that gets things done can fool you. It doesn't mean that they can do other things that you need. A great meeting planner may know how to do appointments but may NOT be able to leap into a full assistant position which requires prioritizing for others and high level decision making.

2.5.2 Expertise Trust

Expertise trust occurs when you can depend on someone's special knowledge or ability. There is no one who has special knowledge about everything, but it is vital with any experts with whom you work. You must be certain that their advice is sound and their knowledge current. It is pure Hubris Syndrome to believe that you don't need experts. For example, when engaging a consultant to advise you, you should check that his or her experience includes the kinds of situations your administration or your business may be facing. You need to become acquainted with experts who will give you the real situation you are facing and the whole picture whenever you ask them, or even before. You test expertise trust by double-checking the information you are given until you feel confident in someone. That is especially important when you are in other countries where your gut feelings may not be as accurate.

2.5.3 Political-savvy

Political-savvy trust comes from knowing that your team and colleagues understand workplace or political norms and how to play the organizational or political game. It is bound up with confidentiality and discretion and is important in any colleague with whom you work in confidential ways. Being great at getting things done, or being experts in their field is no guarantee that colleagues deserve political savvy trust. Your creative staff member who can come up with great off-the-wall ideas may not realize the importance of keeping these low profile so that her staff doesn't think that they're a done deal until the ideas have been vetted and passed by others.

2.5.4 Structural Trust

Structural trust is needed whenever you work with people from elsewhere in your company or your party. It comes from knowing that someone in another department can put the interests of the entire organization, or party before his or her own, and give credit to others rather taking total ownership. Since resources are often stretched and different departmental interests often don't coincide, developing total structural trust is tricky. You can generate a good working trust by establishing clear frameworks in advance, rather than taking blind leaps of faith. You should agree on how to resolve conflicts among departments and groups before the need arises. If you have a policy or procedures in place that will help your team members 'play fair' when they work across the white spaces on the organization chart, it will be easier for everyone to develop trust.

The rules in place make it easier to work together, but loyalty is a mixed bag. Family members and long-term friends are attractive choices. President John F. Kennedy used his brother Robert as his closest advisor. Luckily they had great trust in each other and a first class education with worldwide experience and a superb network. Using a family member may be comfortable but not necessarily the right choice for everyone.

Each occasion for dealing with others, however low-key, is a chance to test their trustworthiness. Give new people a chance to prove themselves. If someone breaks your trust once, you should be wary of asking for his or her support with anything important in the future. But try not to get hung up on a single incident; you're looking at behaviour over time. Telling you something you do not want to hear is not a break in trust, it may be what you want and need. It shows how trustworthy someone is since it is in your best interest to get a heads-up about other ways of thinking. *Watch out if you only want agreeable opinions.*

Think of the ways new colleagues can earn your trust then open those paths for them. Trust develops over time. Be conscious of earning and granting trust as you work with people. If you need to get tough feedback you may want an outside consultant or coach if you are wary of hearing anything negative.

2.6   Decency

The American presidency was shaped by the values and ideals of the first president, George Washington. He had the ideals of patriotism, selflessness, and emotional self-mastery. These came with Washington's faith in public service that echoed the Ancient Romans, especially Cato. Serving one's country was his highest ideal. Washington talked about the conflict with England not in terms of America or justice. He fought in the name of goodness, honesty, rectitude, and decency. Washington personified rising above the fray when he rode around his plantation in Virginia on his horse to obtain a perspective of all he surveyed. He endeavoured to take the same perspective in public office. Since the political currents and rivalries were at least as strong, the first US president stayed above them all.

How did he do that when there were double crosses, fierce rivalries, false news, and a yearning to go back to the divine right of kings? What gave George Washington the strength to deal with the same issues facing the office in the modern era? Washington was clear that the republican way of government had to remain. No matter how often he had to solve the disputes between Hamilton and Jefferson or had to deal with John Jay's reluctance to do his duty, he maintained the general morale and endeavored to consistently do the decent thing for the new country. When he heard the cheering crowds, Washington worried about how he could live up to what people expected of him. He felt that there was a moral burden for him to govern with compassion.

The US Presidency had an early role model to emulate for the country's beginning, yet a recent holder of the position was more reminiscent of the days of kings than a constitutional office. After the initial inauguration, he was concerned that the attendees were fewer than for his predecessor. The most recent photographs of his inauguration on January 20 showed low attendance. At his insistence, his staff provided a much more crowded photo taken of the Women's March on January 21. That was reminiscent of Phillip IV of France having his image inserted into a painting of a military victory instead of his brother who won the battle in The Netherlands. Typical of a hubristic leader, he had to be the best and have the best, even by lying.

Since kings can make most things happen by proclamation, the new President began using the presidential version called *executive orders*. Evidently, some of these may not have been consistent with the US constitution. Less than a week on the job he had moved on more objectives than his predecessor had in years. Hubristic leaders like to keep moving, sometimes becoming manic. They can be impressive in their speed. Yet, informing those around them first would be the decent thing to do.

For his inauguration pageantry, he had had built something special in his country's capital. In order to have it ready in time this hubristic leader had authorized around the clock construction work to finish in time for his photo op and publicity. He lived up to his hubristic reputation when he refused to pay the legally required overtime. Paying for what he requested would have been the decent as well as legal thing to do. Just starting his time as a powerful world leader, he was in the full-blown Hubris Syndrome. He obviously had not a care for the details resulting from his actions.

2.7   Humility

Humility is the capability of being humble and letting others take credit and not tooting your own horn. It is the opposite of egotism. Typically, leaders are not heavily admired if they are humble. Amazing but true, leaders who are brash and braggarts are seen as confident. Humility is associated with religious meekness. In actuality, humility is a reflection of emotional intelligence in leaders who can regulate their own emotions and get along with others. They allow others to shine and even invite them to take the limelight and more.

Like few leaders the world has known, Lincoln proved that any leader's first and greatest victory is always that over his own ego and pride. For him, humility was the maturing of what we now call emotional intelligence (EQ), controlling and putting aside your own strong feelings. This president always kept his values and goals in mind; what he did was for the greater good. He judged every action through that lens. He was the opposite of hubristic.

Leaders can be commanding to others with their words, their tone of voice and the strength of their oratory. Lincoln commanded himself first. And with his self-command he practiced humility. Instead of diminishing his rivals, who had made fun of him and his awkward appearance, he acknowledged their skills and capabilities. He was humble enough to admit that he was learning on the job every day.

A visitor to the US needed a dose of Lincoln's humility. Dimitri was a foreign leader visiting the United Nations on First Avenue in New York City. It was an important visit. His interpreter was confused working with him. He was carefully turning Dimitri's Russian into English for the audience. The interpreter's work was for naught: Dimitri immediately answered questions in English before the interpreter could get a word in edgewise. Yet when the audience asked for specifics, Dimitri said in Russian, "I don't understand the questions. They make no sense."

Dimitri spoke in such a commanding tone that everyone paid attention. He sounded like a general. He was a powerful orator who was so strong that everyone wanted to know him and align with him. In fact, the American President was always complimenting him. Then he would turn around and compliment the President. He would raise one eyebrow when questioned and would say "I've created jobs in my country and I can help you do the same in your country."

He was over the top egotistical; this has meant glamour and glitz and having the best dachas, or country homes, best limos and beautiful, subservient women surrounding him. One of his personal goals was to garner a position as the head of a US company the way Gerhardt Schroder did in Russia at Gazprom. He needed to appeal to Americans who might be put off by his manic kind of Attention Deficit Disorder (ADD) which kept him constantly on the move amassing fame and fortune.

Dimitri thought ego was just great, that it was what keeps the world moving. When he was told that he should act with more humility he answered that he did not want to be a monk, unless it was Rasputin who was ruthless and strong. Since he was self-absorbed, Dimitri loved his own swagger and his success with land grabs and women. When he was asked to tone down his bragging and intolerance to prepare himself to take on a US leadership position he got some guidance. After all, the US political leaders said that he was very smart; his attitude was the only thing that needed a change. He could learn new ways of acting. Here are the areas he worked on:

1. Being genuinely thankful for the work that others did on his behalf.
2. Showing thanks by recognizing others' capabilities.
3. Helping out friends and acquaintances regularly.
4. Being modest about his achievements.
5. Giving others credit.
6. Encouraging teamwork and mutual support.
7. Developing a set of values, in addition to self-interest, as a guide to making decisions.
8. Soliciting input from experts, team and colleagues to make decisions.
9. Being willing to wait to check with others rather than act impetuously.
10. Practising meditation for calming purposes. Even doing this for short periods of time makes a difference.

You know that you are developing humility if you are kind and courteous and speak well of people who have spoken ill of you. It takes humility to hire enemies as Lincoln did if they are the best for the job. The key for humility is to make decisions based on the highest possible good for all. This can be a big change for a leader caught in the Hubris Syndrome. It can take a longer time period with supporting successes to initiate the process of transformation for a leader. There are skills and behaviours that change relatively easily. Humility is not typically one of them. It is usually developed as a result of childhood and tough life experiences.

Steel needs to be tempered in very hot fires. Great leaders need to be tempered with real life experiences. Just as a cushy and easy life doesn't encourage humility, great leaders can learn from overcoming obstacles. But their learning from their lessons of experience on the job, whilst always supporting people, is exactly the way that great leaders learn.

2.8   Self -Awareness

Self-awareness is developing a conscious knowledge of your own nature, feelings, desires and actions. Being self-aware means knowing your motivators and determining whether they're reasonable and your actions make sense. Sometimes, having this trait can really make the distinction between success and failure. David was a successful young entrepreneur in a major US city. His father, Julius, had provided him with enough money to get a foothold in the family business. At the same time he had introduced Dave to his own circle of friends and contacts. But Dave had different motives and expectations than his father. He floundered a bit in the early days and made many mistakes.

He realized that he needed some hard, non-biased advice. That was when he engaged an executive coach and thinking partner, something he had not done before.

The steps he took:

1. Working with a thinking partner, he took the MBTI Type Indicator and had the executive coach conduct feedback interviews with his team. The most useful inventory of all was the *Motivation Questionnaire* which revealed what gave him energy and motivated him [Niche Consulting 2005–2017].
2. With his new knowledge, David built a team to complement his skills and preferences. His team was very much like a stock portfolio with some steady stocks and some risky ones.
3. With self-awareness, he assessed his team with new eyes.
4. He learned to observe himself by creating a "David 2" who could stand outside himself and watch his actions and sense the feelings that he had.

5. Having become more self-aware, he was able to find ways to improve.
6. David learned new ways of thinking within himself. He learned to ask why more than once whenever he made a decision. That was tough.
7. Learned to tune out his auto-pilot of strong reactions.
8. Although he was not enamoured of meditation he was willing to reflect on his actions in his life for short periods every day.
9. Learned to consider others when making decisions by checking with some of those concerned.
10. Had his team take the same inventories he had taken.

How did *The Motivation Questionnaire* [Niche Consulting Ltd] reveal his motivators to David in four key areas?

1. Energy and Dynamism—where the person gets their energy from and "what drives them"
2. Synergy—how important environmental comfort factors are in maintaining their motivation
3. Intrinsic motivators—coming from doing the job itself
4. Extrinsic motivators—rewards and fame.

Since David was motivated and energized by extrinsic appreciation he now could determine which of his team could and would complement his needs. Specifically, David saw that he:

- Was motived by time pressure
- Liked to be on the go
- Invested energy readily
- Liked challenges
- Overcame challenges
- Competed to beat others
- Hated failure or losing
- Must be in charge
- Liked to control
- Loved making money

- Loved recognition
- Must always have status and respect, and be seen as the best.

David realized that what he needed was a team to support him in his personal motivational needs. That would certainly help him to be successful. Without his new awareness he would have charged forward without thinking. Just in case, his executive coach worked with him to relax and reduce the manic hubristic pressure that propelled him to keep moving. Although he stayed in the Hubris Syndrome, with his pause for self-examination he was ready.

2.9   Empathy

Empathy is the ability to understand and share the feelings of another. It is the ability to sense other people's emotions, coupled with the ability to imagine what someone else might be thinking or feeling. Compassion for suffering can lead to empathy. Empathy can mitigate or deflate the Hubris Syndrome. Elaborating on specific jobs and their associations, most jobs in the current century are based on the opposite of empathy, called systematizing, like law, engineering, and computer science. These are traditionally considered male jobs. Empathy jobs like nursing, education and service jobs are traditionally considered female jobs.

Companies that are better at empathy do much better financially. The 2016 Empathy Global Index was published in the Harvard Business Review. The source of this global index was Empathy Business, a UK-based firm "Committed to bringing empathy to business", and 2016 was the 3rd year that they had published the Empathy Global Index. This timely article laid out how the index had determined the empathy value of more than 170 companies. The Empathy Business Global Index broke down empathy into: ethics, leadership, company culture, brand perception, and social media. The metrics included softer people ratings like CEO approval ratings from staff, ratio of women on boards, and number of accounting infractions and scandals. The index focuses on varied global companies, with an emphasis on U.K. and U.S. companies and 10 Indian companies. The soft details were harder to find publicly available in every country, though these factors mattered greatly. Facebook rose to the top slot as a result of its focus on improving its internal culture and the introduction of its Empathy Lab, put in place by an accessibility engineer. In true empathetic fashion the Lab stands in the shoes of others. It's clear that practices in companies that promote a focus on empathy actually lead to economic growth.

The Empathy Lab puts employees at Facebook into the shoes of those who are differently abled, in different cultures and countries. Those use all sizes and types of devices and degrees of connectivity. Empathy is working for this company. Thinking of the varied purposes of the Empathy Lab there are always many opportunities to practice empathy at work and in politics. Lack of empathy is not only the province of men. Anyone can suffer from lack of empathy, and later pay for it. Carly Fiorina became the CEO of a technical company started by engineers in a Palo Alto Garage. This was a shock to a company culture based on teamwork that believed in innovations in technology. HP was a company that totally believed that it had a "cultural ecosystem grounded in the past but relevant for our present and future." There was a clear correlation between financial success and global empathy index.

When I met Carly at a formal dinner, this CEO was dressed in an elegantly short-skirted suit; she had flown to the event in her own airplane. With her jet setting lifestyle, she never connected with her company or its culture. And especially did not understand her employees. With little empathy, she didn't understand that her employees were proud to travel economy class. They did not understand her outrageous salary package. When Carly was pushed out of HP for not meeting any of her challenges, her severance package was around 42 million.

Here are some examples just like the one above from which you could learn:

1. A high level executive moved into a 100 year old company in a European location. Mindful of the mistakes others had avoided ignoring the importance of the company traditions, he made sure that he honoured the past of the company and the technical culture.
2. At a Hong Kong investment bank, a native of New York City was using his successful New York techniques to push his staff to

perform. When he noticed employees not working hard enough he made fun of them by yelling at them down the hall or even across closed doors. He was always noisy and cursing. His employees hated him. What he was doing was publically making them "lose face", or look bad, in front of others. This is really painful for Asian employees and is difficult for others. Working with empathy, he later learned to give neutral feedback, instead of criticism. All feedback and coaching had to take place in private in the boss' office.

3. A company in China had a Chinese boss in charge with some American born Chinese and Americans working for him. The boss was experienced and well educated in the west. The boss was really upset with his American employees when they talked back to him, and they with him. Putting the boss and his employees into each other's shoes they both learned what was happening. It is normal for Chinese parents to conscientiously and constantly criticize their children. They even call their children names to exhort them to improve. So it seemed normal for the boss and not for the subordinates to be criticized. They learned to change the way they talked to each other.

4. Empathy must play a part in the way we talk about disabilities, ethnicity, religion, skin colour and anything else we can't change. Think of the Empathy Lab. Facebook did not call it anything like equal opportunity. It was all about feeling for and understanding others. The kinds of put downs that children, and some hubristic leaders use are often about characteristics that are not really changeable and therefore shockingly painful.

5. The head of a famous software company was taken to a struggling hospital for the victims of polio. Although not particularly empathetic, he was shocked at the magnitude of suffering he saw. He felt compassion for the sufferers he met. After thoughtful consideration, he realized that he could make a difference for not just one hospital but rather many hospitals on a huge scale.

A useful way to empathize with others who have disabilities or disease is to talk with them and learn more about them. And to generally better your ability, start off by working on empathizing with fictional characters of different ages, background and locations. That's a safe and private way for hubristic leaders to practice empathy.

To know where you are starting from rake the "Reading the Mind in the Eyes" test Appendix 1 [Baron Cohen 2003] or take the Empathy Quotient test [Baron Cohen 2003 Appendix 2]. A lot more research will help us understand, value and use the power of empathy for good as well as profit and Return on Investment.

3   Cure

Performance Reviews and Other feedback create an opening for the Cure. If an employee is confronted with a mediocre performance review or difficult 360-degree feedback it can provoke a realization of his or her actions. This may be the best time to get a wise and neutral advisor or mentor to assist the leader in understanding the nature of the feedback. It is difficult for the employee's direct boss to do the feedback and coaching since a boss or a board is focused on performance. A big help in companies is to have People Principles so that there is a baseline of behavior that is expected. Businesses can fire a hubristic leader when needed. The People Principles enabled a company to weed out over the top hubris.

Decades ago I was privileged to participate in the development of a company's People Principles as part of their Business Principles. Their people principles, focused on honesty, integrity, and respect, may not have looked very different from other companies. What was different was that the entire company discussed what honesty, integrity and respect meant on a day-to-day basis. One of the most basic rules, that didn't change or suffer from misinterpretation, was that no foul language or rudeness would be tolerated. The repercussions made it clear that bad behavior would not be tolerated. To make sure that the principles were enforced equally across the company worldwide, an infamous senior executive, to his great surprise, lost his position. He then went to four different US companies. One of them asked me how they could work with this difficult character. In conversation with them it became clear that this already wealthy executive was not worth working with.

For instance, respect was expected at every level. Every single employee was expected to treat other employees at any level with good manners and respect. Therefore, a Managing Director, a very senior employee, was to treat a car driver, a secretary, a cook, or a cleaner with the same respect and careful manners as he would his superiors. In situations like this, it becomes very noticeable how much subordinates need to flex to work with executives sucked into the Hubris Syndrome. It is probably preferable to not hire such executives. The People Principles of honesty, integrity and respect are the minimum that anyone, in any institution, deserves and expects.

It's easier to control the behavior of hubristic executives in the fairly controlled environment of a business, even though it might be global. The control of a political candidate is much more difficult. With the still, small voice of conscience it's tough to move a hubristic person to abide by "people principles." The punishments are not as important, severe, nor clear to politicians. Although the US looks as if it has more checks and balances with Congress and the Judicial Branch in place, a parliamentary system can "fire" a Leader more efficiently with a party no confidence vote. Which is highly necessary for preventing extremely hubristic, out of control leaders from remaining in power.

3.1   When It's Too Far Along…

How to combat power that corrupts, is probably one of the most important questions. Historically, kings and queens are those in whom all power is invested. Examples of corrupting absolute power include Roman emperors who declared themselves gods, most kings and queens, and Napoleon Bonaparte (who declared himself an emperor). The US founding fathers tried hard to put mechanisms in place to stop US Presidents from becoming dictators or monarchs.

Behavioral research in universities and organizations has shown that when people feel powerful, or indeed powerless, it influences their perception of others. Power goes to our heads and corrupts our minds. It allows us to let those with power to influence others and push them around. It turns out that power along with having much money make us believe that what we do is always the right thing.

In addition, if you don't take the perspectives of others into consideration, you augment your hubris. That often makes it easier to take rash and impulsive actions that might make you seem decisive, but usually constitute the worst decisions. This image causes others to obey, even though that person might have not done the smartest thing. "This means that people with power not only take what they want because they can do so unpunished, but also because they intuitively feel they are entitled to do so. Conversely, people who lack power not only fail to get what they need because they are disallowed to take it, but also because they intuitively feel they are not entitled to it." (Resnick 2013).

Just taking power positions with your body, body language, gives you the feeling of entitlement. Standing over someone, posing with outstretched hands, or stalking around them makes you feel more powerful by increasing testosterone and lowering cortisol hormone levels. Power and taking power positions tend to put us into a manic state. These make us "feel expansive, energized, omnipotent, hungry for rewards, and immune to risk—which opens us up to rash, rude and unethical actions." (Keltner 2016).

Listening to others is one of the hallmarks of good leadership. When we feel less powerful we are more likely to listen to others and to look for consensus.

3.2 How to Free a Manic Mind to Listen

Sitting at the same level as someone else, relaxing and leaning toward them all help us to listen and tone down the deafness of power. Power tends to turn off our brains. When we get into a reflective mode, rather than a talking mode, we are better able hear others. Even more important, when we can become aware of our feelings and thoughts we get out of the manic influence of power. Those of us who engage in daily meditation, focusing on breathing, find it an effective way to tone down a manic "monkey mind" and focus on listening.

There are many approaches to meditation to tone down a manic mind. In conjunction with Harvard University and Massachusetts General Hospital, Jon Kabat-Zinn created practical ways for leaders to calm the mind and deal with hubris. His courses and books are useful and practical. With practice, his approach can be done in just a few minutes and still make a difference.

In a similarly practical way, Simon Sinek has created books about the keys to leadership that works by paying attention to your followers. His latest book: 'Leaders Eat Last' explains how good leaders inspire loyalty by caring for their troops. I've been getting regular leadership guidance from his Notes to Inspire, his leadership snippets, and from his Ted talks. They are all designed to counteract the Hubris Syndrome by connecting with followers with compassionate and benevolent leadership that is much more effective. Another practical website, Charter for Compassion, offers guidance on empathy and generosity. Both of these are key antidotes to the Hubris Syndrome.

Moments of surprise, life's traumas, tough feedback, and change are openings for the leader to become aware of the trap of the Hubris Syndrome. When a Senator remarried an astute and independent woman, he admitted that his young children helped him to practice his skills of empathy and compassion. Children have a way of making us learn. Nevertheless, each of us is responsible for our own cure. Traditionally, advisors have always been available for rich and powerful leaders as guides and truth tellers. Most importantly, remember that the Hubris Syndrome cure is in the hands of the hubristic leader.

References

Alford, Henry. "Is Donald Trump Actually a Narcissist? Therapists Weigh In!" Vanity Fair 11 Nov. 2015: n. pag. Web.

Baldoni, John. "How to Recognize (and Cure) Your Own Hubris." Harvard Business Review 08 Sept. 2010: n. pag. Harvard Business Review. Web.

Belisle, Marc. "These Psychologists Issue Nation Dire Warning About Donald Trump." ReverbPress. N.p., 27 Mar. 2016. Web.

Berglas, Steven. "Rooting Out Hubris, Before a Fall." Harvard Business Review. N.p., 14 Apr. 2014. Web.

Brooks, David. "Donald Trump's Sad, Lonely Life." The New York Times 11 Oct. 2016: n. pag. Print.

Bunch, Will. "The Greek Tragedy of the Billionaire Who Fracked up Pa." The Inquirer. N.p., 03 Mar. 2016. Web.

Ciampa, Dan. "When Charismatic Leadership Goes Too Far." Harvard Business Review. N.p., 21 Nov. 2016. Web.

Collins, Jim. How the Mighty Fall: And Why Some Companies Never Give in. New York, NY: Jim Collins, 2009. Print.

Geneen, Harold, and Alvin Moscow. Managing. New York: Avon, 1993. Print.

Goodwin, Doris Kearns. Team of Rivals. N.p.: Simon & Schuster, 2005. Print.

Holiday, Ryan. Ego Is the Enemy. NYC, NY: Portfolio, 2016. Print.

"In Quotes: Italy's Silvio Berlusconi in His Own Words." BBC News. N.p., 02 Aug. 2013. Web.

Keltner, Dacher. "Don't Let Power Corrupt You." Harvard Business Review Oct. 2016: n. pag. Harvard Business Review. Oct. 2016. Web.

Kernberg, Otto F. Borderline Conditions and Pathological Narcissism. Reissue Edtion ed. N.p.: Jason Aronson, 1995. Print.

Large, David Clay. "The Developing World Thinks Hitler Is Underrated." Foreign Policy 5 Oct. 2016: n. pag. FP. Web.

Love, Reggie. Power Forward My Presidential Education. New York: Simon & Schuster, 2015. Print.

Maccoby, Michael. "Why People Are Drawn to Narcissists Like Donald Trump." Harvard Business Review. N.p., 26 Aug. 2015. Web.

McKirdy, Euan. "Fools Are Everywhere: The Court Jester Around the World." CNN. N.p., 30 Sept. 2016. Web.

Otazo, Dr. Karen. Truth About Being a Leader. N.P. Financial Times Prentice, 2007. Print.

Otto, Beatrice K. Fools Are Everywhere: The Court Jester Around The World. Chicago: U of Chicago, 2007. Print.

Owen, David, and Jonathan Davidson. "Hubris Syndrome: An Acquired Personality Disorder? A Study of US Presidents and UK Prime Ministers over the Last 100 Years." Brain: A Journal of Neurology 132.5 (2009): 1396–406. Web.

Owen, David. The Hubris Syndrome: Bush, Blair and the Intoxication of Power. York: Methuen, 2012. Print.

Resnick, Brian. "How Power Corrupts the Mind." The Atlantic. N.p., 09 July 2013. Web.

Sager, Carole Bayer. They're Playing Our Song: A Memoir. New York, NY: Simon & Schuster, 2016. Print.

Smart, Bradford D. Topgrading: How Leading Companies Win by Hiring, Coaching and Keeping the Best People. 1st ed. N.p.: Prentice Hall, 1999. Print.

Appendix

COGNITIVE SYMPTOM QUESTIONNAIRE   Date: ....

PATIENT'S NAME: ....   YOUR NAME: ....

Please select your relationship to the patient:
SPOUSE -- CHILD -- SIBLING -- FRIEND / NEIGHBOUR -- CLIENT

Please select how often you spend time with the patient?
DAILY -- MOST DAYS -- WEEKLY -- LESS THAN ONCE A WEEK

How long have you known the patient? .... Years

When did you first notice the symptoms? ....

Please indicate whether you have noticed the RECENT ONSET or worsening of any of these signs of
MEMORY DIFFICULTY

1. Failing to pass on messages	Not really	Sometimes	Definitely
2. Forgetting about recent events	Not really	Sometimes	Definitely
3. Forgetting something they were told a few minutes ago	Not really	Sometimes	Definitely
4. Forgetting appointments	Not really	Sometimes	Definitely
5. Inability to concentrate	Not really	Sometimes	Definitely
6. Saying the same thing over and over again	Not really	Sometimes	Definitely
7. Difficulty thinking of words they want to use	Not really	Sometimes	Definitely
8. Easily getting lost	Not really	Sometimes	Definitely

Continued:

Please indicate whether you have noticed the RECENT ONSET or worsening of any of these

signs of

MEMORY DIFFICULTY

1. Failing to recognize a place they have visited before	**Not really**	**Sometimes**	**Definitely**
2. Forgetting the names of people and places	**Not really**	**Sometimes**	**Definitely**
3. Forgetting characters' names while watching a TV programme	**Not really**	**Sometimes**	**Definitely**
4. Forgetting what day it is	**Not really**	**Sometimes**	**Definitely**
5. Getting the present mixed up with the past	**Not really**	**Sometimes**	**Definitely**
6. Deciding to do something and forgetting after a few minutes	**Not really**	**Sometimes**	**Definitely**
7. Forgetting to do something even though it is in front of them (e.g. taking pills)	**Not really**	**Sometimes**	**Definitely**
8. Forgetting to buy things that they went out shopping for	**Not really**	**Sometimes**	**Definitely**
9. Mislaying things they have just put down	**Not really**	**Sometimes**	**Definitely**
10. Forgetting what they watched on TV yesterday	**Not really**	**Sometimes**	**Definitely**

Please indicate whether you have noticed the RECENT ONSET or worsening of any of these signs of
LANGUAGE CHANGE

1. Not talking very much	Not really	Sometimes	Definitely
2. Using simpler language	Not really	Sometimes	Definitely
3. Asking what certain words mean?	Not really	Sometimes	Definitely
4. Using words incorrectly (e.g. "table" for chair)	Not really	Sometimes	Definitely
5. Long pauses while trying to find words	Not really	Sometimes	Definitely
6. Distortion of speech	Not really	Sometimes	Definitely
7. Stuttering	Not really	Sometimes	Definitely
8. Difficulty following the thread of a conversation	Not really	Sometimes	Definitely
9. Repeating back things that other people have just said	Not really	Sometimes	Definitely
10. Using the same expression or catchphrase	Not really	Sometimes	Definitely

On this page we would like you to provide information about repetitions in speech.

Repetitive speech can take a number of forms: some people use a particular word over and over again when they are talking.

How often do you hear REPETITIONS OF A 'FAVOURITE' WORD?

Many times a day   A few times a day   Hardly at all/Never

Are there any specific circumstances (e.g.: in company, on the phone, when stressed, particular times of the day)? If so, please specify:

Can you recall any examples of frequently repeated words? If so, pleas   e write up to three of them below:

1.   2.   3.

Others repeat familiar catchphrases (e.g. 'at the end of the day'; 'it takes all sorts"), or statements (e.g. 'it's very cold today').

How often do you hear REPETITIONS OF THE SAME PHRASE OR SENTENCE?

Many times a day   A few times a day   Hardly at all/Never

Are t here any specific circumstances   (e.g.: in company, on the phone, when   stressed, particular times of the day)? If so, please specify:

Can you recall   any examples of frequently rep   eated phrases or sent   ences? If so, please write up to three of them below:
1.

2.

3.

Some people may also ask questions repeatedly (e.g. 'what day is it today?'; 'what time are we leaving?').

How often do you hear REPETITIONS OF THE SAME QUESTION?

Many times a day   A few times a day   Hardly at all/Never

Are t here any specific circumstances   (e.g.: in company, on the phone, when   stressed, particular times of the day)? If so, please specify:

Can you recall   any examples of frequently rep   eated questions? If so, please write up to three of them below:
1.

2.

3.

Please indicate whether you have noticed the RECENT ONSET or worsening of difficulties with any of these

EVERYDAY SKILLS

1. Writing	Not really	Sometimes	Definitely
2. Using the telephone	Not really	Sometimes	Definitely
3. Handling money or paying bills	Not really	Sometimes	Definitely
4. Driving (if applicable)	Not really	Sometimes	Definitely
5. Household chores	Not really	Sometimes	Definitely
6. Not completing activities once started	Not really	Sometimes	Definitely

Please indicate whether you have noticed the RECENT ONSET or exaggeration of any of these

BELIEFS

1. Being suspicious of people or accusing them of things	Not really	Sometimes	Definitely
2. Seeing or hearing things that are not there	Not really	Sometimes	Definitely
3. Odd or bizarre ideas that cannot be true	Not really	Sometimes	Definitely
4. Thinking that other people are living in the house	Not really	Sometimes	Definitely
5. Thinking that a family member has been replaced by an impostor	Not really	Sometimes	Definitely

Please indicate whether you have noticed the RECENT ONSET or exaggeration of
any of these types of
BEHAVIOUR

1. Frequent crying or sadness / depression	Not really	Sometimes	Definitely
2. Appearing anxious or fearful	Not really	Sometimes	Definitely
3. Appearing restless or agitated	Not really	Sometimes	Definitely
4. Rapid shifts between different emotions	Not really	Sometimes	Definitely
5. Socially embarrassing behaviour	Not really	Sometimes	Definitely
6. Treating strangers as if they are close friends	Not really	Sometimes	Definitely
7. Acting impulsively without thinking	Not really	Sometimes	Definitely
8. Being unusually cheerful or energetic	Not really	Sometimes	Definitely
9. Exaggeration or boastfulness	Not really	Sometimes	Definitely
10. Argumentative and easily irritable	Not really	Sometimes	Definitely
11. Engaging in rigid routines or 'rituals'	Not really	Sometimes	Definitely
12. Hiding or hoarding things	Not really	Sometimes	Definitely
13. Wanting to eat a lot of sweets, cakes or chocolate	Not really	Sometimes	Definitely
14. Eating the same type of food every day, or eating food in an exact order	Not really	Sometimes	Definitely

Please indicate whether you have noticed the RECENT ONSET or worsening of any of these problems with

SLEEP

1. Disturbed night-time sleep	Not really	Sometimes	Definitely
2. Sleeping a lot during the day time	Not really	Sometimes	Definitely
3. Loud snoring at night	Not really	Sometimes	Definitely
4. Long gaps (ten seconds or more) between breaths	Not really	Sometimes	Definitely
5. 'Acting out dreams' while asleep	Not really	Sometimes	Definitely
6. Sleep-talking	Not really	Sometimes	Definitely
7. Sleep-walking	Not really	Sometimes	Definitely
8. Waking in the night and getting dressed, thinking it is morning	Not really	Sometimes	Definitely

Please indicate whether you have noticed the RECENT ONSET or exaggeration of
any of the following changes in

MOTIVATION

1. Less enthusiasm for usual interests	Not really	Sometimes	Definitely
2. No interest in doing new things	Not really	Sometimes	Definitely
3. Loss of interest in socialising	Not really	Sometimes	Definitely
4. Loss of interest in friends and family	Not really	Sometimes	Definitely
5. Withdrawn, not initiating conversation	Not really	Sometimes	Definitely
6. Indifference to other people's worries or concerns	Not really	Sometimes	Definitely
7. Loss of affection	Not really	Sometimes	Definitely

Do you think that he/she has any AWARENESS of or INSIGHT into his/her problems?

Memory problems	AWARE	UNAWARE	DOES NOT HAVE THESE PROBLEMS
Language difficulties	AWARE	UNAWARE	DOES NOT HAVE THESE PROBLEMS
Changes in behaviour or personality	AWARE	UNAWARE	DOES NOT HAVE THESE PROBLEMS

THANK YOU FOR COMPLETING THIS QUESTIONNAIRE!

Your answers will assist with diagnosis, but also help with our research when they are combined (anonymously) with those relating to other patients. Please indicate whether or not you are happy for your responses to be entered into an anonymised electronic database.

We are happy for the information on this questionnaire to be stored in an

anonymised database ....
                    Signature (patient)   Date

               ....
                    Signature (informant)   Date

We <u>do not</u> want the information on this questionnaire to be stored in an

anonymised database ....
                    Signature (patient)   Date

               ....
                    Signature (informant)   Date

Index

© The Editor(s) (if applicable) and The Author(s) 2018
P. Garrard (ed.), *The Leadership Hubris Epidemic*,
https://doi.org/10.1007/978-3-319-57255-0